Inside the Liberal Arts

Inside the Liberal Arts

Critical Thinking and Citizenship

Jeffrey Scheuer

ROWMAN & LITTLEFIELD
Lanham • Boulder • New York • London

Published by Rowman & Littlefield
An imprint of The Rowman & Littlefield Publishing Group, Inc.
4501 Forbes Boulevard, Suite 200, Lanham, Maryland 20706
www.rowman.com

86-90 Paul Street, London EC2A 4NE, United Kingdom

Copyright © 2023 by Jeffrey Scheuer

All rights reserved. No part of this book may be reproduced in any form or by any electronic or mechanical means, including information storage and retrieval systems, without written permission from the publisher, except by a reviewer who may quote passages in a review.

British Library Cataloguing in Publication Information Available

Library of Congress Cataloging-in-Publication Data

Names: Scheuer, Jeffrey, 1953– author.
Title: Inside the liberal arts: critical thinking and citizenship /Jeffrey Scheuer.
Description: Lanham, Maryland: Rowman & Littlefield, [2023] | Includes bibliographical references. | Summary: "Scheuer guides us through the moral and conceptual heart of the liberal education ideal"—Provided by publisher.
Identifiers: LCCN 2022044488 (print) | LCCN 2022044489 (ebook)
 | ISBN 9781475869873 (Cloth) | ISBN 9781475869880 (Paperback) | ISBN 9781475869897 (epub)
Subjects: LCSH: Education, Humanistic. | Critical thinking—Study and teaching (Higher) | Democracy and education.
Classification: LCC LC1011 .S367 2023 (print) | LCC LC1011 (ebook)
 | DDC 370.11/2—dc23/eng/20221107
LC record available at https://lccn.loc.gov/2022044488
LC ebook record available at https://lccn.loc.gov/2022044489

For Jack, June, Clementine, and those to follow.

Contents

Acknowledgments	ix
Preface: Inside the Liberal Arts	xi
Chapter 1: The Liberal Arts Idea	1
Chapter 2: The Liberal Arts and Triangular Citizenship	15
Chapter 3: Gateways to Critical Inquiry	25
Chapter 4: Language Lessons: What We Need to Know About Words to Think Well	39
Chapter 5: The Range of Rationality	57
Chapter 6: Defining Critical Thinking	69
Chapter 7: The Spectrum of Critical Thinking	83
Chapter 8: Analytic Thinking 101	97
Chapter 9: Analysis and Ambiguity	109
Chapter 10: The Uses of Complexity	121
Chapter 11: Truth and Consequences	133
Chapter 12: The Two Riddles of Causality	149
Chapter 13: Morality and the Liberal Arts	165
Chapter 14: Democracy and the Liberal Arts	181
About the Author	193

Acknowledgments

I can't enumerate all the people who have helped me in writing this book. The largest group, of course, has been other writers, and there is no greater canon in the English language than that of modern British philosophy. Among the names that stand out for me are Stuart Hampshire, Bernard Williams, and J. Renford Bambrough. Further inspiration came from such writers as Rolf Dobelli, Robert Grudin, Douglas Hofstadter, Emanuel Saner, Martin Minsky, Harvey Siegel, and Herbert Simon—to name just a few who buoyed me in my solitude.

On a more personal level, a chance remark by my friend John Delman was a crucial trigger, prompting me to join him in a course on Ludwig Wittgenstein, whose later work proved deeply informative as I wrote this book. For commenting on one or more chapters or passages, I wish to thank (among others) Elle Bisgaard-Church, Barbara Frankel, Chase Fuller, Charlotte Z. Rotterdam, and Richard Sclove. For expert editing of the whole, I'm indebted to Richard Osterweil and Maxine Phillips, and for general editorial counsel, I thank Bud Bynack.

Hans Oberdiek first infected me with a love of philosophy, and he remains among the most exasperatingly reasonable people I've ever known. Likewise, my thinking and reading have been guided and improved by the insights and stunning erudition of my friend Mitchell Cohen.

Early encouragement from Ariella Foss was greatly appreciated. Gregory M. Britton was exceptionally kind and helpful at a critical point, as was Petra Hardt of Suhrkamp Verlag. William Germano provided wise and timely advice, and Nicholas Lemann generously shared his ideas about liberal education.

For constant support and encouragement along the way, I especially thank Heidi Rotterdam, who remains at my side through thick and thin. She has provided thoughtful conversation and emotional intelligence on demand, as have Michael Bergmann, Barbara Esgalhado, Adam MacLean, Lewis

McDuffie, Raphael Mostel, and my children Winifred Scheuer Bonebrake and Jeremy Scheuer.

I have also benefited from the insights and ideas of (among others) Alfred Bloom, Daniel Brudney, Ana Diz, Maurice Eldridge, Cynthia Graae, Jay Hyams, Franz Leichter, the late Victor Navasky, the late Gretchen Salisbury, and André Spears. Communications with professors Ben Berger, Richard Eldridge, and T. Kaori Kitao of Swarthmore College, and John McKinnon of St. Mary's University, were invaluable.

Dan Bessire has been a tireless source of ideas, research, and supporting materials. For further research and assistance, I thank Molly Adea, Jean-Luc Banchereau, Lea Banchereau, Donna Drewes, Jessica Mendes, Mary Ellen Kennel, Mary Glen Fredrick, and Stephen Viksjo, and Dan Strassburger. Michell Thurmond and Mary Devlin Sobel, with their usual skill and grace, bore burdens on my behalf that enabled me to complete the work.

At Rowman & Littlefield, Carlie Wall and Nicole Carty provided expert editing, and without Tom Koerner, this book might not have come to fruition. Finally, I want to thank Gary, Keith, and Ron, who for many long seasons have kept me in the game.

Preface

Inside the Liberal Arts

> As no better man advances to take this matter in hand,
> I hereupon offer my own poor endeavors.
>
> —Herman Melville, *Moby-Dick*

A few years ago, I traveled with my son to the West Coast to look at a small liberal arts college that was not unlike the one I had attended in the East thirty years earlier. A late-spring snowfall had just coated the nearby mountains when we arrived at the campus. My son liked what he saw, and he ended up studying there. Coincidentally, his college had been my own second choice, and while my undergraduate experience was memorable, his fir-clad Oregon campus might have served me just as well as my Quaker arboretum in Pennsylvania.

What struck me most of all, in looking through the catalog of his college-to-be, was how much its curriculum resembled that of my alma mater—not then, but a third of a century earlier. Whereas my school had vastly diversified its course offerings—and its student body—since that time, the curriculum of my son's college was like mine in a time capsule: it had hewn to a narrower and more traditional approach to the "liberal arts."

I put "liberal arts" in quotation marks here not in disparagement but to emphasize just how ambiguous and problematic the term is, despite its wide usage, and also to highlight the fact that it embraces the different paths that two otherwise similar institutions have taken over the past generation. There remain crucial overlaps, of course. My college hasn't abandoned philosophy, literature, or the classics. It has merely added, among other offerings, Arabic, Asian studies, Chinese, cognitive science, computer science, environmental studies, film and media studies, gender and sexuality studies, interpretation theory, Islamic studies, and Japanese.

Both schools are avatars of academic excellence, and both can claim the mantle of a liberal arts college. More than anything else, it was seeing the contrast between two viable models—triggered by a sense of déjà vu in a course catalog—that prompted me to consider a series of interlacing questions about the meaning of liberal education and how it relates to critical thinking and citizenship. This book is the result.

So much for the genesis of the work. What about its form and destination? In brief, it began on what seemed like twin tracks, in response to the two original questions: What are the liberal arts, and what is critical thinking? But those tracks quickly converged as it became clear that they are really one and the same question. The universe of human knowledge is the universe of reason. It is useful to treat them as distinct entities, and I do so throughout the book. But as I hope to show, they are in fact two sides of the same coin. Some of what we call rationality or critical thinking applies beyond liberal learning. But it is also the very essence of liberal learning.

As I further discovered, there are many good books defending the liberal arts against their critics. And there are many good books about thinking, for the general reader, the philosopher, and for other students and scholars. But there are none that show how deeply the liberal arts and the study of thinking are connected.

Until now.

Inside the Liberal Arts is not a work of scholarship per se, nor is it a study of colleges, public or educational policy, or pedagogy. Its twin purposes are intertwined, if not inseparable: to elucidate the concepts of the "liberal arts" and "critical thinking," including how they lay the groundwork for full citizenship, and to guide readers toward becoming critical thinkers in the highest sense. In the process, the book identifies and explains some of the core concepts that connect the various liberal arts disciplines, forming a unified system of thinking and learning, with a common ancestry in philosophy. The aim is to provide a high baseline of intellectual literacy centered on critical thinking, as well as a map of the structure and purpose of liberal learning. In other words, to provide keys to the "ivory tower"—a trope I am unafraid to embrace, although I might choose another building material—and also the blueprint of that proverbial tower of learning.

I address in passing the ongoing conversation about the future of the liberal arts. That conversation is old and vital. It is ongoing of necessity, because any democratic culture is a dynamic, evolving organism in a state of perpetual crisis—a state of continual and contested change—and higher learning is an essential part of that process.

Broader discussions of the liberal arts are especially important at this moment, and they hover around the central questions of what we mean by the terms "liberal arts," "critical thinking," and "citizenship." All are essential to democracy. But it isn't my goal to add to the impressive stack of recent works on why liberal learning is important. Rather, this book is intended for anyone interested in those underlying questions: for all learners and seekers, including students, educators, and aspiring scholars who, like me, are still in the process of occupying their minds.

Reed College in Oregon and Swarthmore College in Pennsylvania were, in the 1970s, and remain today, institutions given over to scholarly rigor, open inquiry, and the joy of learning. In this they are not unlike many other American colleges and universities. Although Swarthmore has changed in ways that Reed has not, those core values remain intact at both institutions. Each pathway has its strengths and drawbacks, yet both are models of the liberal arts ideal at its best: an ideal that combines intellectual breadth, academic excellence, and moral and civic responsibility.

These institutions of higher learning and others like them across the country, large and small, public and private, collectively represent the signal achievement of American civilization: a beacon of intellectual empowerment to the nation and the world. Within their halls, in their classrooms, and along their walkways, students are challenged to discover how the liberal arts and critical thinking combine to promote citizenship in its fullest form: creativity, enterprise, intellectual and social mobility, and thoughtful engagement with the society those students are preparing to change, preserve, and make their own.

Chapter 1

The Liberal Arts Idea

> The value of a college education is not the learning of many facts but the training of the mind to think.
>
> —Albert Einstein

This is a book for all aspiring critical thinkers and citizens, including current, former, prospective, and lifelong students of the liberal arts. It aims, above all, to answer these three questions: What is critical thinking? What are the liberal arts? And how are they connected?

As we shall see, none of these terms has a single unambiguous definition, and one of the first tenets of critical thinking is the recognition that we can't ignore received definitions—but we can't always be slaves to them either. Definitions are sometimes malleable, but only up to a point. (We don't normally debate the definition of a "circle," for example, but we do debate the definitions of "art," "freedom," "justice," "education," "thinking," and "human nature.")

Mastery of such definitions is a point of departure. Definitions lend a measure of certainty and precision to shared discourse, but they are neither our masters nor our slaves. Rather, they are our tools. Certainty and precision are precious but limited commodities. More about that later.

Everything—almost everything—is a question of balance, and balance isn't just a matter of locating a stable fulcrum or striking a medium between extremes. It takes more mental work than that, as we explore the fifty-plus shades of gray in the world and try to locate useful truths or working hypotheses, however temporary or clouded by uncertainty, probability, or ignorance. We can't spend all our time thinking or balancing either; there's more to life.

The purpose of this book is not to plumb ancient questions in depth or to advance arguments about them. In that sense, it isn't a scholarly or academic work. Its intention is rather to explore some of those questions—to help *you* to think and argue about them. It will show how critical thinking forms a coherent system of inquiry that transcends particular disciplines and organizes the vital intellectual project we call the "liberal arts." Critical thinking is both the spine and the soul of that project.

The ideas, techniques, and principles in the book are not a set of tricks or shortcuts. They can't be applied without effort. They are not a substitute for reading, writing, talking, listening, or reflecting, and they don't replace learning about kinship, demand curves, or Cézanne. Rather, I hope these tools will help you to place your lifelong learning in a series of organizing frameworks by mapping it onto a wider universe—the universe of the liberal arts—and empower you to think more deeply, broadly, and clearly.

It is often said (typically without much explanation) that the liberal arts promote critical thinking. There's an important truth lurking in that statement, but what exactly does it mean, and how does it happen? *Inside the Liberal Arts* systematically connects the dots to answer those questions. It is both a primer on advanced critical thinking (or what I will call "critical inquiry") and a conceptual map of liberal learning. That map covers the range of basic tools for critical thinking, as well as certain buttressing concepts that further underscore the commonalities across the disciplines. Those "gateway concepts" of the liberal arts include language, rationality, analysis, truth, causality, and complexity.

As we study this map, we will look first at critical thinking, as a byword for rationality. Next, we'll explore each of the remaining gateway concepts in turn. Finally, we'll consider the complicated role of morality and moral reasoning in the liberal arts, concluding with a brief look at the external political context of how the liberal arts fit into a democratic society. As such, *Inside the Liberal Arts* is not a defense of liberal education. Other writers have defended the idea very capably. It is rather an exploration and explanation of the underpinnings so often lacking in liberal learning's defense.

THE LIBERAL ARTS IN CRISIS

Faced with the rising challenge from the STEM disciplines (science, technology, engineering, math), the liberal arts ideal is on the defensive in the United States. But warnings about the decline of liberal learning are hardly new; Jacques Barzun, the renowned scholar and dean at Columbia University, pronounced the liberal arts tradition "dead or dying" in 1963. A quarter century earlier, in 1938, James L. McConaughy asked in the *Journal of Higher Education*, "Is the Liberal-Arts College Doomed?"[1]

These educators may have spoken too soon, but they foresaw trends, and by some measures liberal learning is indeed worse off today. The number of residential liberal arts colleges on the traditional model has fallen, as curricula shift toward the STEM disciplines, although few are closing their doors. Students want jobs, not debt—and who can blame them?

The conversation around the liberal arts hasn't changed much either. It often sounds like this: "Many students and their parents now seek a clear and early connection between the undergraduate experience and employment. Vocationalism exerts pressure for substantive changes in the curriculum and substitutes a preoccupation with readily marketable skills." The problem described here is contemporary, yet these words were written by Donald L. Berry in 1977.[2] And we may still be having the same debate in 2077.

The liberal arts ideal continues to have its eloquent defenders, however, and there's evidence that good jobs do go to liberal arts graduates—eventually.[3] Despite the popularity of business and technology courses, students haven't abandoned the liberal arts in droves. According to the National Center for Education Statistics, degrees in the humanities, in proportion to all bachelor's degrees, declined just 0.1 percent from 1971 to 2010, from 17.1 percent to 17.0 percent. And in 2016 a leading educator observed that, "of the 1640 private, nonprofit institutions in the United States, only 33 have closed in the last 20 years."[4] So much for being doomed.

But this book mostly avoids questions of policy, politics, and culture, important as they are. It addresses these questions: What do we mean by the "liberal arts," and why should one study them at all? Why do we fall back on two standard answers—critical thinking and citizenship—and what is the connection between them? The aim here is to explore the forms of critical thinking that the liberal arts crucially entail. This book charts a course through the empire of liberal learning. It isn't the only such course, and the liberal arts aren't the only empire of learning. But the unifying ideas and techniques presented here identify skills and insights that are useful across the whole—and in life itself. In fact, that's the point of it all.

The liberal arts form a broad rubric, giving rise to many interesting questions that cannot be addressed here. The economic, cultural, technological, and pedagogic issues surrounding the liberal arts in this digital century—what subjects should be taught, how they should be taught, who should be educated, and how education should be funded—are beyond our scope. Nor will the notion of citizenship be explored in detail; we need only consider its conceptual outlines to see how it fits into the larger picture.[5]

Likewise, we won't be considering in depth the purported rationale for a liberal education as a means of developing ethical intelligence, or the kindred notions of developing character, the idea of well-roundedness, the skills of moral reasoning, or the virtues of living and learning in communities. However, these moral questions are indeed relevant to liberal education, and we won't ignore them entirely.

CULTURAL CONTRADICTIONS

A final demurral: The increasing pressure on liberal arts colleges to prepare students for careers (or to explain why they don't do so), reflected in Donald L. Berry's remarks, is also beyond the scope of this inquiry. However, because of the urgency of careerism as a threat to the liberal arts, two points are worth noting before we continue.

First, the conflict between vocationalism and the liberal arts represents one of the oldest and deepest fissures in American culture. It traces back to the alternate visions of Thomas Jefferson, the United States' first great apostle of education and founder of the University of Virginia, and Benjamin Franklin, the practical genius who valued learning but largely disdained the formal education of his day. (Franklin nevertheless founded an academy in Philadelphia that became the University of Pennsylvania.) The schism resurfaced in the late nineteenth and early twentieth centuries in the controversy between Booker T. Washington, author of *Up from Slavery*, who advocated skills training for African Americans, and W. E. B. Du Bois (*The Souls of Black Folk*), a forceful proponent of liberal learning.[6]

A variant of the same debate is found in the early twentieth century in the opposing views on citizenship and democracy of John Dewey and Walter Lippmann. And it continues to play out today across the information spectrum of education, old and new media, publishing, and popular culture. In its bluntest form, it is a conflict between knowledge and money, and between alternative visions of social mobility—visions that are in continuous conflict in democratic market societies.

We Americans didn't invent this controversy, however. Like liberal learning itself, it originated in ancient Greece, in the divide between the Sophists and the Socratics. The practical-minded Sophists advocated skills and specialized learning, whereas Plato's ideal curriculum (drawing on the teachings of Socrates) stressed dialectical reasoning and the analysis of concepts pertaining to the mind and society, thus laying the groundwork for philosophy, critical thinking, and the modern liberal arts. (Plato disdained both democracy and the arts—but nobody's perfect.)

The second point about this conflict is that pressures on schools and students for job-readiness do little or nothing to advance either personal or national prosperity, but they do a great deal of ambient damage to the culture of learning, always a fragile thing on these shores. Treating students as "customers," who only need to be taught immediately marketable skills, is just one form of such damage: a heady blend of ignorance and philistinism, with some class snobbery in the mix.

Ignoring or denying these underlying cultural contradictions impoverishes public discourse. Encouraging a course of education that teaches students to think, a crucial skill in an information-based economy, is not elitist. Rather, prejudging who gets to choose that course of education is elitism.

The careerist mentality ignores the values of liberal learning that go beyond the ability to get a good job right away or to make money. It ignores a democratic society's need for engaged citizens, and for freedom, innovation, community, and creativity in all spheres. It ignores the importance of the broader conversations that constitute a culture and the need for such general knowledge and core intellectual skills as depth, breadth, and clarity of thought and communication.

The demand that the liberal arts provide immediate career preparation also ignores the fact that greater certainty about finding a job right out of school doesn't necessarily equate with certainty about finding a better-paying job, a more secure or satisfying job, or one that leads to a steeper arc of personal success or fulfillment. It ignores the long-term benefits of liberal learning, which include breadth of vision, mobility and longer-term income, career satisfaction, and contributions to society. In short, it's ignorant of all the ways in which liberal learning promotes civic and cultural as well as economic growth, both for individuals and for society as a whole.

Before moving on, let me put the point more bluntly. This book doesn't defend the liberal arts; it explains them. Of course, we also need skills training of all kinds. But the liberal arts open doors to a wider range of careers, to lifelong learning, and to fuller preparation for citizenship than does education for particular skills. As such, liberal education isn't a form of elitism but the very opposite. If you're a student or parent worrying about tuition cost and student debt, you can hardly be faulted. But if you are looking at the liberal arts and asking, "What's the payoff?" you may be asking the wrong question.

Not everyone needs, wants, or can make use of the intellectual transformation that a liberal education offers, and there are other paths to useful and rewarding citizenship. We are all citizens in different ways, to different extents, and at different times in our lives. But all who are inclined should have the opportunity to occupy their minds. If most of the United States' cultural, economic, civic, and intellectual elites are beneficiaries of liberal education, that's a reason to open the gates to the garden, not to close them. It's also a reason to think it's a fruitful garden. Whether to open those gates to diverse cohorts of young people is a moral question. How to open them is a political question. What grows in that garden, how to harvest it, and why—that's what we're focusing on here.

WHAT ARE THE "LIBERAL ARTS"?

During the past century and a half, the United States has emerged as a superpower while adhering to a predominantly liberal arts–oriented model of higher education. Yet the term "liberal arts" is a complicated and antiquated one, yoking together two words that don't obviously belong in harness and may not be ideally suited for hauling their intellectual load in the twenty-first century. It isn't exclusively or obviously related to freedom in the modern sense, or to the arts, and the plural form is awkward and misleading.

The liberal arts rubric embraces dozens of commonly recognized fields of study, and new areas of inquiry have emerged along with interdisciplinary and cross-disciplinary study. What unites them under that rubric is what this book is about: the bundle of tools and techniques for thinking clearly, consistently, rationally, and critically. So let's look at the origin story.

The Western idea of the "liberal arts" dates to Latin writers of late antiquity, but the underlying questions about humanity, nature, and knowledge go back to the Greeks. "Liberal" comes from the notion of freeing the mind, but its original meaning wasn't the modern sense of the term. As Katie Billotte writes, "The Latin *ars liberalis* refers to the skills required of a free man— that is the skills of a citizen."[7] Slaves and women need not have applied, although male slaves sometimes served to tutor the young. The Greek term *Teknê*, although translated as "art," meant a practical skill or form of applied knowledge and had nothing to do with our modern notion of art or aesthetics.

Originally there were seven liberal "arts": the classical "trivium" of grammar, rhetoric, and logic, later combined with the medieval "quadrivium" of arithmetic, geometry, music, and astronomy. Of the seven, only music is an "art" in the contemporary sense. These subjects formed the basis for the system of higher education that emerged from the monasteries and cathedral schools of medieval Europe, beginning with the universities at Paris and Bologna during the twelfth century—the preadolescence of modern Western civilization. The original "arts" were supplemented in the later-medieval curriculum by philosophy, jurisprudence, theology, and medicine.

The eighteenth century saw a revival of the idea of liberal learning among such Enlightenment thinkers and philosophers as Jean-Jacques Rousseau, Immanuel Kant, and Denis Diderot. This revival embraced a web of new ideas: the exaltation of reason as a counterpart to empirical knowledge; an emphasis on pedagogy for citizenship and the moral education of the student; a visionary conception of an educated public, at a time of widespread illiteracy and political absolutism; a belief in the unity of knowledge across the arts and sciences and the centrality of philosophy itself, as reflected in

Diderot's *Encyclopedia* and Jean le Rond D'Alembert's introduction to it, the "Preliminary Discourse to the Encyclopedia."

Clearly the liberal arts model has evolved since then, and neither "liberal" nor "arts" adequately describes what we consider a liberal education. Yet we take for granted what is meant by the term; we define it, in effect, by patterns of usage and context, irrespective of the separate meanings of the two words and without much consideration of their joinder. Linguistic conventions have their purposes, and it may not be feasible to abolish the suboptimal term "liberal arts." However, the reasoning leading to such choices, and careful attention to language in general, are quintessential liberal arts practices. In fact, the question of what we mean by "critical thinking" and the "liberal arts" is a paradigm case.

There are at least three tacit, and overlapping, conceptions of the liberal arts in current usage. They form a kind of definitional wedding cake that is layered, nourishing, tasty, and widely shared. The whole "cake" assumes different outward forms, but they all serve a common general function of enrichment and mark a crucial rite of passage to a new life.

The broadest layer, typified by American liberal arts colleges, embraces the ideal of an integrated curriculum encompassing virtually all nonprofessional higher learning, from the natural and social sciences to the humanities and the performing arts. It's often associated with small, residential colleges—but you can also get a liberal education at Harvard or Wayne State. It's more about you than the school. In addition to this comprehensive sense of "liberal arts," a second common usage implicitly emphasizes the humanities and social sciences, while excluding (but not denigrating) the natural sciences. And at the top of the cake is a third, still narrower sense of the term that implicitly focuses on the humanities.

Any of these implied definitions may be valid in particular contexts, as long as we're clear about what we mean; yet the comprehensive one, which is invoked when we speak of "liberal learning" in general or a "liberal arts college" is arguably the most useful overall. At its best, that comprehensive vision (the base of the cake, so to speak) recognizes both the value and the limitations of such categories and the consequent need for interdisciplinary learning. In fact, some of the most exciting current scholarship is happening between the traditional disciplines, not within them. That base-layer conception also acknowledges the important distinctions that the traditional disciplinary boundaries reflect, and the value of focusing attention on particular (established or emerging) disciplines. We can have it both ways. In fact, critical thinking demands that we have it both ways.

Free and flexible minds are trained to recognize what we don't know from birth: that many areas of inquiry are interconnected and many boundaries are

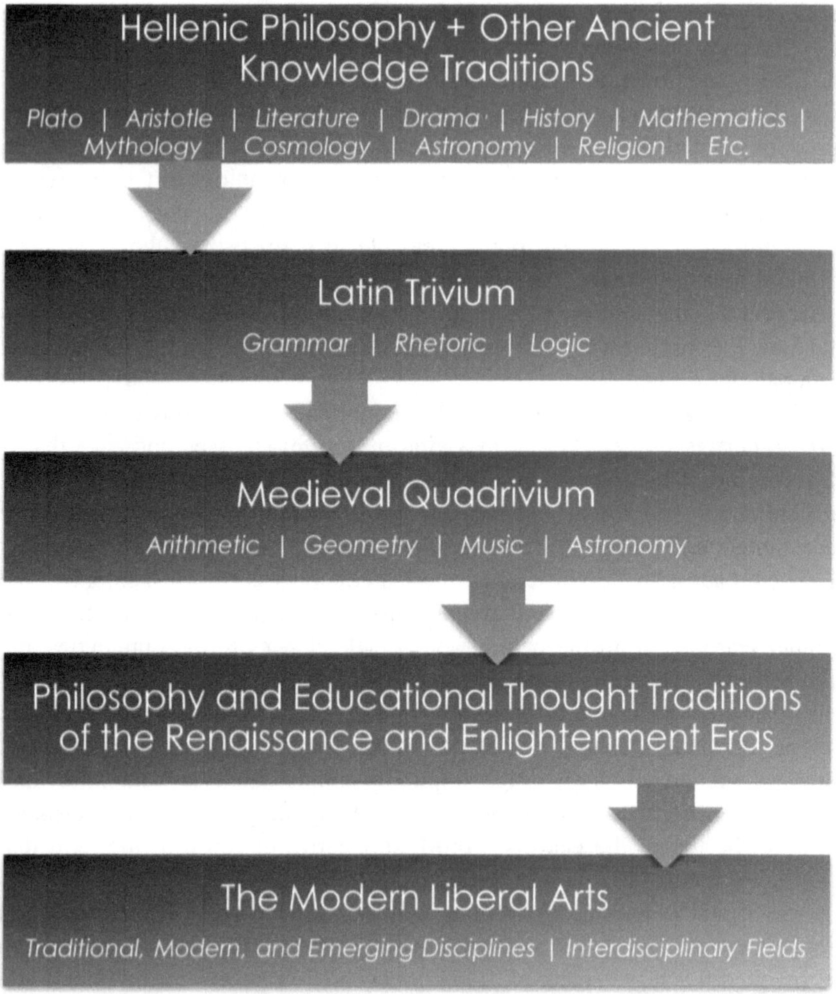

Hellenic Philosophy + Other Ancient Knowledge Traditions
Plato | Aristotle | Literature | Drama | History | Mathematics | Mythology | Cosmology | Astronomy | Religion | Etc.

Latin Trivium
Grammar | Rhetoric | Logic

Medieval Quadrivium
Arithmetic | Geometry | Music | Astronomy

Philosophy and Educational Thought Traditions of the Renaissance and Enlightenment Eras

The Modern Liberal Arts
Traditional, Modern, and Emerging Disciplines | Interdisciplinary Fields

Figure 1.1. The Emergence of the Liberal Arts Tradition

porous. Concepts and categories are instrumental and practical; using them without obscuring underlying connections is a hallmark of higher-level thinking. They are tools for the distinctions and connections that we need to make because everything is connected to, and defined in terms of, something else.

Thus, for example, climate change and biodiversity can only be properly understood as both distinct and related phenomena. Likewise psychology and neuroscience, economics and econometrics, literature and nonfiction, the scientist's view of nature and the poet's, or whatever can be usefully related to, but not conflated with, something else. In modern art, we explore the differences between Impressionism and Post-Impressionism, but also the commonalities, causal influences, and historical continuities. All knowledge is relational, and relations are connections without identity, commonality amid difference.

Similarly, depth and breadth of understanding are complementary qualities, not contradictory ones. The comprehensive liberal arts ideal is tied to the notion of breadth and well-roundedness: learning to think in more than one way, about more than one thing, and attaining a clearer sense of the overall landscape of knowledge. Such breadth is valuable as a foundation for later specialization, not to the exclusion of it.

In fact, two intertwining assumptions, among others, underlie the modern liberal arts tradition. One is that every academic discipline has unique questions to ask, and thus its own techniques and forms of knowledge, which account for its existence as a discipline. The other is that each discipline is linked to others through common questions, techniques, and ways of knowing. Critical thinking, properly conceived, is central to that shared epistemology, or theory of knowledge: a set of intellectual skills that apply across the disciplines of liberal learning.

The tools of critical thinking are what hold together the three-tiered wedding cake. Citizenship is the form of community that it nourishes. Paul H. Hirst makes the point more precisely: "Whatever else a liberal education is, it is *not* a vocational education, *not* an exclusively scientific education [and] *not* a specialist education in any sense." It is rather "an education based fairly and squarely on the nature of knowledge itself."[8]

THE NATURE OF KNOWLEDGE

This idea of "the nature of knowledge" cuts to the very heart of the liberal arts (let's leave the cake aside for now), and in doing so it immediately implicates philosophy, which is centrally concerned with knowledge and thought. Philosophy is the mother of most areas of liberal learning, and midwife to many others. Those other disciplines contain it in their DNA—largely, as I will suggest, in the form of critical thinking and the "gateway" concepts that buttress it.

Thus, what we archaically call "the liberal arts" actually begins not with the Latin trivium and quadrivium but with the Greeks, who asked the first systematic questions in the Western world about nature, knowledge, value, and society. Ancient philosophy, through the development of rationality, including formal logic and analytic discourse (originally known as "dialectic"), evolved as a system for organizing and understanding the known world—nature, human nature and behavior, culture and imagination—and the eventual (useful but not immutable or impermeable) divisions between the sciences, social sciences, and humanities.

In other words, human knowledge is a system; and the defining feature of any system is that it contains separate but interacting parts. This is true whether we're talking about gears in a watch, organs in a body, phases in a natural cycle (such as photosynthesis, metamorphosis, or evolution), instruments in an orchestra, institutions in a community, or realms of knowledge. The liberal arts form such an evolving system, consisting of stable but impermanent areas and modes of inquiry that merge at some points and divide at others, adapting to cultural shifts while sharing a common language and assumptions, and overlapping knowledge bases and techniques. This interconnection of parts is also reflected in how we use language—another prototypical system. We ourselves are stable but mutable entities. So, for that matter, are families, communities, civilizations, and planets.

However else we may define the liberal arts, as a system of learning, there is no uniquely correct approach or methodology, and no text, thinker, or institution that perfectly exemplifies the idea. The liberal arts are not just a domain of inquiry, a set of learning tools, or a single value or idea; rather, the liberal arts are a group of ideas that share what Ludwig Wittgenstein called a "family resemblance," exhibiting, in various permutations and degrees, a common set of attributes.

Liberal learning doesn't aim primarily to inculcate practical skills, or dump data into students' brains, though it may teach a useful fact or two. Rather, it promotes both domain-specific knowledge and the intellectual skills of critical thinking. In doing so, it also presents a panoply of organizing ideas and the habits of curiosity and questioning; an openness to diverse perspectives; a capacity for seeing relationships, patterns, and systems; an appetite for analyzing things in terms of their constituent parts and their connections to other things and to larger wholes; and the ability to judge when it's time to stop analyzing and smell the roses.

Critical thinkers tolerate uncertainty, ambiguity, complexity, and divergent values while also looking for usable truths, workable consensuses, deeper understanding, and clearer communication. They recognize that these intellectual values can't be achieved in any final sense, that they can't be codified in any final form, and that they can't always be achieved at once, and trade-offs and compromises are necessary in learning and thinking as in life. But those intellectual values are unlikely to go out of fashion.

DECONSTRUCTING THE IVORY TOWER

Overall, then, this book might be considered a kind of intellectual X-ray of the liberal arts, revealing their internal skeletal structure, as opposed to an MRI of the soft tissue of particular fields. But it's more than just a conceptual map. Instead, you might think of it as a guidebook for your active development as a thinker. The concepts we'll talk about are a set of navigational tools (and an imperfect set, like any other) for intellectual voyagers. You will form your own mental maps and revise them as you continue on your journey.

Another common metaphor of higher learning is that of the ivory tower. It's a somewhat tarnished trope, having acquired a pejorative connotation of splendid isolation and detachment from the world. Why embrace it? Because higher education is indeed (somewhat) isolated and detached from the world, and necessarily so—isolated in the best sense. It's primarily about learning and not about other forms of doing. But that doesn't preclude studying real-world problems, learning from internships, holding a job, playing a sport, performing community service, engaging in politics, or going about other worldly activities.

In fact, the ivory tower trope is entirely consistent with ways of learning that immerse the student in off-campus communities—or learning at home on your own time. It merely emphasizes the more focused environments that are also important to learning, such as the campus, the classroom, the laboratory, the library, or your study.

Again, the tower metaphor is not about relevance or irrelevance; all education is relevant to something, and relevance is relative. What the tower evokes is a step-by-step climb with a more rewarding view the higher you ascend: a panorama of the "real world" that remains with you through life along with the skills you've acquired—the metaphorical muscles developed in climbing. The purpose of critical inquiry is to create such a sturdy stairway to citizenship. A corollary notion is that while all learning about particular subjects is important, learning how to think well is all-important. Liberal education at its best means acquiring a range of critical thinking skills; there is no single point or plane of absolutely essential content.

Of course, on the climb to becoming a more critical thinker, you will learn much else as well, including domain-specific knowledge and skills: facts and frameworks, rules and methodologies, arguments and controversies, causal schemes and contextual relations. And you'll find that the boundaries between skills, facts, and conceptual knowledge are often fuzzy. You may study art, physics, sociology, or French colonial literature and put that knowledge to good use; we each follow a different route up the tower. But it's not just about the subject matter, and no matter the subject, if the teaching and learning are rigorous the mental-fitness benefits are the same.

Such rigor is important everywhere, from classrooms, laboratories, or studios to meeting rooms, courtrooms, boardrooms, engine rooms, and construction sites. As Ralph Waldo Emerson wrote in his seminal essay "The American Scholar," "We all know, that as the human body can be nourished on any food, though it were boiled grass and the broth of shoes, so the human mind can be fed by any knowledge." Mastering the skills and concepts of critical inquiry enables you to think about—or to learn to think about—anything.

Consequently, another corollary is that branching out beyond Western culture and its so-called canon isn't just crucial for any wider map of human knowledge. It is also just as likely to promote critical thinking, as long as it is approached critically and without an unexamined agenda—for example, one that is reflexively either pro- or anti-Western, or shaped exclusively by narrow frames or assumptions. Reflexive thinking is uncritical: a wall, not a gateway. Nor is critical inquiry the sole province of elite thinkers or institutions; it is rather the hallmark of higher learning at its best, anywhere. The ivory tower that you climb may be at your public library, or it may be a stack of books scrounged from elsewhere. It worked for Lincoln.

NOTES

1. James L. McConaughy, "Is the Liberal-Arts College Doomed?" *Journal of Higher Education* 9:2 (February 1938): 59–67.
2. Donald L. Berry, "The Liberal Arts as Attitude," *Journal of General Education* 29:3 (Fall 1977): 228.
3. A January 2014 study by the AAC&U (Association of American Colleges and Universities) titled *How Liberal Arts and Sciences Majors Fare in Employment* finds that—along with a wider perspective on the world and better communication and critical thinking skills—liberal arts majors outearn, at the peak earning ages, those with professional or preprofessional academic backgrounds.
4. David L. Warren, president, National Association of Independent Colleges and Universities, letter to the *New York Times*, May 12, 2016.
5. A more in-depth study of democratic citizenship, on the other hand, would raise the questions of who should be educated and what they should learn.
6. See, for example, Michael S. Roth, *Beyond the University: Why Liberal Education Matters*. New Haven, CT: Yale University Press, 2015, ch. 2.
7. Katie Billotte, "Conservatives Killed the Liberal Arts," Salon.com, September 14, 2012. Retrieved from www.salon.com/ 2012/09/14/conservatives_killed_the_liberal_arts/#.

8. Paul H. Hirst, "Liberal Education and the Nature of Knowledge," in R. D. Archambault, ed., *Philosophical Analysis and Education*, 13. London: Routledge & Kegan Paul, 1965.

Chapter 2

The Liberal Arts and Triangular Citizenship

> Democracy has to be born anew every generation, and education is its midwife.
>
> —John Dewey

The liberal arts have traditionally been defended as being integral to two interconnected goals of democracy: critical thinking and citizenship. That relationship is not accidental, and such arguments are indeed compelling—once it's clear what is meant by those terms. The meaning of critical thinking, and how we go about it, will be the main focus of the remainder of this book. But first, we need to see how it relates to citizenship.

The subject of citizenship can be treated rather summarily here because our concern isn't how citizenship succeeds or fails, or the various forms it may assume, but its general connection to liberal learning. This doesn't require, for example, that we review the tortured history of the struggle for citizenship in the United States, or the fraught question of the legal definition of "citizen." What we need, in other words, is a clear overall conception of citizenship's nature and purpose. We can leave the rest to political thinkers.

Recall that the idea of democratic citizenship is implicit in the origins of the term "liberal arts": Two millennia ago, that term referred to the requisite skills of a Roman citizen. Let's add a general definition to that: "citizenship" refers to how we relate, as individuals, to larger communities. It refers mostly to positive interactions of mutual give-and-take, not to harmful, annoying, or criminal behavior; belonging to a gang isn't citizenship but its opposite.

Armed with that general definition, we can see that (like the liberal arts) democratic citizenship in the modern context divides rather neatly into three general forms, each of which is advanced by liberal education. That's because there are three broad ways in which we, as individuals, participate in larger communities. And like many interesting objects of critical inquiry, those three forms are both distinct and connected. In other words, they form a system. The concepts of the liberal arts and citizenship are alike in being both comprehensive and systemic, referring to a social ecology: of communities of knowledge and of broader communities, respectively. And both depend on participation by informed and thoughtful citizens. The three main dimensions of that ecology (as depicted in figure 2.1) are civic, economic, and cultural.

The civic dimension embraces a wide range of activities from voting and jury service to political advocacy and dialogue, demonstrating, organizing, volunteering with or supporting nonprofit organizations, and other forms of democratic participation. What unifies all these activities is the focus on making or unmaking laws and policies, choosing or replacing lawmakers, and influencing other citizens toward those ends.

The second dimension is economic citizenship, which means being a productive member of a community, whether working in a factory, farm, home, office, garage, or boardroom. Robbing banks doesn't count. Economic citizenship also involves being a critical consumer and seeing the underlying connections between the political and economic (and scientific and technological) spheres. Consider how computers and personal devices, for example, have increased opportunities for individuals to be informed and to participate—in addition to their downsides.

The third kind of citizenship (and the particular focus of the humanities) is engagement with the various ideas, values, customs, traditions, events, and conversations that constitute a culture. The arts, popular culture, religion, and

Figure 2.1. Triangular Citizenship

sports are all potential venues for such cultural conversations. Perhaps it's no coincidence that many liberal arts colleges were founded by religious sects or that they sponsor cultural events and campus organizations and field sports teams. Like the campus itself, all are important forms of community that can enhance civic skills and buttress communities of learning.

This three-cornered model isn't proposed simply because it forms a powerful justification for the liberal arts. Other geometric schema could serve that purpose. The triangle reflects the actual connections between politics, economics, and culture in society at large and the connections we as individuals have to the world on all three levels. In short, the triangular model works better than, say, a conception of citizenship as having one, two, or fifty-eight basic forms. It fits the case.

Of course, it's not quite that simple; models never are. The three types of citizenship interrelate in subtle as well as obvious ways, and they are neither mutually exclusive nor, perhaps, jointly exhaustive. They are rather the most visible dimensions of the ecology of democratic life. One could argue for a variety of other forms alongside or subsumed within that triad: for example, corporate citizenship; environmental, informational, or moral citizenship; or civic engagement through leadership, teaching and mentoring, spiritual guidance, or military or other public service.

Like all models, in other words, triangular citizenship simplifies by assimilating diverse ideas and activities to broader categories. And when we look at a more complex version of the triangle (figure 2.2), we can see important influences and interactions among the three general types, running in both directions. For example, economic and civic citizenship are related through laws, regulations, and policies that affect the economic sphere, whereas, in the opposite direction, economics affects politics and law in areas such as corporate lobbying and private campaign finance. The economic realm affects the cultural one through foundation grants, philanthropic gifts, and endowments to nonprofit organizations such as colleges and universities. And conversely, the arts, and culture in general, affect the economy through spending and job creation.

Meanwhile, the cultural realm affects the civic insofar as the arts and popular culture generate social commentary and help to shape the political climate. Reciprocally, the civic realm affects the cultural by defining the limits of speech and expression, as well as by promoting the cultural commons through public and nonprofit (tax-exempt) support for the arts, museums, libraries, and other cultural institutions.

More broadly, the civic and cultural dimensions of society intersect in establishing the overall scope and tenor of public media and debate. Such discourse is civic in the sense that it includes important public conversations about the democratic sphere (the laws and the lawmakers). But it's also

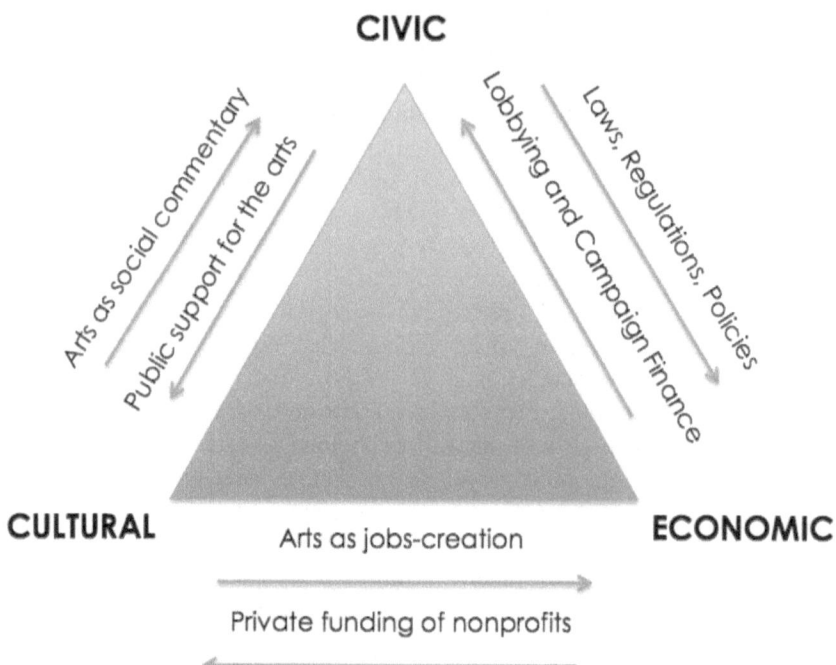

Figure 2.2. Triangular Citizenship

cultural in that it isn't state sponsored, state originated, or state influenced. It's an information free-for-all that includes formal and informal dialogue, new and old media, facts, spin, lies, rumors, opinions, and just about everything else we read, hear, or see in the arts and popular and commercial culture. A college or university, although not a strictly democratic community, is at once a training ground for democratic participation; an economic enterprise with paying customers, whose seemingly exorbitant tuition fees still may not cover the costs of educating students; and a cultural institution, where those students experience the arts both as objects of study and via direct engagement as creators and audiences.

Most social activity falls under at least one of these three rubrics or on a spectrum between them. What the three rubrics have in common is that they connect individuals to the wider community and the public good. Caring for oneself, one's family, or one's pet is a good thing, but it isn't citizenship per se; it's a special, more intimate form of community. But caring about a neighbor or neighborhood, a cause or organization, or a remote community of people you've never met is citizenship. Walking your dog isn't an act of citizenship. Cleaning up after your dog is.

Moreover, the boundaries between high culture, pop culture, civic culture, and economics are often fuzzy—as any day at the ballpark or night at the opera will attest. Running an art collective, a nonprofit theater or orchestra, or a college is an economic as well as a cultural activity, and it has a civic dimension as well. Economic activities have political effects and implications and vice versa. Being a productive citizen can benefit others (although not all forms of profit-seeking qualify) and may facilitate civic participation in the other domains.

In sum, all three types of civic engagement are internally diverse and spill over into one another. All promote active stakeholding in society that involves give-and-take: individual and societal contributions and benefits. Citizenship in all its forms is a two-way street. Indeed, this idea dovetails with our general definition of citizenship: any activity that benefits oneself and others in tandem within a common culture, whether civic, economic, cultural, or otherwise.

The aim here, however, is not to parse the idea of citizenship. It is to understand the role of liberal learning in fostering vibrant and prosperous communities with broad and deep participation, and public conversations marked by fairness, inclusion, and (where critical thinking comes in) intellectual rigor. These core democratic values are at least as important in the twenty-first century as they were in the Roman republic of *ars liberalis*.

Two key points follow from the citizenship triangle. One is that education (formal or otherwise) underlies, and largely determines the quality of, public participation in all three sectors. That's because all three are essentially information driven, ideas driven, and values driven. They don't run on natural gas. Second, given the breadth of the citizenship model, education has *no other public purpose* than to promote one or another form of citizenship. Without education, none of those forms of citizenship is possible, and neither is democracy itself.

DEMOCRACY FIRST: THE PRIMACY OF THE CIVIC REALM

Having outlined this triangular model of democratic citizenship, I'd now like to tilt that triangle a few degrees by adding some extra moral and intellectual weight to the civic dimension, to suggest its limited primacy over the other two. What "limited primacy" means is this: Whereas all three corners of the triangle are vital to a democracy, the civic realm is in an important practical (if not logical) sense paramount. We all want a healthy economy and a vibrant culture along with our political freedoms, but without those freedoms, the rest is compromised. Basic democratic values—such as political equality, inclusion, fairness, civil rights, and open government—are uniquely instrumental to the values associated with material and cultural wealth: they provide the legal framework that shapes the other two domains.

The formal nature of law, its universal scope and potential reach into all areas of society (including where it is properly silent), are what give it disproportionate influence; the law—and ultimately, the citizenry—has the final say. What it should say, how much influence it should have on those spheres and in what ways, are exactly the kinds of things we argue about in a robust democratic culture. To be sure, cultural and economic factors play into the nature of democracy too, shaping our individual lives and values perhaps more directly than the law. We express our personal interests in terms of the jobs we hold, the things we buy, the people we hang out with, and the events we attend, as well as in the voting booth or on social media.

Democratic governments don't produce art, media, or popular culture—or diapers or ball bearings. Rather, they must protect our ability to generate those things. But the legal-political system is the ultimate mechanism of structural stability or change that governs our culture and our economy. It isn't just an accessory to cultural and economic enterprise but the very framework of debate: a continuing referendum on their nature and limits. Along with providing for national security and other essential services, such as roads and schools, sponsoring those debates is the essential democratic function. Democracies have no higher function. That's why the civic realm deserves some extra weight in the triangle of citizenship—not because voting or canvassing is more fun than drawing a paycheck or going to a museum.

Analogous to the primacy of civic democracy is the primacy of certain civil rights—freedom of speech, assembly, and the press—*within* democracy: other rights, and all democratic discourse, are predicated on them. As Alexis de Tocqueville put it, "The sovereignty of the people and the freedom of the press are . . . two entirely correlative things." Freedom of the press, he concluded, "is the principal and . . . the constitutive element of freedom."[1]

A mature democracy is a self-regulating system of citizens: it must constantly attend to the quality of its laws and institutions for promoting appropriate forms and levels of freedom and equality. And "it" here refers to the people and their representatives, not some abstraction or disembodied force. What counts as appropriate? That is for the people to decide and redecide, within the evolving legal and constitutional framework. What matters most of all is an engaged and informed public, and a government accountable to them—not the quality of opera, the level of taxation, or the number of corporate mergers.

Ironically, however, democratic governments have little power to ensure an informed and engaged public; that's largely up to its citizens. We can advocate for better education, better media, or longer public library hours, or we can do nothing. Education, media consumption, and participation are how we get informed. In democracy, as in life, everything interrelates.

THE LIBERAL ARTS TRIFECTA

What has all this to do with the liberal arts? The answer is now clear. By emphasizing rigorous critical thinking, liberal learning promotes engagement in *all three sectors* of citizenship. And to the extent that the civic sector is primary and conditions the other two, a liberal arts education is the widest and most effective route to citizenship. It isn't the only route, or the only good route, but it's the one with the most bearing on civic knowledge and participation in all three spheres.

The same intellectual skills that constitute rigorous critical inquiry also inform democracy, because both are ideally rational, truth-centered, fact-based processes of thinking systematically within communities. Citizenship and rationality are thus integral to one another, as forms of community (like a common language) whose members do not necessarily share other values or traditions. Citizenship is rationality in its public democratic form. The aforementioned portable intellectual skills apply equally to business and economic enterprise, culture and imagination, and civic engagement. But we're citizens first, and artists, bricklayers, scientists, or investment bankers second.

That said, we have no formal or legal duty to be good citizens (other than a duty to obey the law), though we may well have moral duties as citizens. Many of us, by choice or otherwise, fail to exercise the most precious and concrete right we have: the right to vote. But even the most passive citizens have rights and duties vis-à-vis the wider public. And whatever our personal or tribal proclivities, we can't use the same roads, drink the same water, breathe the same air, attend the same schools, enjoy the same protections, or share the same culture without incurring certain debts to one another and to the common good.

The triangular model doesn't depend on any particular ideal of what it means to be a citizen, or any ideology. It's minimalist for a reason: because democratic cultures don't define us; they're a matrix for collective and individual self-definition. They don't dictate how we should live our lives, who should govern, or how they should govern; rather, they're designed to empower us to make those decisions collectively. We engage, as individuals, in various forms of elective social behavior. Most of us pay taxes, but we each have our own unique heat map of types and levels of citizenship. Unless you're a hermit, simply having a pulse means you are part of concentric communities, from family to neighborhood to nation to planet.

> Every citizen doesn't need to do everything, but each one of us can do one thing.
>
> —Marie L. Yovanovitch[2]

Education, likewise, isn't one-size-fits-all. A liberal education isn't for everyone, nor is it essential for anyone, in order to be a good citizen. A life spent in service to others is exemplary of citizenship even if that citizen is illiterate. But triangular citizenship completes the picture of what liberal learning is all about. It's about being a citizen, potentially, in all three dimensions. There is nothing else for it to be about.

Even if some of us limit our civic engagement by choice or necessity, society as a whole still needs robust activity in all three dimensions. We can survive without many of the goods and services we create, and not a few of the Broadway musicals, but without markets for goods and services, laws and public policies, ideas, opinions, and works of imagination, our lives would be impoverished and self-government impossible.

CRITICAL THINKING AND CITIZENSHIP

What does critical thinking have to do with active citizenship? In a word: everything. Critical thinking is rationality, and rationality—thinking based on shared and transparent rules and reasons—is the beating heart of both learning and democratic life. It is the basis of all communication, including language itself as a system of symbolic, phonetic, and grammatical rules, and thus of all learning and public discourse: it is how we navigate our way as individuals in society.

Another word for this sphere of shared experience is "intersubjectivity." We think "subjectively" in our dreams, our inner lives, private conversations, therapy sessions, or in diaries that no one else reads, and we reason "objectively" in those realms (such as logic and mathematics) where the truth is singular—that is, where it's based on following shared rules and there is no room for choice. But we are also (family-bred, socially formed, historically conditioned) individuals, with needs, desires, and personal and social goals that we cannot advance without thinking and talking in groups.

And so, we think publicly—intersubjectively: in classrooms, boardrooms, committee rooms, broadcast studios, social media, football huddles, and elsewhere. Our intersubjectivity, as creatures who live together in communities, imposes the need for baseline forms of rationality, such as implicit rules of order and civility, and those embedded in the shared symbolic systems of math, logic, and language itself.

Now that we're on the subject of thinking (and we'll be staying on it for quite a while), let me emphasize one more point as a segue to getting down to the business of exploring critical thinking. Conceptual thinking—thinking in generalities, thinking abstractly, thinking critically and rationally—is not an abstruse or arcane activity. It is intrinsic to all thinking, all learning, and all democratic citizenship. This is not just because the sole purpose of education is to promote triangular citizenship. It's because both are rooted in language and the need for rule-based, fact-based, intersubjective discourse.

We often distinguish between two kinds of reasoning or rationality: practical (or instrumental) and conceptual. On one hand, any effective action in society (even robbing banks or hacking computers, the very antitheses of citizenship) is based on rational deliberation, whether it's personal strategizing or coordinated planning in groups. To get on in the world with any degree of efficacy, one must be a (somewhat) rational agent. Of course, we aren't equally rational or equally disposed to use our rational faculties. But, except when acting in total isolation (as when fishing alone), we need to factor in the ways in which we cohabit the planet with others. That's practical reasoning: reasoning about how to achieve personal or shared ends.

Conceptual rationality, on the other hand, is about how we model the world in order to understand it, communicate about it, and act within it. Concepts such as democracy and justice, freedom and equality, community and neighborhood, family and education, compel us to think in political terms and to see larger wholes and deeper patterns than what is immediate to us. Conceptual thinking and rational behavior in communities—most of all the kind of rational behavior we call democratic citizenship—are distinguishable but never separable.

Obviously, we need both kinds of rationality. The hemispheres of thought and action are nominally distinct but always intertwined. In fact, without abstract thinking (including ideological thinking and rational ways of acquiring knowledge and adjudicating value conflicts), we could scarcely be politically conscious at all. Even irrational and antisocial behaviors or prejudices are based on the abuse of (otherwise indispensable) abstractions such as race, sex, religion, or ethnicity. Demagogues use language rationally to achieve their ends, even as they appeal to the irrational in their audience. Scholars or scientists can sometimes explain how these ideas enter our heads and hearts, but they can't alter or dispel them. The tinkering of geniuses can't bring down (or keep in place) Confederate monuments. Democratic citizens must argue about such things.

In short, whatever our beliefs or values, we don't just think about ourselves or our families. We also think about neighbors, friends, colleagues, public figures, and more broadly about groups, movements, issues, problems, and threats. All of these are abstractions; all words are abstractions, and abstractions are rational tools. Rationality is thus as integral to active citizenship as it is to brewing coffee. It's the essential ingredient for locating ourselves in the world, expressing our interests, and thinking and acting in communities.

Whatever our other commitments, we are also parts of larger wholes: communities with shared needs, internal differences, common and limited resources, and roughly similar circumstances (human). Democratic cultures, however flawed, give rational order to competition and cooperation in pursuit of such ends. Without abstract and systematic thinking, starting with the use of a shared language, we would have little traction in those pursuits, either in learning or in the wider world.

As noted in chapter 1, Americans tend to gravitate, by choice or necessity, toward either of two broad paths of learning: the more skill-based vocational path or the more academic one of liberal education. There are gradations in between, to be sure. STEM learning, for instance, is something of a hybrid. Although academic in nature, its perceived vocational advantages, degree of specialization, and emphasis on applied skills often set it apart from the liberal arts. American culture celebrates practicality, at times to a fault. Practicality is a fine thing; the ingenuity of the Wright brothers in their bicycle shop put the world of organized science to shame. But we aren't just inventors or tinkerers, and it's foolish to pretend that ideas, controversies, or contested values are mere nuisances that happen along and get in the way of "practical solutions." They are the essence of democracy.

Any complex society needs a range of educational paths. It needs productive workers of all kinds: pilots, farmers, teachers, hairdressers, gravediggers, and technicians as well as artists, teachers, and all-around good citizens who help others and stay out of jail. But for all the importance of vocational and STEM learning, a liberal education (whatever its economic risks or benefits) prepares students for all three forms of citizenship. That's worth thinking about.

NOTES

1. Alexis de Tocqueville, *Democracy in America*, Vol. 1 (trans. George Lawrence). New York: Harper Perennial Modern Classics, 2006, Part II, chs. 3–4.

2. Marie L. Yovanovitch, "These Are Turbulent Times. But We Will Persist and Prevail," *Washington Post*, February 6, 2020. Retrieved from https://www.washingtonpost.com/opinions/2020/02/06/marie-yovanovitch-ukraine-ambassador-american-institutions-need-us/.

Chapter 3

Gateways to Critical Inquiry

> Critical inquiry is the process of gathering and evaluating information, ideas, and assumptions from multiple perspectives to produce well-reasoned analysis and understanding, and leading to new ideas, applications and questions.
>
> —Critical Inquiry Program, University of South Carolina, Aiken

DEFINING CRITICAL INQUIRY

In the previous chapters we surveyed the history and definition of the liberal arts and their connection to the idea of triangular citizenship. "Citizenship" in the latter sense refers to the civic, economic, and cultural roles of individuals and institutions within democratic communities. As has been suggested, triangular citizenship is the ultimate raison d'être of liberal learning, encompassing everything that we do in the public arena. Strictly speaking, higher learning is neither necessary nor sufficient for citizenship of any given type or degree; Abraham Lincoln was self-educated. But the liberal arts expand the possibilities in all three citizenship domains. Thus, Lincoln sent his son to Harvard.

Having framed the structure and purpose of the liberal arts tradition, we can now ask, What makes that tradition a coherent and unified whole, over and above the many disciplines it encompasses? What is its animating core? As I've already suggested, the simple answer is "critical thinking." However, we still haven't defined "critical thinking." And before doing that, we need to explore several other preliminary ideas.

Spoiler alert: Things may get a bit muddy at this point, but if you bear with me there will be greater clarity downstream. General concepts are necessarily complex ones, especially when they are interrelated, and the concepts of critical inquiry, rationality, and critical thinking are exemplars of that. Their definitions are necessarily imprecise; being both vague and general, their boundaries are porous and their meanings overlap.[1] And yet each of the three terms is useful and all are widely used. Often what differentiates them, beyond those overlapping definitions, is their connotations or the different contexts in which we use them. Any such usage, as one philosopher aptly notes, "may be valuable for the light it sheds and dangerous because of the shadow it casts."[2] Acknowledging this predicament of complexity is our point of departure.

Relating these concepts isn't a simple matter of fitting them together like the pieces of a jigsaw puzzle or countries on a map, with clear and unique boundaries. We can't view them as separate and unrelated ideas, but neither can we conflate them. Instead, we need to tease them apart without masking their connections. And that method of understanding is analytic thinking.

As we'll see in due course, a range of types or levels of thinking have evolved in the West along with, and inseparable from, liberal learning. For now, we're broadly equating those forms of critical thinking with rationality: the use of rules and/or reasons in thinking. The concept of critical inquiry usefully describes that spectrum of rationality as a whole, *within the liberal arts context*. In other words, there are other modes or applications of rationality—"practical" rationality in everyday life, problem solving, computing, mathematics, business, medicine, architecture, space exploration. "Critical inquiry" is a convenient name for the various forms of rationality that are used within the liberal arts: the whole toolbox of liberal learning.

That said, there's nothing wrong with the definition of critical inquiry proposed above by the University of South Carolina, Aiken. It's a plausible one, if a bit vague. Our definition is somewhat narrower: by focusing on the toolbox of critical thinking, it emphasizes "well-reasoned analysis and understanding." It implies, but doesn't foreground, the process of "gathering and evaluating information," without which there isn't much to think about.

THE TYRANNY OF TERMINOLOGY

Most conceptual terms are, in fact, useful compromises. That's why we need analytical reasoning: to make those compromises as clearly and efficiently (and as transparently) as possible. For example, the terms "rationality" and "critical thinking," as commonly used, are nearly synonymous. Each has particular applications and contextual shadings, but there is no obvious distinction between them that applies across the board, effecting a neat logical division, or that doesn't obscure more than it reveals.

Because of this tyranny of terminology—the breadth, vagueness, and interconnectedness of concepts—we need to analyze them using critical tools. And to begin that process often means resorting to stipulative definitions—that is, definitions based on logic and convenience that announce, "This is how I'm going to use the term." Authors don't get to rewrite dictionaries or dictate usage. But in dealing with general and gelatinous concepts, dictionaries don't get us far enough. Stipulating definitions involves no sleight of hand, invention, or make-believe. Nor does it allow us to make any term mean whatever we please. It's rather a strategic and plausible delimitation of meaning for the immediate purposes.

To be useful, a stipulative definition must satisfy at least three basic conditions: it should be clear; it should be used consistently; and while it may be broader or narrower than other uses of the term, it shouldn't contradict them or mean something entirely different. Using "critical inquiry" as an umbrella term to cover the spectrum of critical thinking in the liberal arts meets those conditions and also works on other levels. The words "critical" and "inquiry" each bring something important to their marriage: "critical" implies questioning and self-questioning, while "inquiry" suggests searching and learning. The breadth and vagueness of "critical inquiry" makes it all but useless without stipulating a definition.

The term "liberal arts" is similarly tricky. It's in the awkward plural form, combining two independently ambiguous words. And it can be defined in at least two quite different ways. Methodologically, it refers to the various kinds of rational or critical thinking we're identifying with critical inquiry, and substantively (recalling the wedding cake analogy), it denotes the various subjects and disciplines in which such thinking is applied. We're focusing here on the methodological side. Thus, critical inquiry is the common intellectual currency, in various denominations, that enables deeper and broader understanding of any particular field, be it history, sociology, or Japanese literature.

Thus defined, critical inquiry equates with the values of intellectual rigor: clarity and consistency; adherence to the rules of logic and the guidelines of informal logic; a commitment to the pursuit of truth, however contextually defined; and the refusal to take things or words at face value and willingness to look below surfaces. In short, it embraces the array of intellectual best practices that are conducive to flexibility of thought and breadth and depth of understanding. Figure 3.1 outlines schematically what we'll be covering over the next six chapters and beyond. Critical inquiry combines rigorous *systematic* thinking (thinking according to shared rules) with *systemic* thinking (about how things are related and how they are distinct); we'll explore that distinction further in due course. And it applies across disciplines, methodologies, and cultures.

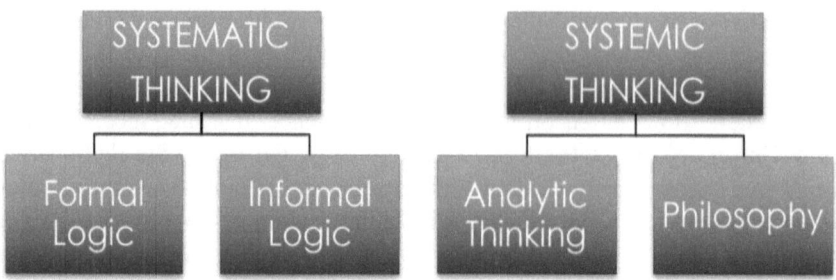

Figure 3.1. Systematic Thinking

THE USES AND LIMITS OF PHILOSOPHY

As a toolbox for thinking, critical inquiry naturally resembles its parent discipline, which is philosophy. And so, before proceeding, we need to briefly consider how philosophy fits into the liberal arts universe. More than a century ago, Bertrand Russell wrote that "many men, under the influence of science or of practical affairs, are inclined to doubt whether philosophy is anything better than innocent or useless trifling, hair-splitting distinctions, and controversies on matters concerning which knowledge is impossible."[3]

There's nothing wrong with being scientific or practical, but Russell identified an all-too-common caricature of philosophy as something esoteric or irrelevant. We can demolish that caricature by understanding philosophy's actual role in liberal learning. It is the parent of most of the liberal arts disciplines—and stepparent to the rest—for reasons that are closely intertwined: historical, conceptual, and methodological. Saying this doesn't "privilege" philosophy or Western thought in general; it's a matter of historical fact. But it's important to see why it's a fact. That's the conceptual and methodological side.

Philosophy's foundational role in Western learning was logical and inevitable given its nature and function as the attempt to think systematically and organize knowledge. Philosophical thinking is by definition *general* thinking. Its business is to ask the broadest questions: for example, about the nature of mind, knowledge, reality, and value. Those questions, in turn, led to narrower ones that gave rise to other disciplines: for example, about art, religion, economics, psychology, or language. And in all those fields, the larger questions recur and the methodological rigor of philosophy is necessary.

> You are no doubt well aware that of all the liberal arts in high repute philosophy is considered by the learned to be the mother, and "the great original."
>
> —Cicero, *De Oratore*

The Greeks raised basic questions about the mind and the world, questions that previously in the Western world had been raised, if at all, primarily within religious, mythic, and oral and narrative traditions: What is nature? What is real? What is knowledge? What is causation? What is good? How did the world begin (cosmogony), and how is it arranged (cosmology)? Beginning with the surviving fragments of the pre-Socratic thinkers, and continuing with Plato, Aristotle, and other Hellenic schools such as the Sophists and the Stoics, those inquiries merged into the distinctive philosophic tradition that, over time, spun off other disciplines.

In fact, Plato used the term "philosophy" more broadly than we do today; the Greek "love of wisdom" applied to all knowledge, not just to abstract concepts about thought and its relation to the world. In doing so, however, he went a long way toward inventing the discipline we now call "philosophy." Philosophy thus emerged—and has endured by default—as the systematic study of thought and knowledge in general, while offloading more particular questions into independent lines of inquiry. That evolution in Western thought was advanced by Aristotle, who pioneered not only the fields of logic and rhetoric but also physics, and largely invented the study of biology through his work in classifying plants and animals. The influence of Eastern thought was felt when Aristotle's student, Alexander the Great, traveled to India.

Fast-forward now some two thousand years. Economics, political science, psychology, sociology, anthropology, linguistics, semiotics, interpretation theory, cognitive neuroscience: these are just some of the free-standing avenues of inquiry that have emerged as questions about, for example, money, language, social organization, institutions, art, and the human mind and behavior, have evolved along with new techniques for collecting, organizing, and assessing information about them.

To be sure, not all learning comes from ancient Greek philosophy. Western literature begins with Homer and the Old Testament; drama and poetry trace back to Euripides, Sophocles, Aristophanes, Aeschylus, and others. The practice of recording history originates with Herodotus and is advanced by Thucydides, and early mathematics owes much to Archimedes and Pythagoras. Ideas from China, India, the Arab world, and elsewhere have infiltrated and enriched the West. But even the fields and knowledge traditions that emerged independently of Western philosophy need philosophy's generalizing and theorizing tendency and its focus on methodological rigor. That is philosophy's ongoing stepparent role.[4]

And philosophy's filling that role is no accident. Wherever there is general or systematic thinking, there is the footprint of philosophy. Providing the questions, methods, and conceptual apparatus for what would become the liberal arts was (and arguably remains) philosophy's core function. Every field of inquiry asks, within its own domain, basic questions about the nature of knowledge and rigorous thinking. Every field shares certain content-independent intellectual values: truth, logical consistency, systematic thinking, clarity of thought and expression. If you probe deeply enough into any domain of knowledge, including science, you hit philosophic bedrock.

> Philosophy . . . does not have a role in liberal education in the sense that an actor has a role in a play; in the drama of liberal education, philosophy constitutes the very form or structure of the play itself.
>
> —Manuel Bilsky

Thus, far from being peripheral, esoteric, or an "innocent or useless trifling," philosophy is both historically and conceptually the hub of the liberal arts. Understanding its central and centripetal role in thought and learning is where critical thinking begins. In short: all rigorous thinking is critical thinking, and all critical thinking, no matter the subject, is philosophical thinking.

Having acknowledged philosophy's central role, we should also be clear about its limits. It isn't the be-all and end-all of learning. And while the intellectual skills we're equating with critical inquiry represent avenues to more effective and sophisticated thinking—in essence, to more philosophical thinking—they don't require immersion in philosophy proper.

Why not? The most obvious reason is that there are many other things we need to learn and ways of learning them. For understanding the world writ large, thinking is necessary but not sufficient; it is auxiliary to what we think about. Theory is a handmaiden, not a substitute, for other intellectual functions, including observing and fact gathering, testing and analyzing, arguing, criticizing, problem solving, defining, and, not least, imagining and creating. In sum, philosophy is the hub of all learning—but we also need the rest of the wheel, and that wheel is in motion. As knowledge expands and evolves, even the hub moves, though more slowly than the rest.

Thus, while the intellectual ascent we're identifying with critical inquiry owes everything to philosophy, it takes wing by applying those philosophical tools beyond the bounds of philosophy proper. One could even argue that lending its tools to other fields, and to nonphilosophers, is philosophy's most important function. Put more bluntly: philosophy doesn't generate art, or teach us how to read novels, make money, save lives, exercise leadership, plant gardens, or raise children. Nor does it reveal the "meaning of life"; spiritual practices may better serve that purpose. Philosophy doesn't add to the sum of knowledge, at least not in the way that science or social science does. Rather, it adds to the *quality* of knowledge by organizing it, evaluating it, asking deeper questions, and enabling us to think more deeply, broadly, clearly, flexibly, and systematically.

A related point is that philosophers, as expert practitioners of metacognitive thinking, are vexed by certain abstract questions (some very broad, others narrower or more technical) that don't necessarily vex the rest of us. Not being vexed by them doesn't prevent us from becoming better thinkers or citizens. All good philosophers are rigorous critical thinkers, but all rigorous critical thinkers aren't, and don't need to be, philosophers.

A third consideration, which we'll revisit in the next chapter, buttresses the first two. Critical thinking doesn't require that we become philosophers because, as thinking creatures who use language, we're already philosophers, unconsciously and in spite of ourselves. All thought and language, and all learning, has a philosophical component. Improving our critical thinking simply makes us better philosophers.

When we think more critically, we meet the philosophers halfway, so to speak. But meeting philosophy halfway isn't a half measure or a compromise; rather, it's a fitting level of metacognition: thinking about our own thought, in the here and now, on matters ranging from the immediate to the remote, and from the more general to the more particular, across the liberal arts and in public discourse. Intellectual rigor isn't just transdisciplinary; because it's about thinking, intellectual rigor is philosophical rigor: the rigor of logic, clarity, truth seeking, thoroughness, relevance, and precision.

Here you may ask, Why do we need to bother with logic, truth, clarity, and so on? The answer is that these are essential pillars of any civic (nontribal, nonspiritual) community. They are how we interact effectively in any collective enterprise. They are primarily values pertaining to communication, and there are few forms of human community that don't involve communication. Should you now ask, Why community? Well, to paraphrase the old joke about the world resting on a never-ending series of turtles: very clever—but it's community all the way down. All of the alternatives are unpleasant.

SIX "GATEWAY" CONCEPTS OF CRITICAL INQUIRY, GIVE OR TAKE

If "critical inquiry" identifies the tool kit of essential critical thinking skills for liberal learning, many of the tools in that box could be considered methodological. They are content-independent rules and guidelines that help us to think better communally, and thinking is always a means to other ends: understanding, judgment, communication, and deliberate action. But there are other useful items in the critical inquiry tool kit besides the methodological ones. Higher-level critical thinking also involves familiarity with a number of essential concepts that persist over time and range across the domains of knowledge: what we will call "gateway concepts" of liberal learning. Not surprisingly, they are also the progeny of philosophy—and we owe most of them to the Greeks.

These gateway concepts include *language* itself, as the principal medium of thought; *rationality* as a conceptual umbrella covering the varieties of critical thinking; *analysis*, which is one such variety; *truth*; *causality*; and *complexity*. These six concepts, and arguably others, are crucial points of entry to liberal learning. They don't constrain our thinking but channel it in ways that are widely useful or necessary, because they reflect fundamental ways in which our minds organize and engage with the world, regardless of the subject matter.

The obvious caveat here is that there is room for debate about the roster of gateway concepts. Other important conceptual gateways include nature, value, experience, knowledge, art, faith, morality, excellence, power, community, and freedom. Each of these sheds broad light within the liberal arts (and we'll look at how morality and politics intersect with the liberal arts in the final chapters of the book). But they are not gateways of the same level of generality as the six I'm suggesting.

In contrast to these near-gateways or partial gateways, a host of other important ideas—such as government, scientific method, transference, foreshadowing, three-point perspective, opportunity cost, immanent critique, double-blind study, hubris, kinship, or means testing, to name just a few—are important within one or more disciplines or form useful interdisciplinary corridors, but they don't apply across the entire spectrum of liberal learning. Likewise, broad conceptual frameworks such as Marxism, feminism, structuralism, psychoanalysis, critical theory, and hermeneutics constitute sturdy theoretical umbrellas, but they don't cover everything, and where they do apply, they must compete with other frameworks.

Not so the gateway concepts. The idea of *truth*, for instance, notwithstanding its intricacies (see chapter 11), is almost self-evidently crucial to every intellectual arena. Without some shared facts and principles, our minds are rudderless and adrift among the intellectual shoals of relativism, nihilism, and postmodernism. Even in contexts where it is elusive or hard to define, or where uncertainty is rampant, we can't abandon the concept of truth without stumbling into incoherence. It is part of the very grammar of learning.

The same is true (voilà!) for *rationality*. Reasoning is our shared system for thinking and communicating: a set of implicit rules guiding our movement from one thought or expression to another or from thought to action. Rationality is thus a kind of metalanguage, a common grammar of learning and public discourse. As such, it is also a form of community: a unifying force, at least for coalitions of the willing.

Similarly, the concept of *causality* is intrinsic to how we organize the world—part of the architecture of human consciousness. As creatures imprisoned in something we call time, we find the idea of causality necessary for any coherent account of science, history, nature, or morality. Thinking and learning are themselves causal processes. As we do with truth, we argue about what causality is, how it works, the different forms it takes, and how responsible we are as individuals for our thoughts and actions. Often, we have these arguments implicitly, without realizing it, and without resolution. But they are arguments we can't help having.

The concept of *analysis* also qualifies as a gateway because it is the methodological capstone of critical inquiry: the highest form of critical thinking, not just for philosophers but for all of us. In later chapters we will explore what we mean by analysis and how it regulates thinking across the disciplines. As I'll suggest, it involves its own family of intellectual skills, such as establishing clear and useful definitions, making distinctions and connections, forming analogies, and resolving or mitigating ambiguity.

The concept of *complexity* (and its logical counterpart, the simple/complex spectrum) likewise opens a crucial door to liberal learning, one that leads to other debates and alternate ways of organizing experience at a fundamental level. That is because the complexity spectrum reflects something essential about how we perceive—and differently perceive—the structure of things. Indeed, the very term "structure" implies a conception of complexity.

Complexity and simplicity are relative to one another and have reciprocal advantages and disadvantages. Which is better or more useful, or what balance of them, depends on the thinker and what is being thought about—as well as the audience. Calling complexity a gateway concept doesn't imply a bias toward any point on the simple-complex spectrum; rather, it's intended to foreground that spectrum itself. Often, what clear understanding requires is that we commute between the simpler and the more complex.

When we examine the concept of complexity, we'll consider its benefits and drawbacks. We'll see why its use is, to an important extent, elective and contestable, reflective of our individual values and proclivities—and a way of understanding the roots of our intellectual, moral, and political differences. What's non-negotiable for critical thinkers is the need to reckon with complexity versus simplicity as a basic axis of understanding and to see why that spectrum has broad explanatory power.

Finally, we come to arguably the most important gateway concept. Critical thinking, like philosophy, begins but doesn't end with careful attention to *language*. Because we think mainly with words, we can't be critical thinkers without considering words as complex tokens of meaning and the various ways in which they help or hinder us in forming and sharing thoughts. Therefore, we'll begin our survey of critical thinking in the next chapter by examining language as the principal medium of thought.

Like the other gateway concepts, language is almost always central to thought and almost always problematic. Clear and consistent language is essential to philosophy as well, but it isn't a substitute for philosophy, and it certainly isn't (as Ludwig Wittgenstein originally suggested, before radically revising his thinking) the graveyard of philosophy. More to the point, the need for clear and consistent language extends far beyond philosophy. No understanding of critical inquiry can ignore it.

The gateway concepts share certain additional defining features along with their ubiquity as intellectual tools. One such feature is that they continually interrelate and overlap one another. Another is that they tend to raise important questions of a kind that philosophers call "essentially contested." These are questions that can never be resolved by stating factual or logical truths. Instead, they generate a range of possible moral, political, aesthetic, or intellectual responses. (A paradigm case is the question of free will versus determinism in causality.) Because there is no higher principle to appeal to in deciding among such responses, no final consensus is possible.[5] Yet they are questions we can't avoid asking and arguing about.

When we talk about truth, rationality, causality, analysis, complexity, or language, we need to negotiate broad ranges of meaning and make and explain our choices. We need to distinguish between disagreements about facts, where we can achieve some consensus by closer examination of the world, and disagreements on other bases such as values, worldviews, or ways of interpreting facts, where we can't. And the more general the concept (think of freedom, morality, justice, art, education, or knowledge), the wider the room for potential disagreement.

Another defining feature of the gateway concepts, previously noted, is that they are domain independent and apply to all critical inquiry. They are basic structural elements of the liberal arts tradition and reminders that it originated in ancient Greece, largely in what the Greeks called "philosophy"—by which they meant the general love of wisdom.

Beyond that historical lineage, the gateway concepts remind us that all rigorous learning, in whatever culture or tradition, involves some form of metacognition—self-conscious thinking about the nature, types, and limits of knowledge—and is thus inherently philosophical. It's about getting to the bottom of things and identifying their essence, seeing deeply as well as broadly or narrowly, and asking how things are connected as well as how they are distinct. And it's about managing the economy of meaning defined by those competing goals in order to communicate as clearly, fully, and precisely as possible. Again, critical inquiry doesn't urge us to become philosophers, merely to recognize that we are already philosophers and to try to be the best philosophers we can be.

In the following chapters, we'll touch on a number of other ideas that build on the gateway concepts and buttress critical inquiry. We've alluded to some of them already. One is triangular citizenship, which constitutes the broadest and most powerful raison d'être for liberal learning. Another is the notion of intersubjectivity. Others include the distinction between systematic and systemic thinking and the concepts of family resemblance (a contribution of Wittgenstein's); recursion; nonbinary thinking; and binocularity, an idea that applies to truth, complexity, causality, and more.

Some of these terms may be unfamiliar, but there's nothing fancy or obscure about them; they are simply helpful and exceptionally versatile conceptual tools. Understanding them, along with the gateway concepts, nudges critical thinking to the highest level.

SUMMING UP: CRITICAL INQUIRY IS CURVILINEAR

Early sailors used maps of the night sky and the known world to find their way, along with other navigational devices: compasses for direction, astrolabes, and later sextants, to determine latitude. While crude or inaccurate by modern standards, those instruments worked well enough for millennia, enabling navigators to guide their ships at sea. (Navigators on American bombers used sextants to cross the Atlantic as recently as World War II.) Similarly, the tools of critical inquiry enable us to navigate the natural and symbolic worlds with greater precision and success until better ones come along. And most of the ones we use have served for thousands of years.

Beyond these tools of intellectual rigor, critical inquiry is boundless; there are no fixed rules governing its ever-expanding inquiries and conversations. The roster of organizing concepts and buttressing ideas I've proposed is partial and contestable; in the end, they may simply be convenient ways of carving reality "at the joints," as Plato suggests. They are not shortcuts or substitutes for specific knowledge of the way things are, what things mean, or how things work. Rather, they are tools for intellectual navigation that turn students into critical thinkers and citizens.

In equating critical inquiry with rationality and critical thinking, and using the metaphor of navigation, one might be accused of excessive linearity. The world isn't made up of lines, rules, or formulas, just as it isn't made up of maps; the world is fuzzy, fragmented, interconnected, and in flux. Everything is connected, but some things are more connected than others, and all is subject to change. Any sound definition of critical inquiry must encompass other forms of cognition: association, observation and data collection, memory, opinion, emotion, imagination, and all the rest. As Leonardo da Vinci observes in his *Notebooks*, lines don't exist in nature; rather, they are abstractions that artists, architects, cartographers, navigators, and others inscribe on flat surfaces to depict or represent nature, and thus to reach (imperfect and changing) accommodations between the world and the mind.

Like words, however, lines—straight or otherwise—are indispensable for modeling the world. They tell us where the horizon is, when Monday becomes Tuesday, and where Colorado ends and Wyoming begins. But lines are not just connections between points. They are also bifurcations: they have two sides, and while it's either Monday or Tuesday, and you're either in Colorado or Wyoming, such binary thinking is inadequate in many contexts. Like the artist, architect, or mapmaker drawing lines on paper, we use black-and-white words and sentences to depict gray zones and layers of complexity.

Model versus reality, map versus world, binary versus nonbinary: critical inquiry has the power both to create and to bridge such dichotomies. It insists on the continual accommodation between thought and the world, not the predominance of either domain. The only metaphysical assumption is that the mind and the world are always distinct and always connected.

Critical inquiry might therefore be better described as curvilinear: it uses lines to map the world in all its curves, depth, shading, and variety. The map isn't the territory, yet we can't dispense with maps. And to be useful, any map—or any sentence, diagram, graph, chart, photograph, recipe, checklist, playlist, and so on—must somehow represent the territory it identifies. That's its job. We think with words and images and ideas, not with objects or actions. But our representations are seldom perfect or final.

This modeling process is central to higher learning because it's central to all thinking, and thinking is ultimately, and necessarily, a process of blending similarity and difference and of reconciling the linear geometry of the mind with the disorderly curves of the world. That's how we make sense of things, simultaneously adapting to and organizing the flow of conscious experience so that we may act on it with greater efficacy.

That process isn't a triumph over nature or our emotive or imaginative selves but their complement. It isn't an exalted or ennobling activity, and it isn't for an elite few. It's just what we do, as best we can, to grasp the bigger picture, the smaller picture, the more granular or more integrated picture, the more elusive or unobvious picture, the changing picture, the other person's or other culture's picture, as the case may be. It's what distinguishes us as a species, making us better learners, creators, and decision makers—in short, better citizens. It helps to explain why we have books, cupcakes, carpools, museums, and indoor plumbing, while baboons do not. (Robots may have some of these soon enough, but they are products of human thought.)

Thinking, in sum, is quintessentially a process of *relating*: facts, ideas, things, events, processes, people, institutions, the general and the particular, hither and yon, past and present. It is the product of the tools and methods we have devised for modeling the world, making it more coherent and, to the extent possible, more manageable. It's seldom a perfect fit, because thoughts, like maps, are essentially linear, static, and partial maps of a dynamic universe. Yet we muddle through because thinking isn't useless, experience isn't incoherent, free agency isn't entirely illusory, and what is complex isn't inscrutable. Besides, what else have we got?

Thought and action form an endless looping series of semicoordinated, error-prone initiatives, accommodations, recognitions, resignations, course corrections, risks, hedges, guesses, and little triumphs and disasters as we navigate our daily lives. What's clear is that learning to think more clearly, deeply, broadly, and flexibly helps in almost everything we do, except perhaps in love—and flexibility helps there.

This book is about the types of cognition that assume linguistic form: language as thought. It's about so-called rational thought as distinct from, say, more emotive, reactive, or imaginative thinking, or purely functional types of rational problem solving, such as surviving in the woods, fixing a leaky toilet, coding software, or completing your tax returns. It's about abstractions. But abstractions are only fit for human contemplation because they are useful or necessary in some messy context or other. And fitting abstractions to contexts, using them to better manage the world and our knowledge of it, is what critical inquiry is all about.

NOTES

1. Generality isn't the same thing as vagueness. All general terms aren't vague, and all vague ones aren't general. Generality denotes breadth of application; the concept of education is general. Vagueness denotes nonspecificity of range or content; the concept of blueness is vague.

2. Renford Bambrough, "Aristotle on Justice: A Paradigm of Philosophy," in R. Bambrough, *New Essays on Plato and Aristotle*, 165. London: Routledge, 1965.

3. Bertrand Russell, "The Value of Philosophy," in B. Russell, *The Problems of Philosophy*, 111. Oxford: Oxford University Press, 1997.

4. We can exempt certain *practices* (e.g., religious or artistic) from rigor or rationality but not the study of such practices, and philosophy continues to inform other disciplines in many ways. As Subrena E. Smith (https://aeon.co/ideas/why-philosophy-is-so-important-in-science-education) observes, "Albert Einstein's philosophical thought experiments made Cassini possible. Aristotle's logic is the basis for computer science, which gave us laptops and smartphones. And philosophers' work on the mind-body problem set the stage for the emergence of neuropsychology and therefore brain-imaging technology. . . . Science brims with important conceptual, methodological and ethical issues that philosophers are uniquely situated to address."

5. The notion of contestability is, in fact, one of philosophy's most important, if unappreciated, contributions to wider intellectual discourse. It applies to a range of issues across learning and to value systems such as art, morality, and politics. Logically speaking, broad consensus in these areas is possible (depending how one defines "consensus") but highly unlikely to occur.

Chapter 4

Language Lessons

What We Need to Know About Words to Think Well

Words strain,
Crack and sometimes break, under the burden,
Under the tension, slip, slide, perish,
Decay with imprecision, will not stay in place,
Will not stay still.

—T. S. Eliot, *Four Quartets*

WHY WORDS MATTER

We think mainly with words. It might sound better to say we weave our thoughts on the loom of language; but the metaphor breaks down if we subject it to critical scrutiny. If we "weave" our thoughts at all, language is the wool, not the loom. Does that make all our language woolly? We should beware of appealing but inexact metaphors. George Orwell, the patron saint of clear English, would approve. We should always err on the side of clarity—or almost always. Even clarity isn't everything.

So, to begin again: We think mainly with words, and the signs and symbols that stand for them. We use them as building blocks for constructing the more complex meanings that can be achieved with sentences and longer expressions.[1] It is mainly through spoken and written language, gestures, and other symbolic systems (such as math, logic, codes, traffic lights, stop signs, or Braille) that we can communicate at all. "For all but the simplest thoughts," writes the philosopher John R. Searle, "one has to have a language to think the thought."[2]

That much might seem obvious. Most cognition is verbal, though we also express ourselves in other ways, for example when using color, form, sound, or light to create works of art. Music, painting, photography, sculpture, and dance don't directly involve language, but we still need language to talk about them—and for just about everything else.

> I believe that language is the fundamental human institution in the sense that other institutions, such as money, government, private property, marriage, and games, require language, or at least language-like forms of symbolism, in a way that language does not require the other institutions for its existence.
>
> —John R. Searle[3]

Exactly what kinds of thinking occur prelinguistically or extralinguistically (for example, in animals, toddlers, or early hominids) is an interesting question but immaterial here. The relevant point is that human thought and communication take place mainly through language. Likewise, most verbalization is in some way cognitive, the result of a conscious mental process, and not just babble or a precognitive neural response to stimuli. And yet the role of language in our thinking—indeed, the primacy of language as the very medium of thought—isn't simple or self-evident. In fact, although thinking, speaking, writing, and listening are intimately related functions, how they are related remains something of a mystery.

This intimacy between language and thought is a major reason why linguists, psychologists, philosophers, cognitive scientists, and other scholars have had so much to say about language over the past century. And it's why, in order to think clearly about thinking, we first need to think about language itself. To be critical thinkers, we don't need to be scholars or wade into the controversy over whether, or in what sense, thought precedes language. But we do need to appreciate what complicated and even dangerous toys we are using when we play with words, how certain basic features of language condition our thinking, and what can be done about it.

If improving our command of language doesn't actually enhance our ability to think, it at least enhances the ability to communicate thoughts clearly and effectively. And functionally these amount to the same thing—whether it's writing a college paper or making a case in a public forum. What we can think but cannot express may enrich our inner lives, or enable us to live off the land, but it doesn't enrich our shared conversations, where good thinking becomes good dialogue, good scholarship, and good citizenship.[4]

So what exactly do liberal learners need to know about language? First, that language is a flexible, but not an infinitely elastic, tool. It can't walk the dog or take out the garbage, though it may help in getting those jobs outsourced. Clever language alone doesn't necessarily "win" arguments, though it may sway audiences (citizenship, meet critical thinking!).[5] There's a crucial distinction between a sound argument and a persuasive one, as our politics frequently shows.

More specifically, the basic features of language that all critical thinkers need to understand include the following: that it is reflexive, imperfect yet perfectible, pragmatic and economic, complex and multivalent, linear yet often fuzzy, and essentially philosophical. As we consider these features in turn, we'll see how deeply they are interconnected and why careful use of language is a crucial part of critical thinking. The aim isn't to penetrate all the unsolved mysteries of the spoken and written word. It's rather to understand those aspects of ordinary language (excepting perhaps involuntary utterances or primal screams) that illuminate—and may critically improve, extend, or undermine—our thought.

The larger point is that, in liberal learning and civic life alike, clear language is a prerequisite to clear thinking. Words matter because if we use them carelessly, we degrade, or opt out of, important communities of understanding. Conversely, the more carefully we use words, the more mutually beneficial are those interchanges. And that's the beauty part: clear thinking, higher learning, and citizenship aren't zero-sum games but team efforts. They are mutually reinforcing forms of community.

CHASING THE WILD GOOSE OF DEFINITION

Before examining some of the features of language that are key to critical thinking, we need to get some other business out of the way. Language is a system of conventions that allows us to communicate thoughts. Those conventions include grammatical rules, alphabetic and punctuation systems, pronunciation, and definitions. Of these, definitions bear closest examination. They serve as important guidelines for using words, but they aren't the only guidelines, nor do they explain everything that is important. Definitions concern us here because (unlike alphabets or grammars) they are in some respects flexible and negotiable and in other respects rigid and non-negotiable. We can use them as we find them or tweak them for our purposes. If critical thinking begins with how we use language, Ground Zero is how we use and define words.

As a system of conventions linking verbal sounds to meanings, language predates formal or written definitions. Without such conventions there could be no trafficking in meaning. Definitions codify conventional understandings about words, but they aren't written in stone. They are sometimes fuzzy conventions, and they evolve. Yet without any such conventions—in stone or otherwise—there would be little communication.

Some definitions are more exact than others. It's clear what we mean by a "circle," a "sphere," or a "square." But while we all have a general idea of what "blue" is, there is no single definitive shade and no overall idea of blueness except as a band of wavelengths on the light spectrum. Russian has no single word for blue, but separate words for dark and light blue. This distinction can be helpful in some contexts, enabling greater specificity, and less helpful in others, obscuring the connection. All words are in principle definable—but only in terms of other words.

This presents an apparent paradox: meanings are based on their relations to other meanings. The philosopher W. V. Quine, echoing Ludwig Wittgenstein, argues that definitions represent a "correlation between two languages."[6] "Circle," for example, means the same thing as "line connecting all points equidistant from a given point." However, one could also say that definitions are correlations between two distinct *functions* of language.

One is the lexical function, whereby individual words map meanings: they identify objects, properties, relationships, conditions, processes, events, and so on. The other is the discursive function, whereby we use complex expressions (involving multiple words) to supplement and correct for the shortcomings of the lexical function of single words. Analytic thinking involves working with language on both levels, and coordinating those levels.

No two dictionary definitions of the same word are identical, although they tend to coincide. Some definitions have a core of reference that can't be ignored without impeding communication: for example, those of geometric terms such as "circle," "square," "line," "point," or "plane." But other words may have multiple definitions, vague definitions, or contested definitions. "Yankee" means one thing in the American South (a generic northerner), another thing in the Northeast (a New Englander), and a third thing in Great Britain and elsewhere (a native of the United States).[7]

More general concepts, such as "freedom" or "education," tend to have definitions that are more flexible or negotiable, within limits. This is a reflection of their generality, and the fact that formal definitions can't account for all possible meanings or uses of words, or all contexts in which they may be used. We can define "green" as a primary color, but that doesn't distinguish it from "yellow," at least not until we point to some referent as an example, and, of course, all green referents aren't the same shade of green.

> The wild goose of definition is never captured but the chase takes the hunter over the rugged and uneven ground whose contours he needs to survey.
>
> —Renford Bambrough[8]

Time and the vagaries of usage also come into play as we attempt to capture that "wild goose." Received definitions evolve, but they don't change overnight, and we can't change them willy-nilly; they change to adapt to new needs or conditions. "Gay" no longer primarily means happy or festive, no one in the eighteenth century knew about aviation or computers, and no one in the twentieth century knew about twerking or tweeting. We can't ignore or flout current usage, but, per the discussion of stipulative definition in chapter 3, we can stretch it a bit here and there to promote communication, sculpting definitions to suit a particular context or need.

What matters in the end is efficiency of meaning, but there are different kinds of efficiency, and they may compete. It doesn't matter whether I call the thing in my soap dish "soap" or "cleansing agent" or "bunny rabbit," as long as whoever is listening understands me. Most definitions are neither as rigid as those of a circle, minute, mile, or inch, nor are they wholly elastic, which would render them meaningless.

How much freedom we have in using words depends on several factors: the particular word in question, the context, how clear and specific we need to be, how much we want to be understood, and by whom. I might choose to call an "idea" something that leads to action, and a "concept" something that doesn't, but that's just one way of distinguishing between two terms with broad and similar if not identical meanings. You won't find it in a dictionary.

Again, formal definitions take us only so far, and (as noted in chapter 3) to maximize the power of our words we need to obey at least three general imperatives. First, unless there is an ulterior motive (such as manipulating the audience), implied meanings must be clear, not opaque. Thus, one might stipulate, "I'm using 'chair' here to mean the person who runs a committee meeting." Second, we must treat terms consistently. "America" can refer to the Western Hemisphere, North America, or the United States of America, but other things being equal, we can't use it to mean the Western Hemisphere in one sentence and North America in the next. And third, usage must plausibly relate to conventional meanings, even if it is customized in significant ways. If we want to be understood, we can't use "America" to mean "Delaware."

"When *I* use a word," Humpty Dumpty notoriously said in Lewis Carroll's *Through the Looking Glass* (1872), "it means just what I choose it to mean—neither more nor less."[9] Well, not quite. It matters how we define and use words such as "torture" and "terrorism," because those definitions and uses have important legal, moral, and political ramifications. Critical inquiry thus begins with definitions that are clear, consistent, and plausible. Here as elsewhere, we often have to deal with vague but workable boundaries—and vagueness has its uses. By adding clarity, consistency, and a dash of common sense (however that's defined), we can make them work better.

LANGUAGE IS REFLEXIVE AND RECURSIVE

A salient feature of language as a human practice is its reflexive capacity to examine, interrogate, criticize, qualify, clarify, correct, or amend itself. This reflexive function is inherently metacognitive: thinking about thought itself. It goes hand in hand with what's known as *recursion*: language's combinatorial ability to form an indefinite number of unique yet instantly recognizable expressions from a finite number of words and a much more limited set of letters and symbols. That's what makes language such a powerful instrument.

Because of such reflexivity and recursion, we can talk about language and think about thought. Examples include this sentence, paragraph, and chapter. This reflexive process of language-looking-at-itself is where philosophy and all metacognition begins, and the hallmark of all critical inquiry. It involves focusing attention in several directions at once (or in close succession): on our choices of words and expressions; on the connection or disconnection, as the case may be, between those words and what we mean to say; and on the relationship between words and their intended audience. The connection between words and meanings, as we'll see in due course, involves showing what those words conceal as well as what they reveal.

Ludwig Wittgenstein, the enigmatic Viennese-born philosopher, argued early in his career that the proper analysis of language would clear up the questions of philosophy once and for all. In his short and dense *Tractatus Logico-Philosophicus* (1922), Wittgenstein purported to resolve all the big questions of philosophy by revealing them to be linguistic muddles. (His posthumous works, including the monumental *Philosophical Investigations* [1953], take a quite different view.)

Yet in attempting to bring philosophy to a close by, in effect, reducing it to problems of language, Wittgenstein ironically achieved the opposite result, giving the discipline an enormous burst of fresh intellectual energy. Linguistic problems, it turned out, are philosophical problems. They are problems not just about words, but about meaning, knowledge, reality, values, and minds. They *begin* with words. And we all have to deal with these problems at some level as students and as citizens. Despite his early intentions, Wittgenstein isn't considered the greatest philosopher of the twentieth century for having been the last to turn out the lights.

Wittgenstein wasn't the first thinker to examine language, philosophically or otherwise, and neither was Humpty Dumpty. In 1651, Thomas Hobbes wrote in *The Leviathan*, "Words are wise men's counters, they do but reckon with them; but they are the money of fools."[10] Words, Hobbes suggests, can be used to map the world but should not be confused with what they represent nor used as substitutes for understanding, argument, or action.[11]

Another writer, John Wilson, puts it this way: "Instead of using language, we are in a very real sense used by it: we allow words to guide our thinking, instead of guiding our own thinking consciously and critically. . . . The analysis of language teaches us to avoid the pitfalls of language which are only dangerous because we are unaware of them."[12] Complex and general terms, in particular, need to be analyzed in order to be properly understood as markers for ideas.

Ferdinand de Saussure pioneered the formal study of linguistics in the late nineteenth and early twentieth centuries; in Vienna, meanwhile, Karl Kraus and other scholars were practicing what they called *Sprachkritik*: the critique of language, or using language as a mirror against itself in order to identify careless, incomplete, ambiguous, inaccurate, untruthful, deceptive, manipulative, or otherwise imperfect expressions. Thus began the great twentieth-century project of focusing philosophy on what we say.

The idea of studying language wasn't new to these nineteenth- and twentieth-century thinkers. The semantic enterprise is inherently philosophical, because it's the study of thought, and a lot of philosophy, going back to the Greeks, is about how we use words. But it was Wittgenstein, influenced by Saussure, Kraus, and others, who put language squarely on the map of twentieth-century philosophy.

Two closely related ideas are especially significant in this great linguistic swerve. One is the realization that we can grasp both connections and distinctions between language and the ideas that it aims to convey. We can ask what exactly language does, how it does it, what its powers and limitations are as the vehicle of thought; and we can consider how those limitations may be offset and those powers enhanced, using language itself as the tool. We can adjust our language to better suit our messages, our critics, and our audiences. We can make it reveal more and conceal less.

The second idea is the prescriptive side of that one: the notion that language, while intimately bound up with various forms of meaning—facts, analyses, descriptions, calculations, conjectures, memories, narratives, argument, innuendo, artistic expression—must itself be subjected to certain regulatory disciplines. Language must be used self-consciously and critically if we are to see how it shapes and misshapes messages, how it reveals and conceals. We must distinguish our speech or writing from its semantic business;

consider how successfully, and at what cost, it conducts that business; and weigh the possible alternatives.

> Does it matter [what] we say, so long as we avoid misunderstandings in any particular case?
>
> —Ludwig Wittgenstein, *Philosophical Investigations* §48

LANGUAGE IS IMPERFECT—BUT PERFECTIBLE

Language is an elaborate system for encoding meaning in order to communicate. Alphabets, lexicons, grammar and punctuation, pronunciation, body language, style: all are part of the toolbox. But while most of these tools are essential, they are not perfect for every task. If the goal is to perfectly replicate our thoughts in the minds of others, language is structurally imperfect in an imperfect world—"a leaky bucket," as Daniel L. Everett puts it.[13] Its flaws can be mitigated but not avoided or cured.

That's just one reason why philosophy can't, as Wittgenstein originally supposed, be brought to a close simply by clarifying language. We always need to expose the flawed or limited connections between words, expressions, and ideas; to say with sentences what can't be said with individual words; and to say with one word or sentence what we cannot say with another. Whenever we do this, consciously or not, we're doing philosophy.

This structural limitation of language (if one can call it that) is exhibited in at least two fundamental ways. First, all communication is nonideal, because we can't literally reproduce what's on our minds and transpose it intact into the minds of others; speech isn't a forklift. There's inevitable slippage between the intended message and the one received (with some obvious exceptions; there's little room for misinterpreting simple messages such as "Go to bed!" or "One plus one equals two").

For anything more complex, we can at best share a partial and distorted simulacrum of what's on our minds at a given moment. (And can we even fully know what's on our own minds?) If communication were perfect, we would in effect have shared consciousness. And would we even want to board that train, if it ever arrived? Because words never reproduce experience perfectly, they often fail us by simplifying, distorting, and selecting. As Jean Améry, a victim of Nazi torture, put it, "If someone wanted to impart his physical pain, he would be forced to inflict it and thereby become a torturer himself."[14]

Another way in which language is nonideal is economic: we are limited in the dimension of time. We cannot say two or more things at once, or say one thing in different ways. Thus, anything we say potentially obscures something else. This happens much of the time, and we need to say more to qualify or amend the original message.

The need to manage the economy of meaning, given limited time, energy, and audience attention, is another philosophical dimension of language. Even the critical scrutiny of language has its limits; we can't question or qualify everything we say, hear, or read ad infinitum. There is always something more that could be said, or said differently, and we can't say everything. No one wants to hear it all, and life is too short. At some point the class ends, the gavel drops, or your mother yawns.

> There are alternative ways of speaking, and . . . that does not mean that any way of speaking is as good as any other. But it does mean that there is always scope for learning more by making comparisons and contrasts that our language does not make for us.
>
> —Renford Bambrough[15]

But if perfection is impossible, at least there is perfectibility: the capability to make meanings clearer and more complete. We can limit the shortcomings of words by using more words, within those limits of intellectual economy. Critical thinking begins with using language reflexively to examine language, conveying fuller or more precise meanings, and considering how doing so forecloses other semantic possibilities, in pursuit of the competing aims of depth, breadth, and clarity.[16]

Absent the dubious luxury of shared consciousness, we muddle through because language works; it's often better than silence. To be sure, we routinely misinterpret, ignore, misunderstand, or simply forget what we see, read, or hear. Shared knowledge is what we strive for—except when we don't, as when the intended message is manipulative, propagandistic, commercial, hortatory, proselytizing, and so on. Everyday speech is freighted with unconscious motives, and even supposedly objective things, such as facts, figures, rules, artifacts, texts, and images, are seldom understood by different people in precisely the same way. On balance, though, language succeeds, or we'd all keep quiet.

A related point is that, just as there is little nontrivial communication that we can consider ideal, there can never be an ideal language, if by "language" we mean a grammar and a lexicon of words. Different ways of parsing meanings have different advantages and correlative disadvantages. "Nation" means something different from "country" or "state." There are good reasons for making such distinctions, as well as for seeing the connections they nominally obscure. But you can't do both at the same time, and in that sense, no lexicon can ever be perfect, because individual words just can't get the job done.

> [A] grave limitation of language is that it cannot, like music or gesture, do more than one thing at once.
>
> —C. S. Lewis[17]

At best, we approximate our thoughts, feelings, or perceptions when we communicate. (This may be what Wittgenstein had in mind when he remarked, "Language disguises thought."[18]) Individual words can convey particular or general ranges of meaning, but they can't say everything. They can't, for example, be both general and particular at the same time. "Cat" means something different from "this cat." By using complex expressions carefully, and compounding them, we can say much more, and we can show connections and distinctions that individual words conceal. That's why we use sentences, often a lot of them.[19] It is why language, though inherently imperfect, is also almost limitlessly perfectible. As the poet Wallace Stevens observes, "The imperfect is our paradise."[20]

LANGUAGE IS PRAGMATIC AND ECONOMIC

In addition to being reflexive and imperfect, language is radically pragmatic. We use it to convey meaning because for all its limitations it beats the alternatives. The capacity for complex verbal and written communication largely defines us as a species. We breathe because we must; we talk because we can.

Speech is also pragmatic in a narrower, more operational and economic sense. Limited by time and space, and unable to say two things at once, we have to make choices. Virtually every human utterance (with the exception of exclamations like "Ouch!" and certain profanities) reflects such a choice. Again, there are inevitable trade-offs in how we express things. Often we must choose between generality and specificity; between depth and breadth of audience comprehension; between candor, completeness, or accuracy on one hand, and self-interest, tact, or the limits of the audience's attention span on the other.

Languages are also dynamic: they evolve and change, and some usages are arguably better than others in a given context. Unlike Humpty Dumpty, we are the *temporary* masters of language, as well as its slaves. Even when we're insincere or have ulterior motives, such as when selling a product, advocating a plan or idea, or maneuvering for power, we function under the near-universal constraint of needing to be clearly understood. The aim is always to maximize the impact on an audience—otherwise, why bother?

Thus, for example, it might be futile to try to expunge a term such as "liberal arts" from the lexicon, even if it's clumsy and antiquated—even if there is a ready alternative such as "critical inquiry." We can only drive language so far in the directions we deem semantically fitting for our immediate purposes. Beyond that, we have to use more language to fix the flaws or fill the gaps. It's easier to critique a term than to abolish it or dictate an alternative.

As with all critical thinking, a certain intellectual humility comes into play here as well: what Jacques Barzun called "a becoming sense of incapacity."[21] The history of language, Barzun observes, is "a free-for-all." But if we wish to communicate clearly, he suggests, we don't have complete freedom. The duty of writers is rather "to exploit, preserve, and possibly enrich the language." Sometimes it's useful or necessary to split hairs; at other times it's just annoying, or pre-empts more useful mental acts of slicing and dicing; hence the inescapable economy of meaning. The trick is to manage that economy by choosing the best words and using them carefully to shed light where other words cast shadows.

LANGUAGE IS COMPLEX, MULTIVALENT, AND LINEAR

Another characteristic of language that underscores the need for critical thinking is its inherent complexity. We'll say more about complexity later. For now, it will suffice to focus on a few of the ways in which language is complex—and to note again how deeply gateway concepts such as language and complexity are interrelated.

One symptom of language's complexity is the fact that we don't fully understand it. The list of open or disputed questions about language is long: how it is acquired, and how it relates to other cognitive functions; its evolutionary and cultural origins; why there are so many languages, and why they often differ so radically from one another, not just in their vocabularies but in their grammars and how they organize experience.

Such resistance to understanding is a crude definition of complexity, but it's a good enough starting point. The complexity of language, we might add, reflects the complexity of the mind itself as a generator of meaning. Our cars, computers, cell phones, and other devices are also complex, but unlike our capacity for language, they don't live inside our heads. Not yet, at least.

A more specific example of language's complexity is its recursive nature. Starting with a fixed and relatively small set of letters and symbols, and a similarly limited number of sounds, we can form hundreds of thousands of words. And with those words, and a limited set of rules of grammar, punctuation, definition, pronunciation, and so on, we can generate an indefinite range of possible expressions. The ability to form a vast number of relationships from a relatively small set of constituent parts, by combining them according to rules, is a prime example of recursion as a form of complexity.

Language, in other words, is not just a random set of tools; it's a system, and systems are inherently complex. Language is a system in which a limited set of inputs yields an enormous array of possible outputs. For all practical purposes, there's little we can't say; yet most of our expressions, despite their uniqueness and unpredictability, are readily understood. I may utter a unique sentence that has never been uttered before, yet you can instantly recognize the words, decode the grammar, and grasp the intended meaning with little or no conscious effort.

Another way of understanding the complexity of language is in terms of the distance it can mark between appearance and reality: in this case, between words and sentences and their meanings. A sunset looks nothing like the word "sunset," or even like a page of writing describing a sunset. That is because language is encoded: its meanings are embedded in strings of arbitrary sounds and symbols (incoherent to Martians, unless they've done their homework) that we decode using our knowledge of the lexicon and grammatical rules.

Like "sunset," most words are not literally what they represent (the referent), nor are they little photographs of the referent, but rather its symbolic counterpart. This is a basic logical distinction. The word "boat" isn't a boat, nor does it resemble one. In some cases a word *is* what it represents, or strongly influences how we think about that referent, but these are exceptions. "Word" is a word, and the word "black" as printed on this page is black. Onomatopoeias are words that sound like what they mean, such as "buzz," "thud," "splash," or "whoosh." But the list isn't endless.

Language is also complex because it is multivalent: individual words can have multiple meanings, and language in general has multiple uses and purposes. Words and expressions may report or reproduce information, but they may also amuse, enchant, distort, praise, criticize, exaggerate, obscure, or otherwise aim to manipulate an audience. And the challenge of discerning the reliability, authenticity, or completeness of a message, and the intentions of the messenger, further complicates the decoding process. Again, context matters: lies and distortions are more likely to occur in political or commercial advertising than in a math class or a dictionary. This is another way in which appearance and reality can diverge, making careful attention to language essential to critical thinking.

Finally, language is complex in that it is an essentially linear process, while the world is a fuzzy, nonlinear place. Language, in other words, *models* the world more than it reflects the world. We tend to overlook this, because we are accustomed to encoding and decoding unconsciously and allowing for the differences between words and what they refer to. We need reminding that the linguistic map isn't the territory; it's a map of the territory.

Our maps bring a modicum of order to that fuzzy world so that we can share information and act in concert. But when we speak we're essentially mapping a three-dimensional world with a one-dimensional tool that spools out across time and space, word by word. The linearity of language limits us to saying one thing at a time, which is why we need to use words reflexively to compensate for other words and to shine the light of meaning in their shadows.

Modeling a fuzzy, nonlinear world with the linear tool of language doesn't always require exactitude. In fact, vague boundaries in experience need to be respected and described as such, not erased or replaced with arbitrary lines. We can't say precisely where one wave ends, as it approaches a beach, and the next one begins, but that doesn't stop us from talking about waves, or distinguishing one from the next. The philosopher K. Ajdukiewicz explains it this way:[22]

> The Vistula at Warsaw cannot be called a brook . . . the Vistula at its sources, on the other hand, will undoubtedly be called a brook. When however we follow the course of the Vistula from its sources we shall find places about which we shall be unable to decide whether the Vistula at these places is a brook or not a brook any longer.

The point isn't a trivial one. We can usefully identify things—a wave, a cloud, a brook or a river, a culture, an idea—that don't have specific boundaries. The world is fuzzy because things (objects, attributes, processes, patterns, relationships) overlap and interrelate, fluctuate, share attributes and indistinct boundaries, and are not always easy to individuate. Waves and clouds and breezes don't have sharp edges, yet we can still talk about them.

Definitions tend to mark clear, if general, lines of distinction: an apple is not an orange, and war is not peace. There may be clarity at the extremes but not in the middle: some things are art, while others just aren't. But what about the object on the wall of my motel room: Is it non-art, semi-art, bad art? Some things are *like* art, *like* apples, *like* war; others are borderline cases, small-scale versions, pale imitations, causal cousins (thunder/lightning), or logical twins (brother/sister, war/peace, yesterday/tomorrow).

One of the reasons why we use language reflexively is to clearly reflect the very fuzziness of the world. We don't worry about where one wave ends and another begins, or at what point a brook becomes a river, because through language we can express necessary gradations or qualifications and skip the unnecessary ones. Language is linear, yet we can use it to describe a world that is full of curves, fuzziness, and shades of gray.

The point is relevant to all critical inquiry. In every area of learning and public discourse, we need to communicate with a maximum of intellectual order—clarity, completeness, consistency, relevance—and correlatively, with a minimum of obscurity, inconsistency, and needless ambiguity. Yet we also need to describe the world in the messy state in which we find it. We optimize the quality of our thought by optimizing our language.

LANGUAGE IS PHILOSOPHICAL— AND WE'RE ALL PHILOSOPHERS

All of the basic features of language we've identified point to a final characteristic that is highly relevant to critical thinking. Most of our linguistic expressions are complex, based on their recursive structure, and complex linguistic expressions are intrinsically philosophical, because they involve, and can be understood in terms of, abstraction.

By now this shouldn't seem like an esoteric claim. Thinking about language is thinking about thinking, and so is philosophy. When I say, "Catch the ball!" I'm invoking a host of complex, implicit thoughts: a relationship of speaker to hearer, shared assumptions about a habitual act involving the interpersonal transfer of a common mass-produced object, an announced immediate intention to perform an act of throwing, a larger purpose (pleasure, practice, exercise) involving both, a social context and history, and so forth.

Consciously or not, we use language all the time to do essentially the same things philosophers do when they look more generally at thought, being, or value. We negotiate definitions; use abstractions; make generalizations, and commute between the general and the particular; identify parts and wholes; relate nonidentities and construct analogies; make distinctions and connections, and qualify them to describe a fuzzy world in the linear terms of the mind; make arguments by using logic and evidence to build persuasive chains of reasoning; try to resolve or mitigate ambiguity. These are quintessential philosophic skills, and they are precisely the skills that a liberal education, regardless of the subject matter, aims to cultivate to make us better learners, communicators, and citizens.

Ordinary language is usually *somewhat* clear, *somewhat* systematic, *somewhat* abstract, if it isn't gibberish. It reflects the philosophical choices that we make willy-nilly: between specificity and generality, brevity and length, clarity and complexity, depth and range of explanation, breadth of audience and depth of comprehension. We use language reflexively to cast light in the shadows of language itself, using words or expressions to say what other words or expressions cannot.

> If any culture lacked entirely the ability to generalize, it would be incapable of learning human language. . . . Just as every noun is a generalization about things, so every verb is a generalization about events.
>
> —Daniel Everett[23]

Thus, the notion that language—and by extension, critical inquiry as the intellectual structure of the liberal arts—is innately philosophical shouldn't be surprising. This isn't about Captain Ahab on the lurching deck of the *Pequod*, cursing the white whale and discoursing on fate and mortality. Nor does it draw us helter-skelter into the vortex of philosophy proper, fascinating though it is. We needn't fear philosophy the way Melville's whalers feared their fate, as a "speechlessly quick chaotic bundling of a man into Eternity." We're already philosophers because we use language to think and to express our thoughts. A liberal education, by making us more critical thinkers, simply makes us better philosophers.

CONCLUSION: CLARITY IS ALMOST EVERYTHING

If there's one overarching conclusion to be drawn from this survey of the various facets of the prism of language, it's that Humpty Dumpty was wrong. We need to use language carefully in order to think carefully, and that means following its rules and conventions, as long as they serve our communicative needs. Such attention to language is the foundation of critical inquiry. It is also the scaffold on which we publicly execute contradictions, fallacies, bad arguments, conceptual muddles, hopeless ambiguities, misunderstandings, omissions, and gaps of meaning, logic, or information—to the extent we apprehend them.

Words evolve; some wear thin from overuse like old carpets, or smack of manipulation or hidden assumptions (such as when describing a used item as "preowned" or a less-messy divorce as "civilized"). Others atrophy from disuse or fade away ("ice box," "buggy whip"), while neologisms (which may be both useful and hideous: "foodie," "staycation," "dadvertise") emerge as shortcuts to meet evolving semantic needs, or the needs of some marketing guru. We take language as we find it, and we can bend it just a bit to our purposes.

Ultimately it's all about crafting and delivering a message: saying as clearly as possible what you mean, not more, not less, and not something else. Clarity—using the simplest, fewest, and most appropriate words for the message, and organizing them logically—is *almost* everything. Sometimes we have to communicate the lack of clarity inherent in the subject matter, but that's not even an exception to the rule. And clarity is relative to an audience: what's clear to doctors isn't always clear to patients, pilots talk one way in the cockpit and another when addressing passengers, and what's clear to one random listener may be opaque to another.

Pursuing clarity doesn't mean eliminating all vagueness, ambiguity, complexity, or generality. These are intrinsic parts of the verbal and intellectual landscape—along with values, emotions, and intentions. But we still need to be clear about the scope of such generality or vagueness, and that isn't paradoxical. If you're lost at sea and make radio contact with a potential rescuer, you might say, "I'm in the North Atlantic, I saw icebergs a week ago, and I've been drifting south since then." But you wouldn't invent coordinates, or guess at them, for the sake of specificity.

In sum: Words matter, as our primary conveyors of meaning, and meanings are somewhat pliable, somewhat negotiable, and somewhat debatable. They carry practical, intellectual, and moral weight. Using words carefully means being aware of how language does and does not model reality, and using other words to supplement or compensate for them.

Not all philosophical problems are reducible to problems of language per se, and parsing words carefully doesn't solve problems or settle most arguments. But Wittgenstein was right that philosophical problems (like most intellectual problems in the liberal arts) are problems *in* language. And language can best serve learning and citizenship if we recognize its essential nature: reflexive, economic, perfectible, complex, linear, and philosophical.

Part of the job of critical inquiry, then, is to use language to narrow the gap between its own failure and success. It isn't an inscrutable mystery. In fact, it's a fundamentally demystifying process of peeling back our words, and using other words, to reveal deeper, broader, and clearer meanings in all areas of learning. It begins where philosophy begins: with how we talk, what we say, and how we might say it better. We are neither the prisoners of our language nor its masters—not Humpty Dumpty, but Alice.

NOTES

1. As Neil Postman notes (*Building a Bridge to the 18th Century: How the Past Can Improve Our Future*, ch. 4. New York: Vintage, 1999), other communicative "codes" include art and mathematics, and we might also add formal logic; other types of symbolism, from military codes to traffic lights to computer languages; and human body language.

2. John R. Searle, *Mind, Language and Society: Philosophy in the Real World*. New York: Basic Books, 1999, p. 152. Daniel Everett (*Language: The Cultural Tool*. London: Profile Books, 2012, p. 50) adds, "Thinking without language is possible. My dog does it. But non-linguistic thinking does not get us very far. Without language most concepts would be ineffable and unthinkable. No math. No technology. No poetry. Minimal transmission of thoughts from one mind to another. And without language it would be impossible to sequence our thoughts well, to review them in our minds, to engage in contemplation."

3. Searle, *Mind, Language and Society*, p. 153.

4. Intersubjectivity, one of the "buttressing concepts" mentioned in chapter 3, refers to what obtains for any group or community of people (subjects). It is distinct from what obtains "subjectively" for an individual, either in their inner life or when alone in the world, and also from what obtains "objectively" in the world outside of any particular subject.

5. This depends on what exactly we mean by "win"—an example of how language can be tricky. Arguments that sway people aren't necessarily sound—based on evidence and logic. They may simply be more emotionally powerful, more eloquent, or more in sync with the predispositions of the audience.

6. Willard Van Orman Quine, "Two Dogmas of Empiricism," *Philosophical Review* 60:1 (January 1951): 27. Ludwig Wittgenstein (*Tractatus Logico-Philosophicus*. New York: Harcourt Brace, 1933, 3.343) writes that "definitions are rules for the translation of one language into another."

7. The term "Yankee" may or may not have originated as a derisive British label for the Dutch in New York: "Jan Kees" or "John Cheese."

8. Renford Bambrough, "Literature and Philosophy," in R. Bambrough, ed., *Wisdom: Twelve Essays*, 283. Oxford: Basil Blackwell, 1974.

9. Lewis Carroll, *Through the Looking-Glass*. New York: Modern Library Classics, 2002, p. 247. The dialogue continues:
"The question is," said Alice, "whether you *can* make words mean so many different things."
"The question is," said Humpty Dumpty, "which is to be master—that's all."

10. Thomas Hobbes, *The Leviathan*. Baltimore: Penguin Books, 1968, pt. 1, ch. 4.

11. John Dewey (*Democracy and Education*. Hollywood, CA: Simon & Brown, 2011, ch. 11) echoes Hobbes when he writes, "Because of our education we use words, thinking they are ideas, to dispose of questions, the disposal being in reality simply such an obscuring of perception as prevents us from seeing any longer the difficulty."

12. John Wilson, *Thinking with Concepts*. Cambridge: Cambridge University Press, 1963, p. 39. The literary scholar Robert Grudin makes a complementary remark (*The Grace of Great Things: On the Nature of Creativity*. Boston: Houghton Mifflin, 1991, p. 181): "The drama of philosophy lies specifically in the frustrated straining of language to reconstruct the world, and the farce of ideology springs from the illusion that language has succeeded."

13. Daniel Everett, *Language: The Cultural Tool*. London: Profile Books, 2012, p. 276.

14. Jean Améry, *Jenseits von Schuld und Sühne*. Stuttgart: Klett-Cotta, 1977; translated as *At the Mind's Limits* (trans. Sidney Rosenfeld and Stella D. Rosenfeld). Bloomington: Indiana University Press, 1980, p. 33; quoted in W. G. Sebald, *On the Natural History of Destruction* (trans. Anthea Bell). New York: Modern Library, 2004, p. 153. In a similar vein, Drew Gilpin Faust describes in *This Republic of Suffering: Death and the American Civil War* (New York: Knopf, 2008, pp. 208–9) how writers groped to depict the horrors of the Civil War.

15. Renford Bambrough, "Appearance, Identity and Ontology." *Proceedings of the Aristotelian Society* 75 (1975): 73–74.

16. An exception is when addressing a specialized audience. Many specialists use jargon that is poorly understood by the lay public but expedites communication (and doesn't necessarily sacrifice clarity) within their communities of expertise. Thus, clarity as such isn't an overriding goal in communication but rather clarity relative to a given audience.

17. C. S. Lewis, *Studies in Words*. Cambridge: Cambridge University Press, 1967, p. 313.

18. Wittgenstein, *Tractatus Logico-Philosophicus*, 4.002.

19. W. V. Quine describes this phenomenon in his classic essay, "The Two Dogmas of Empiricism," p. 2:

"In logical and mathematical systems either of two mutually antagonistic types of economy may be striven for, and each has its peculiar practical utility. On the one hand we may seek economy of practical expression: ease and brevity in the statement of multifarious relationships. This sort of economy calls usually for distinctive concise notations for a wealth of concepts. Second, however, and oppositely, we may seek economy in grammar and vocabulary; we may try to find a minimum of basic concepts such that, once a distinctive notation has been appropriated to each of them, it becomes possible to express any desired further concept by mere combination and iteration of our basic notations. This second sort of economy is impractical in one way, since a poverty in basic idioms tends to a necessary lengthening of discourse. But it is practical in another way: it greatly simplifies theoretical discourse *about* language, through minimizing the terms and the forms of construction wherein the language consists."

20. Harold Bloom, *Wallace Stevens: The Poems of Our Climate*. Ithaca, NY: Cornell University Press, 1976.

21. Jacques Barzun, "The Retort Circumstantial," in H. Haydn and B. Saunders, eds., *American Scholar Reader*, 205. New York: Atheneum, 1960; New Brunswick, NJ: Transaction, 2011.

22. Kazimierz Ajdukiewicz, *Problems and Theories of Philosophy* (trans. H. Skolimowski and A. Quinton). Cambridge: Cambridge University Press, 1973, p. 37.

23. Everett, *Language: The Cultural Tool*, pp. 242–43.

Chapter 5

The Range of Rationality

> So convenient a thing it is to be a reasonable creature, since it enables one to find or make a reason for every thing one has a mind to do.
>
> —Benjamin Franklin

DEFINING RATIONALITY: THE CORE FEATURES

"Critical thinking" is a broad and nebulous term, and so is the even wider umbrella concept of "rationality." They are nebulous for a reason: like many of the concepts embedded in our thought and language, they cover a lot of conceptual ground and lack precise definitional boundaries. We're not talking about geometry here. Engaging with such concepts is an essential part of critical inquiry (another nebulous term). So to get to the core of our project, which is analytic thinking, we first need to unfold the idea of rationality itself. Then we can properly explore the kind of rationality we call critical thinking.

In the broadest sense, rationality means using the mind to grapple with the world *systematically*—that is, thinking and acting in accordance with rules and/or reasons. Applying those rules and reasons promotes a family of goals: efficacy of action and clarity, consistency, relevance, and coherence of thought. As such, rationality is, like language itself, an essentially communitarian enterprise: a way of achieving axes of common understanding about thought, meaning, and action.[1]

In addition to being systematic and communitarian, a third defining feature of rationality is that *there is no universal model of what it means to be rational*. Most philosophers agree that it isn't reducible to a singular method or principle, nor does it have a single goal beyond sharing understanding of how we think and act in the world.[2] Outside of formal logic, mathematics, and other symbolic systems (such as alphabets, codes, or computer programs), there are no objective standards for achieving consistency, clarity, coherence, relevance, and the like.

One paradigm of rationality is scientific rigor. It includes, on one hand, recognition of the known (and so far as we know, universal) laws of nature, such as the laws of gravity, motion, and thermodynamics. On the other hand, science also depends on the rational methodology known as scientific method: the systematic process of observing and measuring, experimenting, forming hypotheses, and testing those hypotheses in the natural world. Scientific understanding is a moving target, and science is continually revising itself; some of its most basic questions, such as the exact nature of light, gravity, dark matter, space-time, and the universe itself, remain disputed or utterly mysterious. But rational procedures, and the embodied rationality of techniques and technologies, are our best hope for answering those questions.

A fourth general feature of rationality is that we don't just share it; we need it. Although we use it in different ways and degrees, and with varying degrees of aptitude and success, we all use it, and we can't do without it. Indeed, *consciousness itself entails some rationality*. As the anthropologist Gregory Bateson points out, our perceptions aren't raw undifferentiated data, but data interpreted by our minds: "The very process of perception is an act of logical typing. Every image is a complex of many-leveled coding and mapping."[3] We don't simply absorb sense-data passively; we apprehend structure and coherence in the world around us. We are capable, that is, of recognizing and modeling the world, and therefore of acting to change or preserve it.

"Consciousness" is another essential idea that we struggle to define. It's a seemingly ineffable blend of perception, emotion, and cognition, enabling us to identify things—objects, attributes, processes, patterns, relationships—and thus to generalize about the world and have agency within it. Barring extenuating circumstances such as severe mental debility, we are never purely emotive or sensory beings, nor are we purely rational beings. From deciding what to have for breakfast to where to live, we reason all our waking lives—and arguably while sleeping too.

Thought and action are distinct but intertwined functions. Whether screwing in a light bulb, planning a career, analyzing a concept, or critiquing an argument, we're both rational beings and agents in the world. Acting on reasons is part of what we mean by "act," as opposed to random or nondeliberate behavior. Even a seemingly instinctive reaction such as swatting a mosquito is done for a reason.

To be sure, some reasons are better than others. The best-laid plans, arguments, or understandings may be flawed; we may "act" on reasons we don't understand or can't control, such as genetic factors, chemical imbalance, or past trauma. But the hemispheres of thought and action—and of reason and emotion—remain only nominally distinct. In the words of Jean-François

Lyotard, "There are not those who speak on the one hand, and those who act on the other."[4] Neither are there those who only feel or who only think.

A final defining feature of rationality is that it's radically *instrumental*: a means to our ends and not (in any fundamental sense) an end in itself. It's about doing something, changing something, understanding or communicating something. It doesn't guarantee any outcomes, and it's limited by the relative scarcity of other things that fuel success, such as intelligence, information, time, or your readers' attention span. But it promotes the user's goals.

THREE MODES OF RATIONALITY

We have many ways of using or giving reasons and various ways of parsing them, beginning with identifying which reasons we're talking about and what kinds of thoughts or actions they are reasons for. So one initially useful way of understanding rationality is via the logical distinction between three general (and at times overlapping) *modes* of reasoning: subjective, objective, and intersubjective.

Subjective rationality is pragmatic, instrumental thinking by and for the self: how we organize means and ends in solitude. Lone hunter-gatherers, hermits, or survivalists in the wilderness are subjectively rational in this sense, and so is anyone swatting a fly or changing a light bulb unassisted. They *have* reasons but don't need to *give* reasons. They implicitly seek efficient means to solitary ends, without needing to coordinate or defend them within larger communities. If I want to fish, it's subjectively rational for me to use a rod and bait or a lure. If while fishing in a mountain stream I see a bear, it may be rational to climb the nearest tree. Such actions come under the loose heading of common sense, to which we'll return.

You may prefer to call bear avoidance an instinctual fight-or-flight response. But saving one's own life or minimizing a threat is still a rational thing to do, given our shared human urge to survive and avoid harm, and it involves reasoning about the means to those ends: Up in the tree, maybe the bear can't reach me. Even such survival- or subsistence-oriented reasoning is communitarian in the sense that, although applied in isolation, it's a common response to like situations. We all look for a way of escape when a bear attacks. Similarly, if one wants to catch a bus, it's wisest to wait at a bus stop. And the practical rule of crossing streets at crosswalks isn't just useful *for me* but for others as well. It isn't just a question of "What should I do?" but rather, "What should one do?"[5]

When we think and act socially, on the other hand, rationality is more like a common language (and like language itself): a way of communicating effectively among "subjects" with different perspectives, experiences, abilities, values, or aims. Such intersubjective reasoning may not lead to perfect agreement or understanding; nothing can guarantee that. But with shared reasoning and some shared facts (and the reasoning may be faulty and the facts may be wrong), we can sometimes narrow the range of disagreement and promote common goals.

Part of this vast social side of reasoning can be considered objective: reasoning in cases where there is no meaningful choice, because it is guided by more or less rigid and universal procedural rules for relating things to other things. Objective rationality is thus limited to the artificial symbolic systems we share: logic, mathematics, codes, and to a lesser extent alphabets and grammars. Such symbolic systems serve important functions and have important limitations as well. We don't argue *about* them so much as we argue *with the use of* them. Objective rationality undergirds critical thinking and public discourse. It is almost always part of the thinking process—and almost never the whole.

Intersubjective rationality identifies whatever is social and debatable—whatever we share. Its functions include announcing or explaining goals or ideas; making inferences from experience, or inductive claims about the future based on the past; negotiating conflicts and competing according to shared rules; solving problems in groups; and trying to persuade others to see the world as we do. Discourse in the liberal arts, and across public life, is intersubjective. It is public not private, and draws on but is not limited to objective symbolic systems. When we look at the concept of truth, we'll see a similar intersubjective pattern emerge, because the pursuit of truth, in any shared form, is an essentially rational and social enterprise.

THE LIMITS OF RATIONALITY

There are certain aspects of human reasoning that may at first seem unwelcome or counterintuitive. One is its radically instrumental and pragmatic nature. When we reason together in groups or publicly, our immediate ends—the reasons for reasoning—are communitarian: mutual comprehension, clarity, coherence, consistency, relevance, and so forth. Even when we treat rationality itself as an ideal (as when we say we want "reason to prevail" in public debates or in classrooms, laboratories, and so on), it's because it is instrumental to other ends; there is no other reason why reason should prevail. Rationality is not itself a reason.

Those other ends, however "rationally" we may select, prioritize, or deliberate about them, are ultimately rooted in personal or shared emotional states: drives, desires, opinions, or values. As David Hume famously put it, "Reason is, and ought only to be, the slave of the passions, and can never pretend to any other office than to serve and obey them."⁶ Without some such passions, whether for world peace, scientific breakthroughs, or chocolate cake, there's nothing to be reasonable *about*—and no "self" to reason about them.

We reason our way through ideas, problems, and arguments because clarifying those ideas, solving those problems, or having those arguments serves our other purposes, but we remain essentially end-seeking creatures. Rationality merely expedites those ends. It may help us to prioritize them, but it doesn't create them or substitute for them.[7]

It may even be rational, for achieving certain ends, to act irrationally in respect to others. You may risk your life to save someone else's, and eating junk food or maintaining a sedentary lifestyle may be a rational choice if it's the only way to finish your novel. We can't be rational about whom we fall in love with or what foods we like. Reasoning, in other words, isn't just a dispensable tool; it's always auxiliary to other communitarian goals, such as learning, communicating, producing, or governing.

The means-ends economy of rationality, in fact, leaves much unaccounted for. Morality, for one thing: concentration camps are paradigms of efficiency toward maximally evil ends. Also psychology, which seeks (among other things) to explain how and why we depart from rational behavior. Again, reason doesn't dictate ends. As Hume also wrote, "Tis not contrary to reason to prefer the destruction of the whole world to the scratching of my finger."[8]

Another potentially unsettling feature of rationality is a psychological one implied by Hume's dictum: we tend to overvalue it or exaggerate its role. We exalt reasoning as a general practice (or at least give it lip service), yet it's an axiom of psychology that we are far less rational than we suppose. We're prone to overconfidence, denial, selective awareness, and magical thinking. We miscalculate probabilities, ignore what we dislike, overlook the larger context, value the immediate and the obvious over the more remote (especially as children). We tend to overestimate our own rational capacities and underestimate those of others. We confuse the irrational with what is imprudent, immoral, or merely distasteful. And we underestimate the role of emotions in thinking generally.

Part of being a critical thinker is coming to recognize these hardwired mental tendencies and working to overcome them. Another part is distinguishing between the irrational and the nonrational. My taste in art or food, and my preference among baseball teams, are nonrational, as are most emotions (if we can separate them from perceptions of the world). They are not contrary to reason, although indulging them may or may not be.

No one—not even Spock on *Star Trek*—is a "perfectly" rational creature. We aren't computers. We have different capacities and proclivities to think and act rationally, and we reason through a haze of (often unconscious or conflicting) values and norms, needs, goals, social pressures, and the like.

Our more analytical left brains cohabit with our more creative or imaginative right brains, and both are confined and conditioned by time and space, culture and nature, genetics and personal experience. This doesn't mean we shouldn't strive to think more critically. But self-conscious reasoning clearly isn't all that goes on inside our heads, or all that needs to go on in there. As Shakespeare has it in *A Midsummer Night's Dream* (act 5, scene 1),

> Lovers and madmen have such seething brains,
> Such shaping fantasies, that apprehend
> More than cool reason ever comprehends.

At the same time, it would be wrong to think of left-brain rationality as simply oppositional to right-brain emotion or imagination. Both are intrinsic to human consciousness. As Malcolm Gladwell and others have pointed out, the unconscious isn't just a Freudian stew of irrational or nonrational ingredients. Even in our dreams we explore emotions, entertain ideas, form insights, and occasionally solve problems (or at least work on them). As forms of semiconscious experience, dreams aren't random or wholly chaotic: for all their mystery, they are organized, meaningful stories we tell ourselves, if sometimes for obscure reasons.[9] If I go to bed hungry and dream that I'm in a French patisserie, what's crazy about that?

At times, of course, it's convenient to stress the rational side and distinguish it from emotion or creativity. Impulse, opinion, and fantasy don't help when rescuing a drowning swimmer, flying an airplane, driving a car, or changing a light bulb. Yet we're culturally conditioned to think of rationality as somehow better than emotion, as if they were wholly independent and we could choose between them. We can't choose the type or intensity of our feelings; what we can choose, to some extent, is how much, and in what way, we reveal or express them. Rolf Dobelli echoes Hume when he writes, "Whether we like it or not, we are puppets of our emotions."[10] Which is to say, we are prisoners of our selves.

Although we can and must distinguish between rationality and emotion in the abstract, we should see them as complementary in virtually all human thought and action. The objective fields of logic and math are studied and applied for reasons: to pass an exam, measure the drapes, or design a building; there's always a volitional component based on (often shared) forms of subjectivity.

The imagination is central to who we are as a species—and to liberal learning. Like the use of language (which it often involves), creativity is an essentially rational process: it's at least minimally and informally rule based, not a random outpouring, and it's instrumental to further goals, such as sharing ideas and attracting an audience. Any successful work of art is an organized, structured expression: an embodiment of form as well as information, emotion, values, or references to shared knowledge or memory, communicated to an audience. Like any communicative act, it succeeds only to the extent that it is aware of itself, its audience, and the messages it is trying to convey.

> The rational and the irrational complement each other. Individually they are far less powerful.
>
> —Raymond Tusk, in the Netflix series *House of Cards*[11]

We tend to equate irrationality with behavior that is self-destructive, unpredictable, opaque, fantasy based, or otherwise counterproductive to the agent's own ends or incompatible with the goals and actions of others. But thoughts and actions aren't "rational" or "irrational" in themselves, only as means to ends in a particular context, including the intentions and perceptions of the agent in question.

INFERENCE AND INDUCTION MAKE THE WORLD GO AROUND

Most of our thinking lies somewhere in the twilight zone between deduction and raw perception; indeed, there's no such thing as "pure" perception: it is a mental process of absorbing, sorting, and processing stimuli, nominally performed by each of us alone and differently. Every observation or sensation of the world around us is limited because our minds are singular, limited, and fallible. In this sense we are indeed limited by our subjectivity. Yet we need our imperfect and subjective senses to function.[12]

In daily life, we depend almost entirely on customary forms of (informal) rationality, such as inference and induction, and less on logic or mathematics, unless we're measuring the drapes. Looking at your face, I recognize who you are and infer likely emotional messages. I may ask how you're feeling, but I don't measure your smile or calculate your heart rate. Such inferences and inductions are pragmatic—that is, they work much of the time and they're all we have to go on.

Ordinary life is full of such informal reasoning based on assumptions and judgments about past and present experience, probabilities, and educated guesses. If I get dressed, I'll be warmer; if I bathe, I'll be cleaner. This is subjective rationality at its most mundane. Some of these inferences and predictions are reliable enough to be considered, for practical purposes, certainties. As the philosopher G. E. Moore observed, we all have one body; we are each born in a particular place and time; we live, we have "experiences," and we die.[13] That I will die someday is arguably even a logical certainty, if we define "human being" as something that is mortal. And it would be irrational to bet against the sun rising tomorrow. It's when we confuse our generalizations with certainties, or convert them into rigid stereotypes, that we get into trouble.

We often do need to question appearances—but we can't question *all* appearances. That would amount to questioning conscious experience itself. As we learn beginning in early childhood, appearance and reality can diverge in important ways, but in the end, run-of-the-mill (and often unconscious) inferences and probabilities, not certainties, are what hold the world together. The ability to question or doubt is an important part of critical thinking, but doubting everything doesn't make sense in a world of guesswork. Radical skepticism is a losing proposition, a diseconomy of doubting. We make pragmatic judgments all the time about what is true, real, likely, plausible, or doubtful.

The everyday assumptions and judgments we implicitly rely on, based on the most commonplace elements and boundaries of social existence, constitute the substrate of rationality that we loosely call "common sense." It's hard to define, yet we know it when we see it, and its salient features include practicality and, at times, obviousness. One writer calls common sense "an immense society of hard-earned practical ideas."[14] Another defines it as "largely a matter of widely held and usually unchallenged beliefs."[15] Henry David Thoreau is more blunt, admonishing his readers in *Walden*, "Rescue the drowning and tie your shoestrings."[16] Yet for all its apparent simplicity, common sense can sometimes be elusive. As the famously practical-minded Benjamin Franklin notes in his "Sundry Maritime Observations,"[17]

> While on the topic of sinking, one cannot help recollecting the well known practice of the Chinese, to divide the hold of a great ship into a number of separate chambers by partitions tight caulked . . . so that if a leak should spring in one of them the others are not affected by it; and though that chamber should fill to have a level with the sea, it would not be sufficient to sink the vessel. We have not imitated this practice.

SUMMARY: RATIONALITY IS THE GRAMMAR OF CITIZENSHIP

Again, rational thinking in general is a complex and multifaceted human capacity and cannot be reduced to a single method, strategy, or set of finite rules. It can mean thinking subjectively to advance an end; objectively, as with logic or math; or intersubjectively in a community. It can mean an economy of ends and means, thinking and acting instrumentally to achieve such diverse goals as survival, changing a tire, or raising a family. And it can mean thinking systematically, according to shared and transparent rules or principles, to promote the communitarian goals of clarity, consistency, coherence, and relevance. That's the form we're calling critical thinking and (in the context of liberal learning) critical inquiry.

> The freedom to think is opposed first of all to civil compulsion. . . . Yet how much and how correctly would we think if we did not think as it were in community with others to whom we communicate our thoughts, and who communicate theirs to us!
>
> —Immanuel Kant[18]

As the tacit public acknowledgment of rules and reasons, rationality is the basis for all public communication, for all learning, and for the triangle of civic, cultural, and economic citizenship. It is how we navigate as individuals in society to achieve personal and collective goals. As noted earlier, even demagogues use language rationally to achieve their ends, while appealing to the irrational in their audience.

We may think subjectively in privacy or in solitude. We think intersubjectively (in pairs or groups) when planning a family or a barbecue, or considering an idea, an argument, or a course of public action, as we do in classrooms, boardrooms, bedrooms, committee rooms, broadcast studios, football huddles, or criminal hideouts. The fact that we live in communities imposes the need for baseline forms of intersubjective rationality, such as implicit rules of order and civility and the rules embedded in language itself. Forming such rational communities doesn't impede our personal ends; it simply provides a way of communicating and advancing them. Guided by rules and reasons, that intersubjective realm can even expand, enrich, or transform our little subjective worlds, and that is the very essence of citizenship.

NOTES

1. Calling rationality a form of community isn't a radical claim; on its face, it merely states that rational thinking and discourse are primarily intersubjective forms of communication. But it's also consonant with the "social brain" hypothesis that human interaction itself advances thinking, and with evidence that other intelligent mammals, such as whales and dolphins, also live in defined and stable communities and communicate and interact within (and even beyond) them.

2. "There is not a single philosophical method," writes Wittgenstein (*Philosophical Investigations*. New York: Wiley, 1991, §133d), "though there are indeed methods,

different therapies, as it were." These "therapies" vary according to the purpose and context: solving problems, making decisions (which door to open, which school to attend), describing the world, arguing for one's beliefs, stating or interpreting facts. They may call for logical deduction, inference (generalizing from facts), induction (inferences about the future based on the past), stating definitions, analysis of concepts, and so on.

3. Gregory Bateson, *Mind and Nature: A Necessary Unity*. New York: Dutton, 1979, p. 206.

4. Jean-François Lyotard, *Why Philosophize?* Cambridge: Polity Press, 2013, p. 103; for further discussion of the interconnection of thought and action, see Lyotard, chapter 4, "On Philosophy and Action." Children, and adults who are debilitated or institutionalized, are partial exceptions.

5. While we don't know much about what they're thinking, animals also behave in ways that could be described as subjectively and intersubjectively rational. They may not argue, analyze, or tell jokes, but they cooperate, live in communities, gather food, stalk prey, protect their young, and perform other goal-oriented tasks alone and in groups.

6. David Hume, *A Treatise of Human Nature*. London: Clarendon Press, 1988, Book II, section 3.

7. A fair objection to this, or a broad exception, lies in the fact that most if not all of our ends (like our very personalities) are themselves formed and pursued in a social environment and thus partly conditioned by the need to function rationally.

8. Hume, *A Treatise of Human Nature*, Book III, section 3.

9. Here, of course, the ambiguity of the term "rational" comes into play. A dream may and often does reflect forms of illogic or distortions of reality. But it isn't incoherent or without purpose.

10. Rolf Dobelli, *The Art of Thinking Clearly* (trans. Nicky Griffin). New York: Harper, 2014, p. 199. To say we are "puppets" of our emotions implies that we are helplessly determined by a separate force. (As Hume said, "We can do as we please, but we cannot please as we please.") But the conative stew of values, emotions, and so forth are the self's very core.

11. *House of Cards*, Season 1, episode 12, directed by Allen Coulter, written by Michael Dobbs, featuring Kevin Spacey, Robin Wright, and Kate Mara, aired February 1, 2013, on Netflix.

12. "The fact is," as David Deutsch writes, "there's nothing infallible about 'direct experience.' . . . Indeed, experience is never direct. It is a sort of virtual reality, created by our brains using sketchy and flawed sensory clues, given substance only by fallible expectations, explanations, and interpretations." David Deutsch, "Why It's Good to Be Wrong," *Nautilus*, May 23, 2013, p. 135.

13. G. E. Moore, "A Defence of Common Sense," in J. H. Muirhead, ed., *Contemporary British Philosophy* (2nd series). London: Allen & Unwin, 1925; reprinted in G. E. Moore, *Philosophical Papers*. New York: Routledge, 1959.

14. Marvin Minsky, *The Society of Mind*. New York: Simon & Schuster, 1988, p. 22.

15. John Searle, *Mind, Language and Society: Philosophy in the Real World*. New York: Basic Books, 1999, pp. 11–12.

16. Henry David Thoreau, *Walden*, Vol. 2. Boston: Houghton, Mifflin, 1854, ch. 1 "Economy."

17. Benjamin Franklin, letter to Alphonsus le Roy, 1785.

18. Immanuel Kant, *What Does It Mean to Orient Oneself in Thinking?* Kuhn, Germany: Daniel Fidel Ferrer, Verlag, 1786.

Chapter 6

Defining Critical Thinking

The term "critical thinking" is a bit like the Euro: a form of currency that not long ago many were eager to adopt but that has proven troublesome to maintain. And in both cases, the Greeks bear an outsized portion of the blame.

—Peter Wood

WHAT IS CRITICAL THINKING?

The landscape of the liberal arts can be mapped in a variety of ways. One way is geographically, according to its subject disciplines, from chemistry to literature to psychology; more broadly, it can be understood in terms of domains, per the upside-down wedding cake model of natural science, social science, and the humanities. Such maps are useful, although none of those boundaries are impermeable. But liberal learning can also be viewed in methodological terms: in terms of how we think rather than what we think about. And how we think is the unifying element that connects all those areas of learning.

What should we call that defining feature? "Critical inquiry" is a useful umbrella term for those methodologies. But critical inquiry has its own semantic predicament, being closely related to the concepts of rationality and critical thinking. It's no surprise that there's some confusion around these ideas.

A first step toward sorting out the confusion is to recognize that the three terms "rationality," "critical inquiry," and "critical thinking" all mean more or less the same thing, with different contextual shadings. Like the terms "freedom" and "liberty," for example (and unlike, say, "politics" and "art"), they overlap considerably. As we home in on critical thinking, we'll need to qualify that three-way equation and distinguish different senses of rationality and critical thinking.

The first such qualification is a relatively easy one. "Rationality" is used in both practical and intellectual contexts, and although they may overlap, practical reasoning "in the world" is distinct from intellectual reasoning or metacognition. Practical reasoning is the situational kind that tells us the best means to a given end. If you want dinner, plan it, shop for it, and cook it. If safety's your thing, stop at red lights. Intellectual reasoning (critical thinking, as we're broadly defining it) is reasoning according to a rule or principle. Indeed, critical thinking has aptly been called the "educational cognate" of rationality.[1] But it also applies beyond the academy, across the public square.

We think rationally in the practical sense all the time—almost literally so, unless we are mentally impaired—in everything we do, from building a house to opening a door. So not all forms of rationality involve "critical thinking," but all critical thinking is rational.

The second qualification of the equation between critical thinking and rationality is that critical thinking isn't just the more intellectual and metacognitive side of reasoning, the side that thinks about thought itself; it is complex and heterogeneous. Critical thinking has multiple definitions and definitional components that need to be teased apart, forming a spectrum of different types of metacognition. These qualifications will be addressed in due course; meanwhile, the equation holds as a point of departure.

Above all, critical thinking is a form of *community*. It joins people in a common enterprise of mutual understanding through coherent conversations, bounded by shared rules or guidelines, regardless of whether or how much they may agree about the facts at hand or the values in play. As Heraclitus puts it (Fragment 81), "All men should speak clearly and logically, and thus share rational discourse and have a body of thought in common, as the people of a city are all under the same laws." It's a unifier par excellence. That is what makes critical thinking essential to all learning and all citizenship.

As a species of rationality, critical thinking is also *systematic thinking*: thinking in discrete stages that are linked to one another by some rule or principle, and hence shareable and transparent. The core functions of such thinking, inseparable from its being shared and systematic, are clarity and consistency. But clarity and consistency aren't ends in themselves—just as rationality isn't an end in itself and discourse isn't an end in itself. They are instrumental to a larger end: promoting communities of understanding. We don't talk simply to generate sound waves in the air. As individuals and communities, we are the only ends.

How else is critical thinking distinct from rationality in general? Here we can narrow the focus, because there are several definitional fissures that conform to general usage. Unlike subjective practical reasoning, critical thinking is intersubjective (and sometimes objective). It isn't just means-ends optimization, or whatever someone does for a reason or according to a rule: avoid a predator, boil an egg, fix a window shade, and so on. And unlike philosophy, what we commonly call critical thinking focuses on *an immediately present intellectual object*: my thinking, your thinking, this or that concept, text, image, argument, and so on.

These differences help to explain why educators urge students to become "critical thinkers," not "rational thinkers." Rather than equating critical thinking with rationality in general, with practical reasoning, or with philosophy, we can better describe it as a midrange band of rationality: intersubjective, intellectual but not purely philosophical, and bound to particular contexts and situations.

FURTHER STEPS TOWARD A DEFINITION

Again: What is critical thinking? If there were a single obvious answer to that question, beyond the general attributes just cited, most of the writing on the subject would be unnecessary. Like other general concepts (such as citizenship, knowledge, art, education, the liberal arts) critical thinking can't be reduced to a single essence, process, or attribute. In other words, it's a complex idea, identifying a family of formal and informal rules for intellectual rigor. As a result, it is often cited, without any definition or explanation whatsoever, as the keystone of liberal learning. Like anything else—education, sea salt, witchcraft—critical thinking, in the end, is whatever most people say it is, because that's how language works: usage rules.[2] There is broad general agreement, but no final consensus, about its various forms and attributes.

The word "critical," like "thinking," is used in various ways in everyday speech. It derives from κριτικός (*kritikos*), the Greek term for both "crisis" and "judgment." To say something is in crisis can mean several things: that it is undergoing significant change; subject to controversy; under existential threat from an external source; or internally unstable, owing to its state, contents, or complex definition. In another sense, "critical" implies "urgent" or "necessary," modifying something that prevents or responds to a state of crisis. Changing, threatened, complex: the liberal arts are in crisis, democracy is in crisis, almost anything complex is in crisis. Life is full of crises.

At the same time, "critical" can also denote evaluating or exposing flaws; the impulse to challenge, question, and correct; the will and capacity to interrogate. Criticality in this sense can't be quantified or reduced to specific rules, at least outside of formal logic. But we can note that it's essentially dialogic: one voice interacting with, correcting or being corrected by, another voice. Dialogue imparts added value in the form of direct criticism—an advantage over monologue or multivocal speech. Thus Socrates, in the writings of Plato, mainly opts to have one conversational partner rather than none or many.[3]

This latter sense, the dialogic and evaluative, comes closer to what we most often mean by "critical thinking." It's thinking that is metacognitive (self-aware and self-critical) as well as other-critical and that aims to argue, question, correct, analyze, or explain. In more sophisticated forms, such thinking also includes epistemic questions: the attempt to understand what is and is not known, what we need to know, how we know what we know, and how it all relates to other knowledge. The concept of critical thinking draws from all of these wells of meaning. It is thinking that is systematic—that is, governed by formal or informal rules; aimed at the rigors of clarity, consistency, thoroughness, and relevance—and like philosophy, it's a process of metacognition, referring to thought itself.

The idea isn't new. As I've suggested, all thought, and all language, are essentially philosophical. Philosophy itself is a millennia-old tradition of critical thinking in a broader gauge. But critical thinking isn't the exclusive purview of philosophers. Henry David Thoreau offers one version of it from the solitude of his cabin on Walden Pond:[4]

> With thinking we may be beside ourselves in a sane sense. . . . I only know myself as a human entity; the scene, so to speak, of thoughts and affections; and am sensible of a certain doubleness by which I can stand as remote from myself as from another. However intense my experience, I am conscious of the presence and criticism of part of me, which, as it were, is not a part of me, but a spectator, sharing no experience, but taking note of it; and that is no more I than it is you.

The sense of "doubleness" Thoreau refers to, the business of standing outside oneself and self-examining, is the essential feature of critical thinking that we're calling metacognition.

If the sources of "critical thinking" are ancient, the compound term itself is less than a century old. In 1910, John Dewey defined "reflective thinking" as what happens when "the ground or basis for a belief is deliberately sought and its adequacy to support the belief examined."[5] The term "critical thinking" itself, propounded by Dewey and others, emerged in the 1920s and '30s as the idea of extending the rigor of scientific method and logical thinking into a general model of intellectual rigor.[6]

Over the past century, "critical thinking" has been defined and used in numerous ways, often loosely but at times with almost implausible precision. It enjoyed a spike of general and scholarly interest in the 1980s before leveling off. Yet, despite a general consensus, the extensive scholarly literature on critical thinking can't agree on exactly what it is or how it should be taught.

As one writer notes, "Because critical thinking is a complex skill, any attempt to offer a full and definitive definition of it would be futile."[7] Scholars who have tried to define critical thinking are not blind to its complexity, but they have tended to focus on different parts of the proverbial elephant. We will try to see both the parts and the whole.

LONG-FORM DEFINITIONS OF CRITICAL THINKING

In 2012, the Texas Republican Party platform condemned the teaching of critical thinking, because its purpose was characterized as "challenging the student's fixed beliefs and undermining parental authority."[8] Yes—they condemned it. But the state party's description of critical thinking is accurate so far as it goes: critical thinking challenges fixed beliefs.[9] As for undermining parental authority, independent thinking means independence from parents as well as from anyone else. So another general descriptor of critical thinking, along with systematic, metacognitive, and immediate, is "independent." Thank you, Texas GOP.

More scholarly approaches to critical thinking have tended to produce lengthy laundry lists of discrete intellectual skills. For example,

1. "Critical thinking is disciplined, self-directed thinking which exemplifies the perfections of thinking appropriate to a particular mode or domain of thought. . . . These 'perfections' include clarity, precision, specificity, accuracy, relevance, consistency, logic depth, completeness, fairness, and adequacy." (Richard Paul and Linda Elder)[10]
2. "Instruction in critical thinking is to be designed to achieve an understanding of the relationship of language to logic . . . the ability to analyze, criticize, and advocate ideas, to reason inductively and deductively, and to reach factual or judgmental conclusions based on sound inferences. . . . The minimal competence to be expected . . . should be the ability to distinguish fact from judgment, belief from knowledge, and skills in elementary inductive and deductive processes, including an understanding of the formal and informal fallacies of language and thought." (Glenn Dumke)[11]
3. Critical thinking means "developing the ability to look for hidden assumptions and fallacies in everyday arguments." (V. Ramanathan and R. Kaplan)[12]
4. "The general consensus is that critical thinking (CT) per se is judging in a reflective way what to do or what to believe. The cognitive skills of analysis, interpretation, inference, explanation, evaluation, and of

monitoring and correcting one's own reasoning are at the heart of critical thinking." (Peter A. Facione et al.)[13]
5. "When we become critical thinkers we develop an awareness of the assumptions under which we, and others, think and act. We learn to pay attention to the context in which our actions and ideas are generated. We become skeptical of quick-fix solutions, of single answers to problems, and of claims to universal truth. We also become open to alternative ways of looking at, and behaving in, the world." (S. D. Brookfield)[14]
6. "It is best to think of critical thinking as developing depth in successive layers, without any limit to the possible depth one can achieve." (Robert J. Sternberg)[15]
7. "The mental dispositions increasingly emphasized within critical thinking circles [are] the capacities: to unify and make connections in one's experience; to follow an extended line of thought through propositional, thematic, or symbolic development; to engage in mature moral reasoning and to form judgments of quality and taste; to be attuned to skepticism and irony; and to be perceptive of ambiguity, relativity of viewpoint, and multiple dimensions of form and meaning." (Donald Lazere)[16]
8. Robert H. Ennis, in a classic 1964 essay,[17] defines critical thinking as proficiency in judging whether: "1. A statement follows from the premises. 2. Something is an assumption. 3. An observation statement is reliable. 4. A simple generalization is warranted. 5. A hypothesis is warranted. 6. A theory is warranted. 7. An argument depends on an ambiguity. 8. A statement is overvague or overspecific. 9. An alleged authority is reliable."
9. Finally, this is how critical thinking is summarized by the American Philosophical Association:[18]

The ideal critical thinker is habitually inquisitive, well-informed, trustful of reason, open-minded, flexible, fair-minded in evaluation, honest in facing personal biases, prudent in making judgments, willing to reconsider, clear about issues, orderly in complex matters, diligent in seeking relevant information, reasonable in the selection of criteria, focused in inquiry, and persistent in seeking results which are as precise as the subject and the circumstances of inquiry permit.

It's also possible to take a more personalized approach to defining critical thinking. Ken Bain, for example, describes an actual college student who

learned to question everything. He looked for the assumptions behind arguments and the concepts they employed. He thought about their implications and applications, and asked for evidence, questioning the source and nature of that supporting information. He analyzed the reasoning employed by his classmates and in the source material, noting in particular the way language is sometimes used to distort thought and enflame passions.[19]

Each of these definitional sets is plausible, and none is exhaustive or definitive. Each lists important skills, rules, or goals, which can't all be collapsed into broader categories, and although there's a lot of overlap among them, each list is unique. Nor are they free of vagueness. (Ennis, for example, doesn't define "proficiency" or provide benchmarks for when such standards are met.) Instead, they serve as separate windows on the same complex idea and the disparate, but interconnected, skills it encompasses. They are a paradigm case of family resemblance based on a variety of mental skills and attributes.

There can be no final list because there is no supreme principle or criterion that could generate a single roster of critical thinking skills, much less rank them in importance. Any definition of critical thinking must include multiple elements and reflect multiple, overlapping goals. It is thinking that is clear, systematic, and logical; that respects factual truth and avoids bad arguments and psychological and epistemic traps; that acknowledges and assesses the limits of knowledge; and thinking that is analytical, using language to overcome the limits of language itself.

Whether despite or because of its vagueness and complexity, critical thinking has become a general placeholder for intellectual rigor, particularly among educators defending the liberal arts. And for good reason: it *is* intellectual rigor. Nothing is more important, in liberal learning or almost any other kind, than sound thinking. The meaning of critical thinking remains a rugged frontier, but it isn't impassable or impossible to chart.

Moreover, these varying definitions convey an important irony. In thinking about thinking (outside of logic and mathematics), we can never wholly eliminate the subjectivity that is basic to human experience. We all see the world from our own point of view, however much we may agree on what we're looking at.

As individuals, we implicitly assume that the world is pretty much as we see it. Yet despite experiencing a presumably shared reality, our subjectivity guarantees that we see the world partially, indeed infinitesimally, and often inaccurately. This is not just due to our singularity (you and I can never see the same door in exactly the same way, though we can usually agree that we're looking at the same door), but also to a range of conceptual, perceptual, and psychological errors to which we're all prone. Those errors, however, can be identified and taken into account. Like Thoreau in his hut on Walden Pond, we can sometimes, to some extent, transcend subjectivity.

The irony is that such subjectivity is at once endemic to the human mind and often self-defeating. Ignoring our subjectivity is dangerous, but so is indulging it to the exclusion of intersubjective understanding. Applying the tools of critical thinking isn't an art, based on imagination or creativity. Neither is it a science, in the narrow sense of following objective rules or procedures. It is something else altogether: a gradually acquired body of intellectual habits, strategies, and best practices that bring us closer together.

SUMMARY: THE MULTIPLE FACETS OF CRITICAL THINKING

Several patterns emerge from the above definitions of critical thinking. They overlap significantly, often citing the same discrete intellectual skills, but such overlap is never complete. We can summarize—and to a certain extent organize—this family of critical-thinking tools with an extended list of our own, beginning with the most general features. Some items, you'll note, fall in more than one category.

General Elements of Critical Thinking:

- Thinking metacognitively (thinking about thinking)
- Thinking dialogically and intersubjectively
- Thinking both systematically and systemically
- Using language carefully and self-critically
- Thinking independently and questioning all authority
- Asking questions; probing for flaws of reasoning or evidence; exposing latent conflicts, contradictions, fallacies, concealed interests, or unobvious dimensions such as hidden distinctions, connections, or causes or effects

Formal and Informal Logic:

- Avoiding inconsistency, incoherence, and contradiction by adhering to the laws of formal logic
- Avoiding intellectual pitfalls and unsound arguments by following the guidelines of informal logic and exposing latent contradictions, fallacies, blunders, blind spots, and biases, rooted in logic, argumentation, psychological predispositions, self-interest, political or commercial interests, and so on
- Decoding messages that are biased or intended to manipulate and exposing their manipulative function, thus revealing what the messenger doesn't want you to know; these include bullying, deception, commercial advertising, propaganda, political rhetoric, loose or flawed

arguments, and appeals to raw emotion, or to mysticism or faith, as well as "sociocentric" thinking based on unreflective biases

Epistemic:

- Assessing what we know and how and why we know it
- Distinguishing (where possible) between truth and untruth; between what we believe and what we would like to believe; and between reality and appearance, unreality, fantasy, or illusion
- Identifying unstated assumptions
- Making sound inferences from facts or data
- Exposing hidden or latent causes and effects in experience
- Distinguishing between our mental maps of the world and the territory those maps reflect, while also recognizing the inevitable connections between the model or representation and what is represented

Argumentational:

- Avoiding logical fallacies and contradictions
- Distinguishing between facts and values or opinions, and identifying the contexts in which one or the other is appropriate or necessary
- Distinguishing between what is in our interest and what is in someone else's interest or the public interest (see also assumptions and biases)
- Judging the authority of arguments and sources
- Judging the relevance of particular facts to a particular context

Analytic Thinking:

- Making distinctions within wholes and connections among wholes
- Seeing how connections obscure distinctions and vice versa
- Distinguishing between binary discourses—either/or statements or polarities—and the continuums that such polarities often obscure
- Establishing context (what externally surrounds something) as well as content (what is internal to it); seeing both the "forest" and the "trees"

Again, these core benchmarks aren't discrete intellectual skills so much as general best practices. Assimilating them isn't like learning the multiplication table; it takes practice over time and across many contexts, involving different types of problems, questions, discourses, and situations. Critical thinking is less a body of knowledge than a complex set of mental muscles that require development and constant use. And it applies in every nook and cranny of the liberal arts. Without it, there can be no learning.

THE GHOST OF PHILOSOPHY, AND CITIZENSHIP REVISITED

All of the defining features of critical thinking link it to its intellectual mother ship: philosophy. But whereas philosophy proper is systematic thinking about thought in general, and deals with general questions and concepts such as knowledge, being, and value, critical thinking is systematic thinking applied in the here and now: to your, my, or someone else's thought.[20]

It isn't the rationality of the philosopher excavating big ideas, nor that of the hunter-gatherer seeking food or avoiding predators, nor again is it the end-optimization of the business person, the political demagogue, or the cult leader. Rather, it's the kind of intersubjective rationality through which our minds can meet, as students or citizens, even as our aims, values, or understandings of the world diverge. It is the kind of rationality that hovers over all learning—and all public discourse—as the benign ghost of philosophy, contextualized in the here and now. No one is going to push you through that door marked with the Greek letter Φ for philosophy. But we can't avoid that rendezvous with the ghost of philosophy; it is the set of rules and techniques that animate and unify the liberal arts—and democratic life.

Recall the connection noted earlier between critical thinking and citizenship. Democracy, like education, depends on public discourse, and critical thinking, by lending clarity and consistency to such discourse, is the basic glue of such community, and of almost all language. Clarity means simplicity—except where complexity is required; it means relevance to the topic at hand; and it means transparency—that is, communication not intended to manipulate, befuddle, or deceive.

We can make exceptions in some areas, such as the arts, where certain types and degrees of obscurity may deepen our emotional response to a work. Art has no rational mandate other than to somehow express the artist's intention. But one could also argue that art isn't devoid of or exempt from rationality. Every work of art is intentional, a form of discourse, albeit one that draws heavily on emotion and imagination. Joseph Conrad put it more strongly: "A work that aspires, however humbly, to the condition of art should carry its justification in every line."[21] Art is communication, and communication, however imaginative, also requires reasoning for effective transmission and reception. The artist thinks as much as he or she feels. And we need to think about art, not just feel it.

Art aside, what has all this got to do with citizenship? Everything, if you consider the alternatives to clarity, consistency, shared facts, and the critical tools that underpin them in public discourse. Remove these, and what remain are rumors, rants, trolling, and ridicule, unfounded conspiracy theories, unexplored assumptions, unchallenged assertions, unsupported opinions, and unbridled emotions (and love isn't foremost among them).

There's a place for such uncritical rhetoric in any free society; it must be tolerated—and criticized. Left unchecked, it's inimical to democratic culture. It may satisfy a demand but doesn't promote dialogue, factual agreement, or the understanding of differences. It rewards subjectivity, stereotyping, tribalism, and bias, binding communities that already agree while fracturing society as a whole. Critical thinking, on the other hand, preserves and widens the lanes of public discourse that move debates forward.

NOTES

1. Harvey Siegel, "The Rationality of Science, Critical Thinking, and Science Education," *Synthese* 80:1 (July 1989): 10.

2. One thing critical thinking does not equate with is critical theory. Critical theory is a way of theorizing (rooted in the philosophy of the Frankfurt School) that applies to many social disciplines, such as law, politics, and cultural studies, and that tends to stress complexity and a holistic, post-Marxist orientation. None of what I'm saying about critical thinking is intended either to affirm or deny the value of any such mode of inquiry.

3. It's noteworthy, however, that as philosophy became more developed (and perhaps for that reason) the dialogic form of investigation was largely abandoned by philosophers.

4. Henry David Thoreau, *Walden*, Vol. 2. Boston: Houghton, Mifflin, 1854, "Solitude."

5. John Dewey, *How We Think*. n.p.: CreateSpace, 2011, p. 5.

6. Early appearances of the term "critical thinking" include those in J. W. Wrightstone, *Test of Critical Thinking in the Social Studies*. New York: Bureau of Publications, Teachers College, Columbia University, 1938; and Edward M. Glaser, *An Experiment in the Development of Critical Thinking*. New York: Columbia University Press, 1941.

7. Lisa Tsui, "Cultivating Critical Thinking: Insights from an Elite Liberal Arts College," *Journal of General Education* 56:3/4 (2008): 200.

8. See Paul Krugman, "The Ignorance Caucus," *New York Times*, February 11, 2013, p. A17.

9. It's important to differentiate between "fixed beliefs" about how the world is and basic values; the latter are harder to revise and arguably less in need of revision. And there's arguably more reason for children to examine their emerging values than for adults. As I'll suggest in due course, a range of competing values and interests is part of any moral community, but certain "meta-values" are clear exceptions; we cannot have meaningful dialogue (academic, democratic, or otherwise) without shared commitments to rationality, truth seeking, civility, and concomitant shared aversion

to others, such as violence or systematic prejudice (e.g., based on gender, race, ethnicity, religion).

10. Richard Paul and Linda Elder, *Critical Thinking: Tools for Taking Charge of Your Professional and Personal Life*. Upper Saddle River, NJ: Pearson Education, 2002, p. 361; and as paraphrased by A. Lewis and D. Smith, "Defining Higher Order Thinking," *Theory and Practice* 32:3 (1993): 132.

11. Glenn Dumke, "Chancellor's Executive Order 338." Long Beach: Chancellor's Office, California State University, 1980; quoted in Donald Lazere, "Critical Thinking in College English Studies," *ERIC Digest*, 1980. The order mandated formal instruction in critical thinking across the California State University's nineteen campuses.

12. V. Ramanathan and R. Kaplan, "Some Problematic 'Channels' in the Teaching of Critical Thinking in Current L1 Composition Textbook: Implications for L2 Student-Writers," *Issues in Applied Linguistics* 7:2 (1996): 225–49.

13. Facione et al., "The Disposition Toward Critical Thinking: Its Character, Measurement, and Relationship to Critical Thinking Skill," *Informal Logic* 20:1 (2000): 61.

14. S. D. Brookfield, *Developing Critical Thinkers: Challenging Adults to Explore Alternative Ways of Thinking and Acting*. San Francisco: Jossey-Bass, 1987, p. ix.

15. Robert J. Sternberg, "Teaching Critical Thinking: Eight Easy Ways to Fail Before You Begin," *Phi Delta Kappan* 68:6 (February 1987): 459.

16. D. Lazere, "Critical Thinking in College English Studies," ERIC Clearinghouse on Reading and Communications Skills, 1987.

17. Robert H. Ennis, "A Definition of Critical Thinking," *Reading Teacher* 17:8 (May 1964): 599–600. Ennis eventually added to this list a "super-streamlined conception of critical thinking" (www.criticalthinking.net), which states that a critical thinker:

1. Is open-minded and mindful of alternatives
2. Desires to be, and is, well-informed
3. Judges well the credibility of sources
4. Identifies reasons, assumptions, and conclusions
5. Asks appropriate clarifying questions
6. Judges well the quality of an argument, including its reasons, assumptions, evidence, and their degree of support for the conclusion
7. Can well develop and defend a reasonable position regarding a belief or an action, doing justice to challenges
8. Formulates plausible hypotheses
9. Plans and conducts experiments well
10. Defines terms in a way appropriate for the context
11. Draws conclusions when warranted—but with caution
12. Integrates all of the above aspects of critical thinking

18. American Philosophical Association, "Critical Thinking: A Statement of Expert Consensus for Purposes of Educational Assessment and Instruction," ERIC document ED 315-423, 1990; quoted in Facione et al., "The Disposition Toward Critical Thinking: Its Character, Measurement, and Relationship to Critical Thinking Skill," *Informal Logic* 20:1 (2000).

19. Ken Bain, *What the Best College Students Do*. Cambridge, MA: President and Fellows of Harvard College, 2012, pp. 207–8.

20. On this point, see for example, Richard F. Kitchener, "Do Children Think Philosophically?" *Metaphilosophy* 21:4 (1990): 425–26.

21. Joseph Conrad, "Preface" in *The Nigger of the Narcissus*. London: Chadwyck-Healey, 1897. (Also known as "Conrad's Manifesto.")

Chapter 7

The Spectrum of Critical Thinking

> Logic, n. The art of thinking and reasoning in strict accordance with the limitations and incapacities of the human misunderstanding.
>
> —Ambrose Bierce, *The Unabridged Devil's Dictionary*

LOGIC IS WHERE WE START FROM

Having explored various definitions of critical thinking, we will now take a somewhat different approach and consider different aspects or phases of critical thinking. To some extent these are developmental phases, representing the progression from fewer and simpler thought-regulating ideas to more numerous and more complex ones. But since everyone develops at a different pace and by different routes, it will be more helpful to see them as different forms of critical thinking rather than as phases of development. All of those forms contribute to rigorous critical inquiry, and they constitute the animating core of the liberal arts.

We can begin with the most systematic type of thinking (along with mathematics), which is formal logic. We don't start out in life as logicians, but as a rule-based system with specific, important, and limited purposes, logic is our first stop in surveying the forms of critical thinking. From there we'll proceed to informal logic, which has several loosely divisible subtypes, and then to the more advanced form of critical thinking that presupposes these: analytic thinking. Our first question is, What do we mean by "logic"?

To begin with a capsule definition: formal logic is the study and application of rules governing the relationships between propositions of various kinds, the types of those relationships, and how propositions connect to form valid arguments. As such, logic tells us nothing new or factual about the world. It doesn't tell us whether propositions are true or false, interesting or dull, important or trivial, relevant or irrelevant to a particular argument or line of inquiry. It merely gauges the formal, structural strength or weakness of our thinking: whether the links *between* those propositions are valid; and that's enough. It's the initial baseline of critical thinking. Logicians aren't the architects of thought but its structural engineers.

When we speak of "logical truths," we aren't really talking about truth per se but about logical validity. A logically valid argument may contain false premises and/or false conclusions, as long as the conclusions follow from the premises. Formal logic thus concerns the preservation of truth across argumentative steps, not its discovery.[1] In a logically *valid* argument, the conclusion is true if the premises are true. In a *sound* argument, both the premises and the conclusion are true. Thus, a classic logical syllogism is this: All bachelors are men. Socrates is a bachelor; therefore, Socrates is a man. Or again: All pizzas are round. X is a pizza; therefore, X is round. It's a valid deduction—even though Sicilian pizza isn't round.

For truth, or any approximation of it, we need to consult facts that we can agree on, inferences or generalizations based on facts, and inductive arguments, which are empirical statements of probability about the future based on past or present experience. Inference and induction tell us something about the world but don't carry the weight of necessary (logical) truth. As the philosopher Bernard Williams observes, if you've been swindled at cards multiple times by strangers on a train bound for the racetrack, you might be wise not to play cards on that train.[2] It almost sounds like common sense.

However, logic can't be reduced to a single, simple definition. Like "critical thinking," terms such as "logic," "rhetoric," and "dialectic" have been used over time in various and often overlapping ways. All involve the analysis of language, but for different purposes. We can think of logic as a tree, with a trunk, branches, roots, underlying soil, and a history of growth and entanglement with neighboring conceptual trees.

Formal logic begins with Aristotle. Since the late nineteenth century, more recent branches of logic have focused on its relation to mathematics, another archetypal form of systematic thinking. Logic and rhetoric (which along with grammar form the classical trivium) share a long history and have engaged in a kind of sibling rivalry since their birth. Rhetoric, which focuses on the art of argumentation and persuasion, got a head start, dating back to the Sophists, Plato, and beyond. Logic gained the upper hand in medieval times, while rhetoric enjoyed a resurgence during the Renaissance.

Both are alive and well today, with different but sometimes compatible aims. Whereas logic is about the *means* of speech—above all, formal consistency and avoiding contradiction in using language—rhetoric focuses primarily on the *ends* of speech: the best ways of saying things and winning arguments. Thus, rhetoric is more akin to (and largely subsumed within) the area of critical thinking associated with "informal logic."

Rhetoric has an obvious democratic function, because democracy requires argument and persuasion. But rhetoric also has commercial and polemical functions that are at once inherent in, and potentially inimical to, democracy: the use of deception or manipulation to persuade you to buy something, believe something, or vote for someone—what Cordelia in *King Lear* (act 1, scene 1) calls "that glib and oily art/To speak and purpose not."

Most of us don't remember much grammar from junior high school; we learn it largely by reading, writing, and hearing our mother's voice correcting us. Similarly, in ordinary language, we tend to obey the basic laws of formal logic almost intuitively. Logical contradictions have a way of leaping out at us, because they center on inconsistencies in how we use words, based on their definitions. The rules of logic are like roadside barriers that keep us from going over the cliff into an abyss of nonsense or self-contradiction.

The guidelines of informal logic are more like rules of the road that keep us from straying across the median or otherwise endangering our progress. Those rules, as we've seen, are many and varied, and unlike formal logic, they can't be reduced to a fixed set or system. Critical thinking comprises a spectrum of rational tools, extending from formal logic to informal logic of various kinds, and from there to analytic thinking. That spectrum, in the context of liberal learning, is what can usefully be called critical inquiry.

OTHER SENSES OF "LOGIC"

We should note in passing that we don't always use the words "logic" and "logical" in this strictly logical way; more precisely, we use them in several different ways. For example, there is the informal sense of "logic" that means something more akin to common sense: it roughly equates with what is rational, sensible, practical, acceptable, or obvious. When Cheryl Strayed writes of her hike in the Sierras, "Turning back made logical sense," she doesn't mean it was the *logically valid* thing to do.[3] There is never a logically valid thing to do. But in the looser sense, there is often a logical ("sensible") thing to do. The latter sense is in fact the more common usage in ordinary speech. Formal logic means something quite different.

A third sense of "logic" refers to the internal rules, laws, or patterns that define particular systems or phenomena—for example, when one speaks of "the logic of discovery" or "the logic of globalized competition."[4] To talk about "the logic of something" is to ask the most general questions about it: What laws govern it? What are its parts, and how do they relate? How does it change, and what are its causes and effects? This is the logic of organization;

it's the kind that we'll identify with systemic thinking, as distinct from (but predicated upon) systematic thinking.

Finally, there's another intermediary sense of "logic" and "logical" between the poles of logical deduction and common sense. It identifies a class of relationships—that is, of distinctions and connections—that we make with ease, if not necessity, because they map essential divisions or polarities in our grasp of the world, and accordingly, clear definitional and categorial boundaries. We can call these relationships "logical" because they are basic, useful or necessary, and precisely definable—that is, free of ambiguity. (We might call them, tongue-in-cheek, the informal side of formal logic.)

Among the most common of these relationships are *tautology*, or definitional identity between two terms or expressions (e.g., a bachelor is an unmarried man); *part to whole* (my arm is part of my body, not vice versa); *cause and effect* (biologically, I'm causally related to my parents, siblings, and children); *polarity*, wherein things share a continuum relative to some property, defined by the polar extremes (hot/cold, birth/death, day/night); *analogy*, where properties are shared among distinct phenomena or classes of phenomena (a car is like a bus, both being vehicles; a glove resembles a hand; sound and light are analogous as wave-based phenomena); and *duality* (in contrast to polarity), where there are only two logical possibilities (my arm is either my left arm or my right arm; a person is either alive or dead; and so forth. Some things just come in pairs).

Dualities such as part-whole, form-content, cause-effect, inner-outer, past-future, here-there, you-me, among many others, are indispensable tools of thought. So are the binary distinctions between, for example, distinction and connection, or formal and informal. We might need to refine or qualify them in a given context, but they are sufficiently unambiguous that we can call them "logical" distinctions.

Another such logical relationship is *complementarity* or synergy: where A and B can combine to produce result X, which neither A nor B can produce alone. Thus, a woman and a man can produce a child together, but not alone. The logical counterpart to this case of necessary inclusion would be that of necessary exclusion, where A can produce X only in the absence of B: a spark can cause fire in the absence of water. Finally, let's add Wittgenstein's aforementioned concept of *family resemblance*: a complex form of analogy, where disparate things partake of a set of common attributes, even if no two of them share all attributes or any one such attribute. Wittgenstein's perfect example is the concept of a game.

INFORMAL LOGIC: A PASSING GLANCE AT FACTS AND ARGUMENTS

Logic keeps our thoughts and arguments from falling into contradiction or incoherence, and that's no small thing. It is "no accident," writes Marvin Minsky, "that there are no exceptions to the rules [of math and logic]: *there, we start with the rules and imagine only objects that obey them.* But we can't so willfully make up the rules for objects that already exist, so our only course is to begin with imperfect guesses—collections of rough and ready rules—and then proceed to find out where they're wrong."[5] Formal logic is necessary, but not sufficient, for critical thinking. We also need the more rough and ready rules of informal logic and analysis.

Whereas formal logic is a closed system, like mathematics, informal logic is an open system. In other words, informal logic has no absolute or universal rules. Rather, its rules are based in experience, not in thought alone, and they don't form a definite set, nor do they relate to one another in definite ways.

The Greek tradition of dialectic, of probing a subject via questions and answers, predates the trivium of logic, grammar, and rhetoric by several centuries, and it didn't disappear when those new ways of organizing thought arose. That's because there's more to sound thinking than being logical, grammatical, or persuasive. We also need to talk about facts and values, relevance and clarity, legitimate and illegitimate means of persuasion, and the slew of other helpful, but less systematic, rules and guidelines of informal logic. These rules and guidelines can be loosely categorized as informal fallacies that weaken arguments or propositions, other common epistemic or perceptual blunders, and preexisting psychological conditions that are hardwired in our minds, such as the varieties of bias and delusion to which we're all prone.

We'll begin with a brief overview of arguments, because that's where many of these blunders, blind spots, and biases come into play. But not everything we say can be considered an argument, and argumentation isn't the only mode of expression that calls for critical thinking. So I'll focus here on one crucial distinction that frames most arguments and is a cornerstone of all critical thinking: the distinction between facts and values.

Facts are states of affairs that we can agree to be the case, at least in principle. Values are ideas, goals, opinions, desires, or normative (value-based) principles that we don't necessarily agree on. They reflect states of affairs that we wish to bring about (or preserve, remove, or prevent, as the case may be). Facts and values interconnect in many and often complex ways. But it always helps to be clear which we're talking about by examining the nature of the argument in question.

Asking certain questions can promote such clarification. Whom are you arguing against, and how and why exactly are you trying to persuade them? Why does it matter that you succeed in persuading them? Is the argument strictly factual, or do values, needs, interests, worldviews, or ways of understanding also shape your case? Is it possible you are wrong, or only partly right, about the facts? Are your beliefs based on hard evidence, intuition, generalization, wishful thinking, settled personal opinion, firm principle, or some combination of these? How sure are you of those beliefs—and why does it matter? The urge to persuade is a natural part of both the educational and the democratic process, but on most value questions, the demand that others agree isn't just undemocratic, it comes close to the definition of fanaticism.[6]

Purely factual arguments tend to be less interesting, because they are (at least in principle) resolvable. Vermont doesn't border Rhode Island—you can look it up. But most facts can't be weighed on scales like pieces of cheese. There are facts we disagree on, pending further evidence, and we also disagree on how we interpret them and which facts are most relevant or important. We interpret facts according to preexisting frameworks and worldviews, which is one reason why we never stop arguing. Our value differences may not be readily apparent, but in productive arguments, they are at least partially forced to the surface.

Arguments that have a normative component (whether moral, political, aesthetic, prudential, or spiritual) tend for that reason to be more interesting, more complex, and harder to resolve. Facts may change, and different facts that are equally true (statistics being a notorious example) can be used to support opposing normative arguments. But our values don't change as easily as our factual understandings. Agreement on values may be elusive—we don't change them overnight, or even consciously in most cases—but we can agree on some things, some of the time, and thereby achieve a greater degree of clarity and consensus.

Facts can sometimes be embarrassing to particular value claims, but they seldom, if ever, change hearts or minds. We can survive a lot of embarrassment without reassessing our basic values—the untidy basket of needs, desires, opinions, and ideals that largely make us who we are. Moreover, while "winning" an argument may serve my goals, it doesn't make me right. It may only mean I've defended my views with greater rhetorical skill. Nor does an unsound argument preclude the possibility of there being a sounder argument for the same conclusion.

The relevant facts, if agreed on, may frame or guide such debate, but they won't decide the matter. Democrats and Republicans may argue ceaselessly, but they aren't ceaselessly converting one another. Why do we argue nonetheless? For a number of reasons: Because arguing expresses who we are and may lead to short-term success, because it can clarify our own and our opponents' views, because it sometimes leads to at least limited or fleeting consensus, and because we can't help ourselves. When we disagree as democratic citizens, arguing is all we've got.

INFORMAL LOGIC, CONTINUED: THE MENTAL QUICKSAND OF FALLACIES, BLUNDERS, BLIND SPOTS, AND BIASES

Rigorous argument requires logic, and clarity about facts and values. But there are other tools of critical thinking (many of which we noted in chapter 6 in the search for a definition) that can also be lumped under "informal logic" as warnings against intellectual pitfalls—in arguments or otherwise. These additional tools can be broadly divided into two main categories: epistemic and psychological.

The epistemic side of informal logic deals with the assessment of knowledge. It includes justifying factual claims and examining evidence and assumptions, distinguishing authoritative from nonauthoritative and biased from unbiased information, and distinguishing propaganda or other forms of rhetoric from sincerity and truth seeking. The pitfalls of a more psychological nature include the systematic biases, blind spots, and misperceptions to which the human mind is prone, and which we have to recognize and fight against in order to think clearly and well, because they reflect ways in which our needs, values, or cognitive limitations cloud our judgment. Like errors of deductive logic, these can be minimized with familiarity and practice. There are dozens if not scores of common fallacies to guard against, as intellectual errors that don't involve logical contradiction. A smattering will serve as examples:[7]

- The pathetic fallacy: attributing human traits to something else in nature
- The intentional fallacy: divining an author's intentions, or confusing the work with its author
- The affective fallacy: confusing the work with one's reaction to it
- Ad hominem: attacking the person making the argument rather than the argument itself
- Hasty generalization: drawing a conclusion from a too-small sample of evidence, or ignoring important exceptions to the generalization
- Argument from authority: the flip side of ad hominem, where an argument is affirmed because of who is making it rather than on its merits
- Ad populum: appealing to prejudice or convention rather than to facts or reasoning about facts
- Post hoc ergo propter hoc, or "after this, therefore because of this": in which we infer that because A precedes B, A causes B. Sometimes B just

follows *A* and is caused by something else. Just because I'm older than you doesn't mean I'm your parent; Elvis Presley preceded and influenced the Beatles, but he didn't cause the Beatles.
- What might be called opportunistic determinism: our tendency to believe that when bad things happen to us it's someone or something else's fault, and when good things happen it's more due to our own free actions than to luck or help. Contrarily, when bad things happen to other people we tend to think that it's their fault, and when good things happen to them that it's more due to luck or help.

A full catalog of fallacies would fill an entire book (or more: Philip Ward's *Dictionary of Common Fallacies* is two volumes). But such a book can only partially map the territory we're navigating. So instead, we'll look at two questions that form a useful segue to the final portion of the spectrum of critical inquiry, which is analytic thinking. One is the question of appearance and reality—and whether or how they diverge. The other is the mysterious art of questioning itself.

APPEARANCE AND REALITY

One of the first things an infant learns is to distinguish itself from its mother and from the rest of the world. Another significant step comes several years later, when the child learns the difference between dreams and memories and between fantasy and reality: understanding, for example, when a story or a character is imaginary and doesn't actually exist. These distinctions are the very taproots of our critical capacity.

The sense of self and the sense of what is real don't prevent us from enjoying or learning through make-believe, art, or the imagination. But they reflect the emergence of the mind's crucial triage function of identifying and evaluating the nature and quality of incoming information. The ability to distinguish between appearance (which, as we gradually learn, is sometimes unreliable and never complete) and reality enables our understanding to transcend (and distrust) the here and now. It is a precondition for developing the particular skills we use later in life to weigh information generally and to identify scams, rumors, urban legends, conspiracy theories, and the like.

It isn't the aim of critical thinking to suggest (à la Plato) that the world of appearance is innately flawed or inferior to something else. Everything *begins* with appearances. Captain Ahab is hyperbolic when he proclaims that "all visible objects, man, are but as pasteboard masks."[8] But looking beyond immediate perception or feeling is an essential critical function. Questioning appearances, without dismissing them, is how we organize the world successfully; to say that we can look beyond the visible is simply to say that we can think. And to state the obvious, the "visible" is only what is visible to *us*. Everyone sees the world differently, sees it imperfectly, and sees an infinitesimal fraction of what is out there.

What is unreliable isn't necessarily our subjective and fragmentary perceptions of the world. These may or may not be accurate reports. Sometimes the problem is in our mind, the recipient and organizer of those perceptions—especially when, as in Ahab's case, it's unhinged from certain forms of reasoning. There's a larger available context for appearance that affords a deeper understanding of the world. That wider canvas includes all the other things we do with our minds: reasoning, remembering, imagining, intuiting, inferring, generalizing and abstracting, distinguishing and connecting, seeing causes and effects, patterns and systems, contexts and implications.

As part of that intellectual arsenal, we can think metacognitively in order to identify and counter certain widely shared mental limitations. More generally, we've seen that what we can think and express with words depends on which words we choose, and how we use more words to express what fewer words cannot. Indeed, to examine words at all, especially in complex expressions, is to look beneath the surface of appearances and utterances.

And here's the rub: The greater the variance between appearance and reality, the more complex the world becomes to us. Such divergence, in fact, is one way of defining complexity. It's a kind of complexity that ultimately enriches our understanding and capacity for action. We encounter it all the time. Many forms of humor and irony celebrate unstated or unobvious truths about the world or human nature, or truths that are cloaked as something else.

Malcolm Gladwell has made a career of showing how social phenomena are otherwise than they appear. Power is one example, as Gladwell points out in *David and Goliath*. Strength can mask weakness and vice versa. Scripture concurs: "For when I am weak then I am strong" (2 Corinthians 12:10).

The ability to discern levels of reality and unreality, and alternate ways of representing them, also helps to explain the power and beauty of art. One reason why we humans are addicted to art is because it straddles the boundaries of what we think of as real, and in doing so it offers new ways of thinking and seeing. We don't so much escape from reality through art as we play with its boundaries. We can equally appreciate the true story of the whale ship *Essex* and *Moby-Dick*, an invention based on that event, from which we can arguably learn much more.

Critical thinking, then, is built on the understanding that there is more to the world than meets the eye; that what is usefully called "reality" goes beyond what is evident, obvious, or material; and that learning of all kinds requires the capacity to think anew, think outside the box, and be surprised.

That is why art, imagination, and the capacity to wonder are crucial to early education. They are forms of play that teach us not just to compile or organize facts but also to figuratively reimagine the world and see it in ways that are more layered and complex.

THE ART OF ASKING QUESTIONS

Thinking critically means, above all, *questioning*: scrutinizing one's own thought and that of others. Questioning is the ultimate wellspring of metacognition and dialectical reasoning. Where does this come from? What happens next? What fact or principle justifies this assertion? How should we define this term or understand that idea? What is related to what? Why do we believe something to be the case? Certain kinds of questions recur with regularity, but questioning itself is unbounded.

Plato shows us how to question by example. But even philosophers, who are forever questioning, seldom directly address the question of how to question, because interrogation has no limits other than coherence and relevance to some topic at hand. Questions don't arise out of nowhere or pop into our minds randomly; they arise from doubt, curiosity, uncertainty, and our vast stores of ignorance. They arise, that is, in a particular context, as part of some larger fabric of inquiry.

> Questions arise about something; questions are occasioned. Unless there were something other than questionings there could be no questionings.
>
> —D. Z. Phillips[9]

If we can't define "intelligent questioning" in the abstract, however, we can at least make several general points about it. One is that framing questions isn't a special skill apart from other kinds of critical thinking. Questions arise as we make distinctions, connections, and analogies, as we commute between generalities and particulars, compare and contrast—as we reason, in other words, and find gaps in our understanding. We need to pose them in ways that drive the inquiry forward, by giving it greater focus, broader context, greater clarity, as the case may be. And what "inquiry" means here is simply this: a cluster of related questions.

A related point is that questioning is subject to the same economy as any other mental act. To ask any question is to forgo or defer asking a different one. So our questions, except for simple factual ones (e.g., What is X? Is Y the case? Can I buy you a drink?) must be scrutinized for clarity, relevance, and incisiveness. Good questions are formed when we know what it is that we need to know.

Even questioning has its limits. We can't navigate life effectively by challenging everything, or by questioning alone. Even when groping to understand an issue, a problem, a situation, or a person, at some point we need to make decisions or state beliefs about what is the case. If we are critical thinkers, those assertions will reflect the level of confidence we have in our knowledge. Thus, an important part of the habit of questioning is knowing when (and why) to move on to the next question. Skepticism is both central to critical thinking and, when taken to extremes, a hindrance. It shouldn't blind us to the need for provisional truths, valid generalizations, or best practices, all subject to later revision. Critical thinking means questioning—while acknowledging the limits of time and certainty.

Finally, thinking about questioning brings us to the other end of the critical thinking spectrum from formal logic, which is analytic thinking. We can't think analytically about how things relate to other things without asking questions and giving at least provisional answers to them. Questioning thus reflects the complexity, as well as the limits, of knowledge itself.

We know—or can at least make a good pragmatic case for—certain things: that words and numbers exist, as mental devices; that time as we commonly understand it moves toward the future (although physicists disagree); that gravity keeps things on the ground; and that rivers flow toward the sea. But we can't "know" what beauty or justice is; these are normative issues that facts and logic alone can't resolve. We can only define and analyze those concepts at a high level of generality and argue about the rest. Questioning forms a segue to analytic thinking because analysis is the process of posing and answering questions not just systematically, according to rules and reasons, but also systemically.

The abiding questions first posed in a systematic way by the Greeks—for example, about knowledge and truth, thought and action, freedom and causality—are by their nature answerable in different ways and on different levels. They apply generally across many contexts, which is why they abide. Philosophers ask such general questions because that's their job. Likewise, historians ask one particular range and type of questions, mathematicians another. Psychology, literature, economics, and law have their own distinctive questions as well. In the pursuit of knowledge, there's no end to it—it's questions all the way down. When questioning ends, learning ends, thinking ends, and democracy ends.

CRITICAL THINKING AND CRITICAL INQUIRY

Critical thinking, on any definition, comprises an essential, but diverse and imperfectly codifiable, set of intellectual skills. Collectively, those skills describe a spectrum from logic to the varieties of informal logic traditionally equated with critical thinking, to the final level we are about to explore: analytic thinking. This spectrum maps the trajectory of learning and the increasingly sophisticated ability to inquire, and to organize, evaluate, and expand what we know.

While it presumes logical rigor, both formal and informal, analysis takes thinking to a higher level than avoiding errors, by addressing questions of meaning and value both systematically and systemically. It thus completes the spectrum of critical thinking, the rainbow of skills that, taken as a whole, we're calling critical inquiry.

None of this is cut-and-dried, however. It isn't a Rubik's Cube or jigsaw puzzle with a single solution. Beyond the baseline of formal logic, everything is more or less negotiable as long as we don't abuse language. We may disagree about the range of skills that define informal logic, for example, or which of those skills are most important, or how to teach them. We may differ as to whether basic "problem-solving" skills (or which among them) should be lumped under the rubric of critical thinking. It depends on the type of problem and who's doing the lumping.

Problem solving, like questioning, is an important set of skills, and also an impossibly broad one. Just as there are many kinds of questions, there are many kinds of problems. But problems are simply questions with greater specificity or immediacy. How do you fix a leaky faucet, quell a child's fears, balance a checkbook, choose a school or career, decide whom to vote for, win a round of *Jeopardy!*? Being a critical thinker doesn't guarantee mastery of those skills, and we can't excel in all of them. But as students and citizens, it's where we must begin.

NOTES

1. See, for example, Catarina Dutilh Novaes, "What Is Logic?" *Aeon*, January 12, 2017.

2. B. Williams, "Metaphysical Arguments," in Bernard Williams, ed., *Philosophy as a Humanistic Discipline*, 24. Princeton, NJ: Princeton University Press, 2009.

3. Cheryl Strayed, *Wild: From Lost to Found on the Pacific Crest Trail*. New York: Knopf, 2012, p. 140.

4. Luc Ferry, *A Brief History of Thought: A Philosophical Guide to Living*. New York: Harper Perennial, 2011, p. 213.

5. Marvin Minsky, *The Society of Mind*. New York: Simon & Schuster, 1988, p. 96.

6. Exceptions include those normative matters on which we can't disagree without abandoning discourse altogether—such as truth telling, basic civility, the value of human life, and the general proscription against gratuitous harm.

7. For an extensive survey of such pitfalls, see Rolf Dobelli, *The Art of Thinking Clearly*. New York: Harper, 2013.

8. Herman Melville, *Moby-Dick or, the Whale*. New York: Penguin Classics, 2003, ch. 135.

9. D. Z. Phillips, "Is Moral Education Really Necessary?" *British Journal of Educational Studies* 27:1 (1979): 52.

Chapter 8

Analytic Thinking 101

> Our two most basic intellective functions are the perception of likeness and the perception of difference.
>
> —Robert Grudin[1]

SYSTEMATIC AND SYSTEMIC THINKING

Having considered formal and informal logic as the bases of *systematic* critical thinking, we can now ascend to a higher level for a broader view of critical inquiry—that is, of rationality across the liberal arts. That higher level is *systemic* thinking. And it equates with analytic thinking.

We have seen that systematic thinking moves in linked steps based on rules or guidelines, which create space for intersubjective understanding. To a greater or lesser extent, all scholars and ordinary citizens do this; wizards, mystics, and small children not so much. Systemic thinking goes further by making distinctions and connections to model the world. It's systemic in that it enables us to see the world as the interplay of systems—that is, as entities that must be understood as *both distinct and related*. Calling something a "system" means that it is composed of such interrelated parts and that the system as a whole can be usefully distinguished from those parts. Two engineers sum up the systematic/systemic dichotomy succinctly:[2]

> Thinking systematically means employing a given thinking method consistently and thoroughly. Thinking systemically means thinking about systems and connections—the web of relationships within a system, the relationship of the system to other systems, and the larger system that contains all the systems.

Both systematic and systemic thinking are forms of rationality. Both involve connections in our thought, and both proceed in discrete steps because of the inherent linearity of language (and of logic and mathematics). In the broadest sense, all human consciousness is both systematic and systemic at some level (except in cases of psychosis, hallucination, or other forms of impaired or fragmented awareness). We are all semirational beings who follow rules (such as those of language) in order to communicate. All our thought involves discerning basic relationships within and among distinct phenomena: relationships such as association and dissociation, part and whole, cause and effect, past and present, object and environment.

In fact, we could hardly think at all without thinking systemically; to distinguish between systematic and systemic thinking is already to engage in systemic thinking. Language itself is a system of rules. Other examples of systems include mathematics, music, stories, religions, economies, ecosystems, galaxies, democracies, institutions, games, bodies, minds, personalities, and living organisms. We find systems wherever we look, because structure, unity, and connection are how consciousness works: how our minds order and model the world.

Where systematic and systemic thinking differ is in regard to the kind of connectedness to which they refer. Think of it this way: Systematic thinking is mainly about *how* we think, linking our thoughts over time, space, and conceptual space by using common and transparent rules or guidelines. Systemic thinking focuses on *what* we think about: how we find structure in the world. We'll revisit systems in chapter 12, where we'll see that they are closely related to the gateway concept of complexity. For now, the business at hand is to understand systemic thinking—analytic thinking, as we'll call it—and its essential role in critical inquiry.

MUSIC, RECURSION, AND THE ANALYTIC MIND

Analytic thinking is a response to the general problem of the linearity of language noted in chapter 4: *When it comes to meaning and understanding, we can't have it all at once.* We have to make choices and go down different roads. Sometimes we need to backtrack or digress to explore other roads. And in shared public conversations, this means we need to economize among various (superficially incompatible) goals: depth and breadth of meaning, specificity and generality, clarity and precision.

As Robert Grudin notes, analysis begins with two basic nuclear functions: making distinctions and making connections. It doesn't matter whether we're talking about language in general, critical thinking, the history of commercial fishing, or the social patterns in ant colonies. Distinctions must be made—and so must connections.

Music provides a clear example of this. Consider one of the most famous phrases in the Western classical canon: the opening bars of the fourth movement to Beethoven's *Fifth Symphony*, where a four-note motif (duh-duh-duh-*dummm*) is reiterated one step lower down the scale.

Sequences of this kind are essential to all music: not just alteration of notes (like letters in the alphabet, a finite number of musical notes can be sequenced to generate a virtually infinite number of melodies) but also of tone, rhythm, tempo, volume, instrumentation, key, octave, and so on. Music can be defined as the ordering of sounds to form something other than noise. "Ordered" means that there's a discernible pattern: a similarity among distinct elements, such that they form a system. Music is a paradigm of such order; as Shakespeare observes (*Richard II*, act 5, scene 5),

How sour sweet music is
When time is broke, and no proportion kept!
So is it in the music of men's lives

This process of combining finite elements in different ways to generate an indefinite range of possible meanings or effects is known as *recursion*, and it is basic to all thought. In music, the recursive elements include tone, rhythm, tempo, and the rest; in written language, it's letters, words, and symbols. Although music may have referential or narrative qualities (or may be sung with words), and can be described linguistically, it doesn't express "meaning" in the linguistic sense; it more often beguiles our emotions.

Language can also beguile us, whether it be that of Shakespeare, a gifted political orator, or a demagogue. But music—like any nonliterary art—appeals in terms that are primarily symbolic and nonlinguistic. Those arts are, we might say, an escape from language. Yet, just as any writing, however poetic or inspired by emotion, involves making rational choices with words, composing music involves imposing order on sounds and thus requires the same coordination of reason and emotion to achieve its goals.

Figure 8.1. Music Notation

We note this to remind ourselves that reason in general is not the antithesis of human emotion so much as its natural counterpart and instrumental to its expression. We never really stop thinking or feeling, even though we might think we can; it's not in our power to do so, given how deeply they're intertwined. The conceit that we can distinguish them, however useful or necessary, is one that needs to be examined critically.

In a similar vein, there's a superficial contrast between analytic thinking and other types of cognition—intuitive, imaginative, creative, problem solving, thinking outside the box—all of which are essential in the liberal arts and in daily life. Analysis is not a substitute for those approaches; rather, they are complementary and overlapping. Analysis is at once a creative and a rational process—a search for meaning based on the core associative and dissociative functions. It is "not a purely objective or logical process," as Grudin explains, "but [one that] comprises the faculties of the whole mind."[3] And just as analysts must be creative, creators must be analytical, because all creativity is a public and communicative act.

If one aim of analysis is to determine (primarily through distinctions) the content or *essence* of things—their core elements and structure—a complementary function is to determine (primarily through connections) the *context* of things. Context is what identifies the external relations of phenomena: whatever surrounds or adjoins them, causes or results from them, or otherwise contributes to our understanding of them as parts of larger wholes. Anything we can individuate either has a context or is one.

An apple contains seeds, meat, and skin, but does it have an essence? Well, it isn't a pear. Its context includes being a kind of fruit, the tree on which it grows and the soil in which that tree grows, its resemblance to other life forms, and so forth. Eggs come from chickens; people have families and genetic histories, life experiences, communities, and so on. Historically speaking, the Civil War occurred in the context of the institution of slavery. As we can see, the idea of "context" is inherently general, layered, and complex. A given context includes both obvious elements (this egg came from that chicken, fish live in water) and unobvious ones with uncertain borders. Contextual relations expand outward in generality—in time, space, or the mind—to the point where they cease to shed useful light.

ANALYSIS, SYNTHESIS, AND DIALECTIC

The idea of context raises a further question. The Greek term "analysis" means "taking apart" or parsing what is nominally whole—as opposed to "synthesis," or bringing together what is nominally distinct. Establishing context is a process of synthesis. So what about synthesis—aren't we forgetting half the picture? Not really, because the processes of taking apart and putting together, like essence and context, are opposite sides of the same coin.

We tend initially to consider any thing or idea, any "whole," in terms of its divisible parts. When we analyze disparate facts or data, on the other hand, we look first of all for syntheses: patterns, groupings, categories, generalizations, and so forth. Yet, for most purposes, these aren't distinct methodologies but a single one that moves continuously in both directions: taking apart and putting together, distinguishing and connecting. Thus, we don't need to consider synthesis as a stand-alone mental function, except in those cases (such as cooking or chemistry) where blending different things creates an entirely new thing, such as a cake or a physical reaction. We speak mainly of "analytic thinking" and not of "synthetic thinking." But analysis and synthesis are tandem, and ultimately inseparable, mental functions.

If the analytic process seems at first glance formal and rigid, it is actually the opposite. Analysis is how we model things to achieve a more flexible and hence a fuller picture of the world. Short of imaginative leaps or unexpected bolts of intuition (which likely involve some preconscious analytic thinking), it's about as lithe as our minds can get. And so far as we know, this capacity to think in fluid, abstract terms is a unique attribute of the human mind.

There is inevitably a degree of informality to the analytic enterprise, as there is to any thinking outside of codified, rule-based systems such as logic, math, alphabets, grammars, or codes. But such informality shouldn't be confused with lack of rigor. Beyond those rigidly systematic domains, knowledge is an endless series of conjectures, inferences, compromises, and negotiations.

Another term for the analytic process (albeit one that has acquired some historical and contextual baggage) is *dialectic*. In its original Greek sense, it means the interplay of two or more voices (but typically two) to produce deeper understanding, as in Plato's dialogues. Subsequent philosophers discovered that the benefits of dialectic don't require an explicit interlocutor if the thinking is rigorously self-critical and metacognitive.

Whether it involves two voices or one, analysis is a dialectical process, a back-and-forth. The effect is akin to two lighthouses illuminating each other, each casting light where the other cannot. The pre-Socratic philosopher Heraclitus (Fragment 51) speaks enigmatically of the dynamic opposition between forces working in a common cause: "Men do not know how what is at variance agrees with itself. It is an attunement of opposite tensions, like that of the bow and the lyre."

Because of the linearity of language, dialectic is a stepwise process. Not every aspect of a thing or idea, nor every relationship it implicitly bears to something else, can be revealed at the same time or by using a single word or expression. Dialectical analysis makes those implicit features explicit. This is especially true for complex concepts such as knowledge, truth, freedom, or education, the analysis of which reveals important internal distinctions as well as external connections.

> Conceptual analysis gives framework and purposiveness to thinking that might otherwise meander indefinitely and purposelessly among the vast marshes of intellect and culture. . . . Since the business of analysis is essentially a dialectical business, no statement can possibly be perfect and complete, and in that sense no statement is ever entirely satisfactory.
>
> —John Wilson[4]

The dialectical process thus has no preordained boundaries; it goes wherever and however far we choose to take it. What counts as a full description is an open question, and when our values come into play, there is even more to contest. Oscillating between distinctions and connections, between seeing "internal" parts within things and "external" links among things, we find stable, if impermanent, ways to express deeper meanings. We also achieve broader perspective and become more aware of the sacrifices implicit in how we distinguish and connect things in the first place.

HORSES, ZEBRAS, AND POEMS: A CLOSER LOOK AT DISTINCTIONS AND CONNECTIONS

Our next step is to explore analytic thinking as the keystone of critical inquiry. The critic and historian Louis Menand offers an excellent point of departure in a passage that further demonstrates how all language is essentially philosophical:[5]

> The world is filled with unique things. In order to deal with the world, though, we have to make generalizations. On what should we base our generalizations? One answer, and it seems the obvious answer, is that we should base them on the characteristics things have in common. No individual horse is completely identical to any other horse; no poem is identical to any other poem. But all things we call horses, and all things we call poems, share certain properties, and if we make those properties the basis for generalizations, we have one way of "doing things" with horses or poems—of distinguishing a horse from a zebra, for example, or of judging whether a particular poem is a good poem or a bad poem. These common properties can be visible features or they can be invisible qualities; in either case, we create an idea of a "horse" or a "poem," or of "horseness" or "poetry," by retaining the characteristics found in all horses or poems and ignoring characteristics that make one horse or poem different from

another. We even out, or bracket, the variations among individuals for the sake of constructing a general type.

Whether we're talking about horses and zebras or global warming and the loss of biodiversity, similarities and differences such as Menand describes are basic to all conscious experience. It isn't useful to conflate horses and zebras; among other things, zebras are striped and untamable. But one could imagine having a single, if inefficient, word for both. Analysis reveals the relevant connections and distinctions, then moves on. It isn't rocket science.

> What we ought to aim at is less the ascertainment of resemblances and differences than the recognition of likenesses hidden under apparent divergences.
>
> —Robert M. Pirsig, *Zen and the Art of Motorcycle Maintenance*

We begin to make tacit distinctions and connections in infancy. Newborns come to recognize their mother as distinct from themselves, the father as distinct from the mother, and eventually, the abstract categories male and female. Connections emerge as we acquire the tacit knowledge that Mom and Dad are different, but alike in ways that the kitty or the teddy bear is not. Similarly, we recognize early on the continuity of objects: this is the same person, or the same ball, that was here a moment ago. (This is one kind of thinking we do without language.) Thus, toddlers love to play peek-a-boo, and early play is full of the joy of repetition: a celebration of the world's stability and coherence over time.

As we grow older, we make more sophisticated distinctions. Eventually, we discover that it isn't enough just to cut or paste, that we must do both, and also reveal what they obscure about one another. Renford Bambrough offers an elegant account of this process:[6]

> Good philosophy consists in exhibiting connections and distinctions which have hitherto lain hidden; in drawing distinctions without obscuring connections, and marking connections without obscuring distinctions. . . . It is because all or most ways of marking distinctions or connections between concepts have clear advantages and clear disadvantages that philosophy is so difficult and so controversial. . . . Each of several different uses [of language] may be valuable for the light it sheds and dangerous because of the shadow it casts.

Without this ability to recognize transecting distinctions and connections—in a word, to abstract—we wouldn't be able to use metaphors or analogies as tools of meaning. More fundamentally, we would lack any capacity for meaning beyond pointing and naming. Indeed, without distinguishing and connecting parts and wholes, similarities and differences, causes and effects, and so forth (leaving aside the question of how and to what extent infants or animals think), we arguably couldn't be conscious beings at all—certainly not the kind we in fact are.

As mental constructs, our distinctions and connections are seldom absolute. The only "absolute" relationships are logical ones (or in some cases, natural ones so universal as to border on logical): a bachelor is by definition an unmarried man; a person can't be in two places or times at once; a man can't become pregnant. In ordinary experience, however, there are shades of gray. We distinguish between men, women, and transgendered people while recognizing all as members of our species. We make moral distinctions, such as between justified and unjustified violence, while acknowledging areas of uncertainty or contestability in between.

Moreover, most things prove on closer inspection to be more internally varied, or more externally related, than they first appear. To individuate a "thing" at all is to nominally ignore its inward parts and outward connections. Analysis is the process of revealing what those reciprocal distinctions and connections obscure. That's where complexity enters the picture.

Underlying all systemic thinking is a set of basic, interconnected philosophic questions regarding analysis and synthesis, distinctions and connections, generalities and particulars, parts and wholes, causes and effects, and the formation of stable knowledge. These questions frame the more general query, How do we individuate things and draw useful boundaries in the first place while also recognizing underlying relationships of meaning, continuity, causality, logical character, physical makeup or structure, and the like? How is an apple like a lobster? Both are objects, life forms, and edible for humans. Differentiate at your leisure.

So far as we know, only human minds can achieve this cognitive blend of fission and fusion: of making distinctions and connections while also recognizing what they reciprocally obscure. Analysis enables us to model the world in ways that single words, or our senses alone (if we can even speak of our senses apart from our minds), cannot. We can distinguish wholes, but we can also show how they are divisible or related to other wholes. We can predicate things (X has property Y) and analogize between things.

Think back now to the "wedding cake" model of the liberal arts. It's another example of how analytic thinking is basic to all language, creating stable but not necessarily immutable categories. Our pets may be able to tell us apart from our friends, but only we can differentiate between chemistry, physics, and biology while understanding how they overlap and interconnect. And we can appreciate that fuzzy boundaries may more accurately reflect the curvilinear world we're trying to understand. We can take our fuzzy or furry friends to college, but we can't send them to college.

Analysis is a pathway to understanding things or ideas at a deeper level of complexity; in the analytic context, complexity is the property of having relatively more internal distinctions and/or external connections. The United States is a complex entity composed of fifty states, one district, and assorted territories. Among those parts, we can make a plethora of connections. The United States also relates to other countries through common borders, a common language, alliances, treaties, economic and cultural ties, a shared planet, and so on.

Seen in this light, analytic complexity isn't a gratuitous burden but a by-product of how we model the world to maximize our comprehension of it and traction within it. Analysis involves complexity, but it also fundamentally demystifies things, revealing their deeper essence or broader context more fully than mere appearance, assertion, or definition.

BEYOND BINARY THINKING

An old joke says that there are two kinds of people in the world: those who believe there are two kinds of people, and everyone else. Because logical and linear boundaries have two sides, some of our most basic concepts (such as the logical polarities noted in chapter 6) come in opposing pairs, like animals in Noah's Ark. This brings us to the bane of critical thinkers at the analytic level: binary thinking.

But here's the thing: we can't avoid binaries; they're inherent in our language and thought. It's hard to imagine a linguistic world without hot/cold, yes/no, up/down, then/now, or you/me. Of course, there are intermediate states that need to be identified, but one can't even identify them without first defining what they are intermediate between. So we must both have our cake and eat it. The distinction between "nature" and "nurture" is indispensable, yet it masks complex realities about the developmental processes of living organisms, which further analysis reveals.[7] In short, while we need binaries as natural and logical starting points for thought, they are mapping tools, not the final maps—much less the territory. Binaries aren't the problem; the problem is when we limit our thinking to binaries.

Analysis resolves or at least mitigates this problem. As critical thinkers we can safely engage in binary thinking once we recognize and use those binaries as access points to nonbinary thinking, and thus to more complete and accurate models of reality, models that reflect connections and gradients. The only binary we can't seem to escape is that between binary and nonbinary—but then, perhaps we've just mapped an escape route.

Examples of false dichotomies abound in the media and popular culture. Abortion is framed as being only about a woman's right to choose or only about the right to life of a developing fetus. Public or private enterprise is always good or always bad. Slavery caused the Civil War—or states' rights. Almost everything we say needs to be qualified, and that's what analytic thinking does. It isn't about splitting the difference between black and white but about using such polarities to identify connections and useful shades of gray.

> There is no quality in this world that is not what it is merely by contrast. Nothing exists in itself.
>
> —Herman Melville, *Moby-Dick*

Certain important binaries slice the world into seemingly neat logical halves: mind and body, reason and faith, you and me, normal and abnormal, nature and society. Much of the time, we implicitly recognize that such generalities mask all sorts of exceptions, nuances, and intermediate complexities. Bodies and minds interact in ways that we partly understand, yet we can't even talk about such interactions without referring to minds and bodies as nominally distinct entities. Analytic thinking enables us to commute between those twin goals. Conceptual binaries, when properly used, are limited but not limiting. We need them—and we also need to know how to relax them.

That said, some binaries are more stubborn than others: they resist being dissolved into a single entity or being seen as the poles of a spectrum. Identities, for example, are logically absolute: the eighteenth century isn't the nineteenth century, although they are causally linked in many ways, continuous, and not just contiguous blocks of time; and Ohio isn't Indiana, despite their proximity and other commonalities.

A stubborn binary that crops up in educational discussion is the distinction between practical knowledge ("knowing how") and general knowledge ("knowing that"). Knowing "how" is about using personal agency to change the world—from a plugged-up sink to a mismanaged government agency. Knowing "that" is about facts, phenomena, ideas, conceptual frames, and things we don't directly control. But the distinction isn't immutable or logical; pilots and philosophers alike need to grasp certain facts, skills and procedures, ideas, and contextual frameworks.

Learning "how" is broadly associated with the STEM disciplines and learning "that" with the liberal arts. Yet students in the liberal arts also learn skills: how to think, explain, judge, argue, write, organize, and present ideas. Likewise, STEM learners need to know many things that can't be described as discrete skills or practices. Knowing how to think well is arguably neither a "how-to" skill nor a kind of general knowledge but a third category altogether.

The questions we're raising here about boundaries and meaning are inevitably questions about language: what words and expressions we should use and how we should use them. But they aren't "merely" linguistic or semantic questions. If words were simply placeholders for parts and aspects of reality, analytic thinking and philosophy could be reduced to questions about the use or misuse of language, as Wittgenstein originally supposed. We can't do that because our ideas are more complex—more systemic, and better models of the world—than what can be reduced to words or definitions. A house isn't just a pile of bricks; it's also about how those bricks are used in different ways to form different structures for different purposes.

One of the main things analysis teaches us, then, is that conceptual boundaries are essential starting points. They don't confine us; they are fences that can be moved, opened, tunneled under, climbed over. We don't erect them to hem in our thought but to expand its possibilities. Boundaries, and the connections that span them, unify and organize experience by reflecting the ways in which the world is systemic. As an open, experimental, pragmatic, negotiated process, analysis resembles a more formal and self-conscious version of the important cognitive business of exploring the world that children do, which we call "play."

NOTES

1. Robert Grudin, *Time and the Art of Living*. Boston: Mariner Books, 1997, p. 10.

2. J. Kuprenas and M. Frederick, *101 Things I Learned in Engineering School*. New York: Three Rivers Press, 2013, p. 74.

3. Robert Grudin, *The Grace of Great Things: Creativity and Innovation*. Boston: Mariner Books, 1991, pp. 37–40.

4. John Wilson, *Thinking with Concepts*. Cambridge: Cambridge University Press, 1970, pp. ix, 47.

5. Louis Menand, *The Metaphysical Club*. New York: Harper Perennial, 2002, pp. 121–22.

6. Renford Bambrough, "Aristotle on Justice: A Paradigm of Philosophy," in R. Bambrough, ed., *New Essays on Plato and Aristotle*. New York: Routledge, 2012, pp. 162–65.

7. As Murillo Pagnotta writes (in "The Use and Abuse of 'Information' in Biology," *The New Atlantis*, Winter 2017, p. 107), "When we set aside the simple disjunctions between nature and nurture, genes and environment, innate and acquired . . . we begin to see what makes a living organism the extraordinary wonder that it is."

Chapter 9

Analysis and Ambiguity

> Man is an analogist, and studies relations in all objects.
>
> —Ralph Waldo Emerson, "Nature"

ANALOGIES DRIVE THE MIND

Distinctions and connections are the ultimate quanta of human thought: the mental equivalents of waves and particles. Surrounding those waves and particles are the finer points of analytic thinking: analogies, metaphors, family resemblance, and ambiguity. We'll now examine these more closely, beginning with analogies, including the one implied above: that connections are like waves and distinctions are like particles.

Consider the following historical narrative: A small band of men, driven by a blend of political and religious fervor, if not fanaticism, stage a series of well-planned attacks on American civilians and U.S. military property, causing much destruction and loss of life. To their supporters, the attackers are martyrs; to most others, they are terrorists. The attacks cause national shock and havoc, helping to foment a long and bloody war that will change the course of history. It all sounds familiar, yet this thumbnail account describes two starkly different historical events: the al-Qaeda attacks on September 11, 2001, and John Brown's 1859 raids on Harpers Ferry, Virginia, and elsewhere.[1] The superficial similarities, though not trivial, obscure deep underlying differences of time, place, motivation, and results.

Comparing the two events, and seeing both the similarities and the differences between them, we form a compelling yet superficial analogy. That kind of analogy is also a paradigm of analytic thinking: of division and connection, analysis and synthesis, similarity and contrast. The connections reveal what the distinctions obscure and vice versa. ("Obscure" here doesn't mean to deliberately conceal but rather that we can't both connect and distinguish at once, or with the same words, but must do so in succession.)

Analogies are, as Douglas Hofstadter and Emmanuel Sander argue, "the fuel and fire of thinking."[2] They rest squarely on those two basic cognitive acts, connecting and distinguishing. To think means (among other things) to be able to make and recognize analogies. "The flexibility of human cognition," these authors observe, "relies profoundly on our ability to move up or down the ladder of abstraction, for the simple reason that sometimes it is crucial to make fine distinctions but other times it is crucial to ignore differences and to blur things together in order to find commonalities."[3] The search for analogies "pervades every moment of our thought, thus constituting thought's core."[4]

A perfect analogy would be an identity—two things being exactly the same, and that can occur only in logic or mathematics. Any other pair of analogues must have different space-time coordinates, even if they are otherwise indistinguishable. Yet imperfection is precisely the point: analogies draw attention to what is alike among nonidentities. We think and speak by drawing implicit comparisons and contrasts.

Whenever we consider a word, idea, or event in depth or in context, we explore it analogically. In virtually every case, there is more to be said than "x is like y," beginning with the following questions: How is x unlike y? How is the equation of x and y true, and how is it partial or misleading? How does the context of the equation—including the situational needs and intentions of the speaker and the audience—affect what needs to be added or subtracted? To focus on these questions, and to see how they reflect other features of the analytic process, such as complexity and ambiguity, we need to revisit and extend the gateway concept of analysis.

Consider the idea of "excellence." What do we mean by it? The answer depends on the context. There's academic excellence, journalistic excellence, literary excellence, and excellence at gambling, cooking, or horseback riding. Each case has its own criteria and frame of reference, yet they are all forms of excellence because they share a core of meaning. No matter what the field, we understand excellence as having to do with the pursuit or attainment of high standards of achievement within that field according to the relevant criteria. The connection is general, but not so general that we don't understand it. In any human enterprise, it matters what it means to do it well.

The point here isn't obscure: we need abstractions such as "excellence" to talk and think, let alone to be critical thinkers. And we need analytic thinking to understand different uses of an idea. Ambiguity is rife in language, but it isn't always problematic. Sometimes it's useful for describing the world.

Critical thinking at the analytic level entails recognizing ambiguity and knowing when to try to resolve or contain it and when to preserve it.[5]

Again, everything we think about is an amalgam of similarities and differences in relation to other things. Stories and dreams (the stories we tell ourselves when asleep) make sense to the extent they are connected internally by sinews of narrative and thematic coherence. These may include a central character or characters; one or more narrative points of view; events that unfold in some sort of causal sequence; dramatic moments of crisis, challenge, and change; and recurring themes. We can analyze a story to explore its meanings, up to a point. Unlike an engine, a closed system that can only function or be taken apart or reassembled in a single way, a story is an open system, understood differently by every reader.

The Greeks wrote about the relationships of similarity or analogy (having shared properties) and polarity (the relative presence or absence of a particular property). Both ideas reflect a basic, more general relationship between nominally discrete entities: that of being neither identical nor entirely unalike. That relationship is the gateway to analytic thinking; it identifies an idea that is central to philosophy and to all thought. That's why exam questions often begin with this statement: "Compare and contrast x and y." There may also be a z—but you have to start somewhere. It seems simple enough, at least until we explore more complex relationships, or concepts that are pregnant with internal distinctions and/or external connections that need to be reckoned with. In other words, it's the inherent complexity of things or ideas that impels us to analyze them.

LANGUAGE, METAPHOR, AND ANALYSIS

English and Chinese are both languages, defined by certain general attributes that constitute what we mean by a "language." But they are also very different—more different than, say, Spanish and Italian. Similarly, the United States is a country and so is Canada. Baseballs and golf balls are similar in shape and function, as roughly spherical objects used for particular sports, but you wouldn't want to interchange them during a game.

Recall that any language is an economy, and words and grammar are its currency: the bases for more complicated transactions of meaning. The analogy goes only so far, however, as we look for the distinctions that it inevitably masks. That's why we need language—and not just single words but grammatical sentences that organize more complex thoughts—to create meaning; language is essentially analytical. "Butterfly" means something with wings, but that something isn't a bird. The concept of freedom is both internally complex and related to such other concepts as equality, justice, and democracy.

In dealing with a complex term, we have several alternatives. We can leave it alone and tolerate any ambiguity; analyze it to show how it relates to other concepts and how it is being used in a given context; or invent a new word to fill the vacuum in our vocabulary, a move that has its own costs and benefits.

Creating new words (neologisms) is seldom the most efficient option, but there are exceptions. Think of "subconscious," "meme," "email," "emoticon," "selfie," or "crowdsourcing," all of which have been invented to meet the changing needs of discourse. (A few of them we could probably do without.) And inventions or discoveries have necessitated such new terms as "photograph," "aviation," "uranium," and "quark." Other words (such as "dialectic," "evolution," "ideology," "digital") have evolved to take on new or multiple meanings. Any linguistic innovation nominally (and in the short run) debases the currency of language. But it may also identify a hitherto inexpressible meaning without cumbersome analytic work (such as "emoticon" for "a digital icon signifying an emotion"). Once they gain currency, such neologisms can be effective shortcuts; that's why we invent them.

Metaphors are implicit analogies, stressing the commonality among otherwise unlike things. They are powerful linguistic devices because they expand our sense of one thing by relating it to another. Like all language, metaphors are essentially philosophical, extending thought by revealing connections amid distinctions. In short, they do revelatory analytic work. Poetry typically does this with reference to emotions, senses, situations, or personal experience. Consider Ezra Pound's two-line poem, "In a Station of the Metro":

> The apparition of these faces in the crowd;
>   Petals on a wet, black bough.

The poet Jane Hirshfield builds on this idea in describing an ancient vase with a handle shaped like a leaping tigress:[6]

> To see the tigress hiding in the handle, the handle waiting within the tigress, is to throw off the boundaries of the literal and recognize that even the simplest fragment of existence can carry multiple uses, possibilities, connections. The union, like all metaphor, brings revelation and addition, while it also covers, complicates, veils. Art amplifies intelligence: to experience the tiger's silver-doubled resonance is to join in the leap the mind must take toward a more sophisticated comprehension of the world.

In each case—faces as apparitions of petals, a vase handle as a leaping tigress—the power lies in the resonance between two distinct images. The intentional blurring or juxtaposing of the images is ambiguity of a constructive kind; it's left to be resolved (or to remain ambiguous) in the reader's imagination. The results can expand our vision, helping our minds to "leap." Science also relies on metaphors and analogies; as the philosopher of science Thomas Kuhn observes, a "metaphor-like process . . . plays an important role in fixing the referents of scientific terms."[7]

Whereas art thrives on ambiguity, at least up to a point, analysis is about containing or minimizing ambiguity except where it's necessary. That means identifying areas of likeness and difference—and shedding light in the shadows cast by such likeness and difference, respectively.

> It is a great thing, indeed, to make a proper use of these poetical forms, as also of compounds and strange words. But the greatest thing by far is to be a master of metaphor. It is the one thing that cannot be learnt from others; and it is also a sign of genius, since a good metaphor implies an intuitive perception of the similarity in dissimilars.
>
> —Aristotle, *Poetics* 1459a

A common metaphor for analysis itself is that of "unpacking" ideas. It's a useful enough trope, denoting the reduction of a whole to its constituent parts. What it fails to capture is the inherent fluidity of ideas, which are not like socks that can be added to or removed from a drawer. It's up to us as analytic thinkers to decide what those parts are, how best to fit them together, and how to relate the whole to its larger context. We can "unpack" in various ways, but we also have to repack, and concepts are flexible only as long as such flexibility serves the larger economy of meaning—including conformity to standard usage. That economy is driven by the need to reconcile a variety of goals: clarity and precision, depth and breadth of meaning, audience comprehension, and the contextual need to describe, explain, interrogate, provoke, challenge, argue, or entertain, as the case may be.

CONSCIOUSNESS IS COMBINATORIAL

The ability to distinguish diverse things in the world, and to see both sameness and difference among them, is as old as human thought. It's what makes conscious experience (at least as we know it) possible. Try to imagine the contrary case. If things—objects, events, states of affairs, processes, relationships—didn't share attributes with other things, and the universe were composed entirely of unique phenomena, how could our brains even process them as discrete "things"? How could we make basic logical distinctions such as male/female, up/down, here/there, now/then, and so on? We might liken this predicament to a language with no grammar: it would be largely if not wholly unusable. We can't imagine such a world because all thought is essentially associative and dissociative, an integrated system of meanings.

We can see this in the word "likeness" itself, a term that implies both similarity and difference. During the Civil War, when photography was in its infancy, a photograph of a soldier was often referred to as a "likeness." In a sense, it's a better term than the more scientific "photograph," or measure of light. A photographic image is recognizably "like" the thing or person it represents yet clearly distinct from it. Any form of representation is a map—an abstract likeness—and not a copy or literal reproduction of its subject or an identical twin described by other means. There is no conscious, deliberate thought without abstraction—period. Anything else is instinct or reflex.

Again, analytic thinking is a response to the endlessly recurring problem of discerning how, in a given case, two or more things are both alike and unalike, whether they are more alike or different, whether they resemble or differ from one another in significant ways or trivial ones, and so on. The answer depends on the context and the communicative needs of the person doing the analyzing. How is Melville's fictional *Moby-Dick* like the real incident that inspired it, the staving of the whaleship *Essex* by a whale in 1832? How is bread pudding like rice pudding? How are the liberal arts like, and unlike, STEM learning?

Viewed in this way, analytic thinking is relatively straightforward. It has no deep secrets, enduring mysteries, or complicated tricks. All of the sifting, evaluating, comparing, and contrasting that we do, across the liberal arts and in daily life, can be understood as variations on propositions of the form: $x \approx y$ (x approximates y). If we thought this way all the time, we wouldn't need a liberal education to become analytic thinkers. But we'd still need it to learn about inflation, the American Revolution, and Cézanne.

FAMILY RESEMBLANCE

Comparisons and contrasts aren't always simple and bilateral; in some cases, they involve groups in which the different members don't share all, or even any, of the relevant properties. Wittgenstein identified this relationship by using the analogy of "family resemblance."[8] As a way of understanding complex relations of meaning, it's one of the most important ideas of modern philosophy and of analytic thinking in general.

Wittgenstein wasn't the first to have this insight. More than a century earlier, Emerson wrote in his essay "History," "Nature is full of a sublime family likeness throughout her works, and delights in startling us with resemblances in the most unexpected quarters." Melville also alludes to it in his struggle to classify different species of whales.[9] But let's credit Wittgenstein with fully crystallizing the concept of family resemblance; it's doubtful that he read Melville or Emerson.

Wittgenstein introduces the idea by way of an inspired example: the concept of a "game."[10] There are many types of games that bear little relation to one another, yet we seldom question whether any of these is a "game." Many games are recreational; many involve two or more players or teams; most require particular, definable skills; most, but not all, are competitive and have a goal that constitutes "winning"; most have rules; many involve a score; and so on. But not all games have each, or share any particular set, of these properties. We also speak colloquially of the "courtship game," the "insurance game," the "game of life," a "game of cat and mouse," "gamesmanship," and so forth. We can also distinguish between those senses or uses of the word "game" that are intended to trivialize and those that are not. Analytic thinking is, in Wittgenstein's famous phrase, a *Sprachspiel*: a language game.

Some games are more competitive; some are more rule governed; some are more skill based. Hence Wittgenstein's question: What do we mean by a "game"? One can equally ask, What do we mean by calling something a "concept"? What do we mean by such concepts as art, education, information, representation, money, religion, thought, imagination, representation, society, or life? Analytic thinkers are never at a loss for work.

THE UPSIDE OF AMBIGUITY

Many words, especially those representing abstract concepts, are fraught with ambiguity: "love," "war," "spirituality," "freedom," "morality," "justice," "truth," "excellence," "cause," "reason," "education," and "human nature," to name just a dozen. But all words that aren't proper names are *somewhat* general (and even names are shared). "Dinner" is less abstract, ostensibly referring to something palpable, but it also represents a broad social category, without specifying what's for dinner, where, when, or with whom. We can't fully understand such terms until we analyze how they are being used and in what context.

The crux of the matter is that, because language is linear, and isolated words are seldom adequate as conveyors of meaning, we can't have everything at once. We can only say one thing at a time, and then we must use more words to amend, explain, qualify, amplify, or correct what went before.

Consider, for instance, the term "moral community." (We'll return to it in chapter 13.) Do we mean any community whose conduct we deem to be moral? Or do we mean any group that abides by some rules of conduct—whether a nation, tribe, family, the Taliban, a street gang, or toddlers playing in a sandbox? And are the latter "moral communities" in the same sense as a monastery, a sports team, or a scout troop? How do we distinguish these various senses of "moral," and why don't we have separate words for them? Asking such questions, and identifying areas of consensus and conflict, factual agreement and uncertainty, while working to clarify meanings and mitigate unnecessary ambiguity, is the essence of critical inquiry.

Why "unnecessary"? Because ambiguity isn't always bad or eliminable. As the context dictates, we may need to resolve the ambiguity, limit it, or preserve it. Ordinarily ambiguity isn't useful in more literal and empirical realms such as law, history, social science, journalism, or other nonfiction writing. But in other contexts, it properly reflects what is fuzzy, uncertain, subjective, or value dependent. Nothing ruins a good joke like analyzing it.

Whenever we use or explore the imagination, ambiguity is rife. We can deconstruct a work of art up to a point, but then it becomes tedious and counterproductive. Finding that point is a challenge for scholars and critics. A painting or poem isn't a math problem or a logical proof; there is no single meaning lurking in it awaiting discovery. Rather, it admits of a range of possible interpretations and responses, however personal or imprecise. And it's also there to be enjoyed, an ephemeral blend of the emotional and the cognitive.

Obviousness and obscurity are the twin enemies of artistry. Successful works of art are neither literal reports of the world nor wholly opaque, but are inherently ambiguous and open to interpretation. They provide clues to the artist's intentions but don't telegraph them. We may respond differently to a Mahler symphony or a Rothko painting while agreeing about some of the facts that describe it. We may also be ambivalent. Ambivalence, as opposed to ambiguity, is an attribute of the perceiver rather than the thing perceived: it is uncertainty about how we feel. Ambivalence reflects a complex response, just as ambiguity reflects complexity of meaning and the need for analysis.

Discussing interpretations of art can be enriching, and it promotes skills that are intrinsic to critical inquiry. Those skills include the ability to combine reasoning and factual evidence with personal taste and values, to articulate what may at first seem inexpressible and translate from one medium of expression to another, and to learn how meanings and values are transmitted symbolically through various art forms and cultural traditions. More generally, art promotes the acquired ability to tolerate uncertainty, to learn from diversity, and to both contribute to and benefit from cultural communities and conversations as a form of citizenship.

CONCLUSION: ANALYSIS IS THE CORE OF CRITICAL INQUIRY

To recapitulate, several basic features of the human mind combine to make analytic thinking both possible and necessary. We are self-conscious beings, capable of applying rules and guidelines that improve communication. We are capable of making distinctions and connections—the two nuclear mental functions—and thus we can individuate things and compare and contrast them. We can't imagine not having that capacity, which is basic to all cognition. And we can use dialogue to improve, if not perfect, our thought and that of others.

We don't have to simply leap from one assertion to the next, or stand still, but can proceed in steps and for reasons that are shared and transparent. Those propositions and those steps, like all language, rely on abstractions to map and articulate the complexity of conscious experience. Showing how knowledge builds through dialogue was Plato's singular achievement. "Socrates' changing perspectives [in the *Gorgias* dialogue]," as one commentator writes, "are much like the insights the reader is afforded by the dialogue as both continuously move to higher levels of understanding—rejecting, revising, absorbing each time what went before."[11]

In other words, like a writer or composer, we are capable of recursion, of exploring series of phenomena by distinguishing constants and variables across time, space, or conceptual space. And we can reduce, preserve, or celebrate ambiguity as the situation dictates, to reflect the world as we find it and what we want to say about it.

Finally, a principal theme of analytic thinking as the cornerstone of critical inquiry is that "deconstruction" isn't demolition; it isn't just unpacking and leaving a mess. To analyze is to make distinctions and connections and also to look for the reciprocal connections and distinctions that they obscure. It's an experimental journey into the conjoined interior and exterior landscapes of the mind and the world, landscapes where the content and the context of a thing or idea both matter. And this also means that we are continually looking for ways to improve our cognitive maps. It's a journey composed of an endless series of choices about what routes to follow, what scenery to look at, and how to see it.

At times, for the sake of perspective, it's useful to state or restate the obvious. But perspective itself is amorphous, always evolving, always in need of refreshment, and never perfectly achieved. What is most interesting, revealing, or important in our intellectual wanderings is often the unobvious, and we need to be creative (not just analytical) to look for it. The reality that is masked or distorted by appearance is often more interesting or significant than appearance itself. Analysis may reveal the unobvious truth, possibility, or perspective; the subtler or more complex way of seeing; or the more elusive thing to be seen. It generates more balanced, nuanced, flexible, and durable models of the world.

Literary devices such as irony, symbolism and metaphor, abstraction in art, dreams and fantasy, are all complex modes of communication that differ from a literal mirroring of the world. Yet they depart from the literal in ways that can reveal something deeper or broader. They bring us news beyond the headlines—news that we're always free to ignore, overlook, or misunderstand. No one can say a priori where the bounds of useful discussion lie. Beyond a certain point, analytic arguments can become wearying unless you're a philosopher or Talmudic scholar. The connections may become tenuous or the distinctions too fine. That point, however, is always contestable and context-dependent.

Needless to say, analytic thinking isn't a stationary platform for mental skills that we can learn and then forget about. It's more like a moving train that we can climb aboard for a shared journey in any given direction. Mastering its techniques requires no commitment to any particular beliefs, values, or schools of thought. In fact, it's something we already do unconsciously, albeit less efficiently and more superficially, whenever we use language.

Those techniques constitute the core of liberal learning as a lifelong engagement with questions and ideas: about meaning and value, what's in the world and how we can best conceive it, and how to translate those ideas into words and actions and citizenship. The train never stops and the work is never done. But if you think analytically—which is to say clearly, broadly, deeply, and flexibly—whatever else you need to learn will find its way aboard.

NOTES

1. I am indebted to the author Tony Horwitz for this analogy, which he gave at a 2014 public discussion of his book *Midnight Rising* in West Tisbury, Massachusetts.
2. Douglas R. Hofstadter and Emmanuel Sander, *Surfaces and Essences: Analogy as the Fuel and Fire of Thinking*. New York: Basic Books, 2013.
3. Hofstadter and Sander, *Surfaces and Essences*, p. 30.
4. Hofstadter and Sander, *Surfaces and Essences*, p. 18.
5. I prefer the term "ambiguity" here to "vagueness." Strictly speaking, they mean different things. In the literal or dictionary sense, ambiguity denotes "having two possible meanings," not multiple ones. It involves a choice among alternatives ("an old saw" could mean either a rusty tool or a tired joke), whereas vagueness denotes the lack of such clarity—or as Anthony Flew defines it, is "unacceptable indeterminacy in some relevant dimension" (Flew, *How to Think Straight: An Introduction to Critical Reasoning*. Amherst, NY: Prometheus Books, 1998, pp. 81–82). But the distinction

isn't vital here, and "ambiguity" is more commonly used in the looser sense to denote either vagueness or specific alternative meanings.

6. Jane Hirshfield, *Ten Windows: How Great Poems Transform the World*. New York: Knopf, 2017, p. 99.

7. Thomas Kuhn, "Metaphor in Science," in Andrew Ortony, ed., *Metaphor and Thought*, 533–42 Cambridge: Cambridge University Press, 1993, p. 414.

8. See Wittgenstein's *Philosophical Investigations* (London: Anthem Press, 2021, sections 65–67). For a visual example of family resemblance, see Sean Scully's painting *Backs and Fronts*.

9. Herman Melville, *Moby-Dick or, the Whale*. New York: Penguin Classics, 2003, ch. 32. Of the complicated tangle of similarities and differences among whale species, Melville writes, "It is in vain to attempt a clear classification of the Leviathan, founded upon either his baleen, or hump, or fin, or teeth . . . these are things whose peculiarities are indiscriminately dispersed among all sorts of whales, without any regard to what may be the nature of their structure in other and more essential particulars. . . . In various sorts of whales, they form irregular combinations."

10. Ludwig Wittgenstein, *Philosophical Investigations*. New York: Wiley, 1991, § 76.

11. Anthony J. Cascardi, "The Places of Language in Philosophy; or, The Uses of Rhetoric" *Philosophy and Rhetoric* 16:4 (Fall 1983): 224.

Chapter 10

The Uses of Complexity

The mind is the most complex object known to exist in the universe.

—Marilynne Robinson

WHAT WE MEAN BY "COMPLEXITY" AND WHY WE MEAN IT

What is the best way to teach, and to learn, in the liberal arts? No one formula works for every educator, student, or subject. The problem, we might say, is complex. But two contemporary scholars offer a compelling approach. Julius Taranto and Kevin J. H. Dettmar suggest that the teacher's first task is to simplify the subject matter so that students can gain traction with it.[1] The second task is to make it complex again in ways that students can understand.

Underlying this insight is a deeper one. The axis of simplicity and complexity isn't just useful; it's central to all thinking and learning. That's why complexity qualifies as a gateway concept of the liberal arts, and one that needs to be understood as part of a fuller conception of critical thinking. Accordingly, this chapter will introduce some of the general forms and dimensions of complexity and suggest why they are relevant to critical inquiry.

We understand intuitively the meanings of "complexity" and "simplicity," beginning with the fact that they are the opposite poles of a spectrum. We use the terms routinely without scratching our heads. But a broader definition is more elusive. It isn't obvious what exactly the simple-complex spectrum is a spectrum of, or which pole of that spectrum is intrinsically preferable or more useful. We need both ideas, and the spectrum they span.

Reducing things to their simplest form can reveal elemental truths. As Primo Levi explains in his Holocaust memoir *The Drowned and the Saved*,

> Have we—we who have returned—been able to understand and make others understand our experience? What we commonly mean by "understand" coincides with "simplify": without a profound simplification the world around us would be an infinite, undefined tangle that would defy our ability to orient ourselves and decide upon our actions. In short, we are compelled to reduce the knowable to a schema: with this purpose in view we have built for ourselves admirable tools in the course of evolution, tools which are the specific property of the human species—language and conceptual thought.[2]

Levi implies (and he's echoed by Taranto and Dettmar) that complexity also reveals important truths about the world. We need to "reduce the knowable to a schema," but we find some things to be intrinsically more complex. To begin with science (which has spun off theories of complexity), life itself is based on a threshold level of chemical complexity that enables the formation of organisms. It involves multiple elements that combine in particular ways to generate particular outcomes.

Such chemical complexity is predicated, in turn, on the laws of physics that happen to obtain in our universe: for instance, the exact force of gravity, the mass of electrons and quarks, and the value of the strong nuclear force that holds atoms together. These laws may not obtain in any possible universe; we just don't know.[3] But either way, we're here because complex life is possible here, not just isolated particles. Scientists discovered the different levels of organization that exist in electrons, molecules, and humans. The idea of complexity was invented, in part, to identify such levels.[4]

So what exactly do we mean by "complexity," and how does it fit into our conceptual roadmap of the liberal arts? Let's begin by simplifying. Things that we normally call "simple" are (relatively speaking) more unitary, homogeneous, whole, graspable, or obvious. The word "simple," writes C. S. Lewis, refers to what is indivisible, uncomplicated, or "contain[s] fewer heterogeneous elements."[5] The Latin "simplex," he points out, derives from "simel" (once) and "plicare" (fold): to fold once, not more. The term "atom" in ancient Greek meant what is "uncuttable." We no longer think of atoms in this way, but what is simpler is (relative to the more complex) not combined with, composed of, or related to other things.

In contrast, we identify complexity with properties such as composite, organized, layered, nuanced, unobvious or at variance with appearance, and harder to understand. Calling something (such as the human mind) "complex" implies at a minimum that it has discernible parts. The more parts it has, and the more those parts interact, creating further levels of meaning, structure, or causality, the more complex it is.

LOGIC AND ANALYTIC COMPLEXITY

In the analytic context—the context of symbolic and conceptual systems of meaning—we have equated complexity with a wider array of discernible internal distinctions and external connections. Wittgenstein calls this condition "a complicated network of similarities overlapping and criss-crossing."[6] Yet complexity, like simplicity, can't be reduced to a single attribute or essence. In short, its underlying meanings or definitional components are connected by family resemblance.

Recall that family resemblance is the type of analytic complexity wherein entities share from a common set of attributes without necessarily sharing any given attribute. The family of attributes associated with complexity includes *multiplicity of elements* (such as parts, causes, or rules), and whether or how those elements interrelate; *analytic density* (distinctions and connections, or Wittgenstein's "criss-crossing"); relative *knowability*, or ease of comprehension; and relative *opacity*, or disparity between reality and appearance.

Things, processes, procedures, or relationships may be complex. Medicine is more complicated than knot tying, and languages are more complex than words. We've seen how critical thinking requires balancing the competing communicative needs for breadth, depth, relevance, completeness, and clarity. It is also a continuous balancing of simplicity and complexity.

At least one general feature of complexity could be called "logical," because it identifies a clear definitional boundary: the fact that, at least at first glance, it represents a pole of the spectrum relative to simplicity. Complexity and simplicity are logically inverse and matters of degree. But after that, it gets more complicated.

For one thing, there are no clear polar opposites that define this spectrum. At one extreme, simplicity fails to interpret the world and thus verges on the meaningless. At the other extreme, complexity verges on chaos or obscurity. Thus, there's a sense in which complexity is not in fact a pole but an intermediate band on a broader spectrum between the simple and the unknowable. What we tend to call "complex" is not chaotic or inscrutable. It is in principle knowable or partly knowable.

Another important feature of complexity, though not a universal or logical one, is contestability. This occurs more in human affairs, where values and interpretations differ, than in nature. The degree of complexity we impute to things is at least partly a matter of choice about how to interpret the world. We can interpret things in simpler or more complex ways because we control that spectrum as a tool of meaning. Our choices, within a range of plausibility, can be challenged but never dismissed out of hand. We can't appeal to a higher principle to decide such arguments over relative complexity because there is no higher principle.

That said, of course, the context or purpose at hand may argue for more or less complexity. Some things, we might say, are objectively more complicated than others. Living organisms are more complex than single cells. Pilots need to know how to land a plane, and doctors should know something about the human body. Tying knots is a simpler skill than either of those, but some knots are more complex and harder to tie than others, and the difference can be measured in the number of steps required. But whenever values or factual interpretations enter the picture, the degree of complexity is contestable.

In fact, whenever we identify things as wholes, or as parts of other wholes, we make implicit assumptions about how the world is structured, and "structure" is a byword for the simple-complex axis. This is one of the many ways in which ordinary language is inherently philosophical. Words make things discrete—sometimes too discrete for expressive precision. The purpose of analysis, as we've seen, is to reveal and manage their implicit complexity.

Most everyday things—chairs, people, primary colors, cardinal numbers—are individuated for us either by nature, logic (having clear definitional boundaries), convention, or common sense. They cleave reality in obvious and uncontroversial ways, no matter how connected they may be to other things. One chair may be just like another, but they're still two chairs, and so on. More abstract entities—such as rights, games, human or conceptual relationships, systems, or values—are more difficult to individuate and define; they have more complex contents and relationships to other things.

Indeed, there's a direct connection between complexity and analysis as gateway concepts. Complex phenomena are more internally diverse or externally related: phenomena that are harder to individuate in the first place. Analytic complexity equates with the density of such relations. But it isn't just a question of recognizing more wholes, or wholes composed of more parts. A beach is composed of many grains of sand, but a bigger beach isn't necessarily a more complex one. Complexity isn't just the state of being fractured or compound; it's also about how the parts interrelate or are governed by more than one rule of organization or behavior.[7]

Another important dimension of the simple-complex axis is relative knowability. We equate simplicity with clarity and ease of comprehension, whereas complex ideas demand more of their audience. Again, the context or situation may dictate a common-sense answer. A beach is a beach, until we choose to see it as part of a complex ecosystem.

Finally, the unseen or unobvious tends to be more complicated than the visible or obvious, although the opposite can also be true. Superficial complexities can mask deeper simplifying truths that organize appearances in order to answer questions, tell stories, or reveal patterns or principles. But locating those hidden truths is a complex task. It's a necessary task, because what appears to us in the here and now is by definition limited compared to what we can understand by further examination and reflection, using analytic tools such as generalization, inference, or induction. In fact, functionally speaking there is no "here and now," no conscious perception that isn't informed by such modes of thinking.

Consider, for example, how memory affects and complicates the way we think about ourselves or other people. How much can one know about a passing stranger on the street? How well can we know someone even after a few hours of conversation? What do we know about their unconscious minds—or our own for that matter? Finding what's hidden involves additional cognitive processes and assumptions about what is real or true.

We can access the unconscious only indirectly, through dreams, emotions, Freudian slips, stream of consciousness, intuitions, and the like. We may misunderstand such cues or avoid introspection altogether, and the boundary between the conscious and the unconscious is fuzzy. "Our dreams are toys," as Shakespeare observed. But the emotional truths expressed in our dreams are more obscure than our conscious thoughts.

For all these reasons, the level of complexity we discern and communicate is a paradigm question of critical inquiry. Critical thinking isn't about choosing one or the other, simplifying or complicating. It's about arbitrating and commuting between them—or as Taranto and Dettmar suggest, first simplifying and then showing the way back to more complex levels of understanding.

SYSTEMS AND COMPLEXITY

Systems are, almost by definition, paradigms of complexity: structures for understanding experience in terms of distinct but interacting parts, jointly creating a whole or producing an effect that none of the components could achieve individually. Atoms, human bodies, minds, marriages, wars, games, the weather, languages, economies—these are just a few of the things that we can understand better, or can only understand, as systems. They bear all the markings of complexity: multiple parts interacting within a larger whole, producing sometimes unpredictable outcomes, relatively less clarity or knowability, and a disparity between appearance and the deeper understanding of reality that is revealed by identifying the system itself.

> Examples of systems are water molecules, babies, and galaxies.
>
> —John Searle[8]

Systems are models that provide the traction for organizing and understanding the world. In fact, they *are* that traction. Without systemic understanding, our consciousness would be limited at best. Scientific laws explain why icicles melt in the sun, how fog forms, how tides ebb and flow. But we can never fully describe or predict a system as complex as the weather; omniscience isn't an option.[9] Identifying something as a system of discrete interacting elements at once acknowledges its complexity and simplifies our understanding of it.

The parts of a system may interrelate naturally, as in the case of minds, bodies, ecosystems, galaxies, or the weather; mechanically, as with a toilet or an airplane; or logically or analytically, in terms of their meanings or governing rules, as with language, logic, mathematics, codes, games, or constitutions. Some of these interactions are causal, others conceptual. Some systems are more complex than others, but there are no simple systems, unless one counts the interaction of, say, an arm, a hammer, and a nail.

Systems that are causally complex, changing over time in ways that aren't wholly predictable, are known as "open systems." Examples include personalities, economies, stock markets, and the weather. They involve relationships among heterogeneous and/or indeterminate variables, and as such, their origins and outcomes are more opaque and their explanations less complete. In the words of Karl Friston, they are "not reliably determined by their initial conditions, but by the system's own behavior as it feeds back into the interactions of its component parts."[10] Languages are open systems insofar as finite lexical elements and grammatical rules can generate an indefinite number of potential coherent messages.

Closed systems, on the other hand, are entirely self-organized. They tend to be formal or mechanical and include such things as clocks, machines, computer programs, logic and mathematics: systems whose behavior is solely determined by the interaction of the (relatively fewer and known) parts.

Understanding any system involves gauging how the parts relate to one another and to the whole. We can begin by asking, Why do we individuate it as a system in the first place? What are its parts, how do they differ, and how do they form a whole? What are the system's origins, interactions, and consequent effects? One could ask these questions about language in general, Navajo mythology, the Russian Revolution, the Space Shuttle, or the Affordable Care Act.

> The degree of complexity of organized social systems is a function of the number of system components . . . the relative differentiation or variety of these components . . . and the degree of interdependence among these components.
>
> —Todd R. La Porte[11]

Systems may not appear complex to the casual viewer: you turn a faucet and water runs out of the spigot. But several distinct things make that happen, including energy, pipes, pumps, and tanks, and that system isn't inscrutable to your plumber. Other things being equal, a system that has more parts, or is explained or predicted by more rules, is more complex than one with fewer parts or rules. The rules of chess aren't voluminous, but the different kinds of pieces, each with its own rules of movement, and the astronomical number of possible strategies, moves, and consequent positions, make chess more complex and harder to master than checkers.

Social, mechanical, and natural systems exhibit behaviors over time. Storms, viruses, and economic recessions come and go. Games, wars, and elections are won and lost. Our personal electronic devices malfunction. We can't describe these without using language and other symbolic systems that relate to space and time in less obvious ways.

The liberal arts are an evolving conceptual system for organizing knowledge. That system can be mapped according to categories and disciplines. Complexity is a factor in that mapping, due to the connections and sometimes porous or fuzzy boundaries among the disciplines. The liberal arts can also be ordered methodologically and conceptually by the rules and norms of critical inquiry—the spectrum of rationality qua critical thinking that is the subject of this book. Here the complicating factors include the different forms of rationality itself; the complexity of other gateway concepts, such as truth and causality; and the wild-card role of human values, all of which we'll soon explore.

APPEARANCE AND REALITY REVISITED

As patterns of understanding, systems are by definition less obvious and concrete than visible objects, but they are essential to thought and consciousness because they organize, connect, and explain. And in doing so they reflect another dimension of complexity: the disparity between appearance and reality.

This is especially evident in nature. We can't see atoms or molecules with the naked eye, yet we know they exist. By using technology we can detect a much broader range of the light spectrum (including, for example, X-rays, gamma rays, and ultraviolet light) than the tiny fraction (less than 0.01 percent) that is visible to the naked eye. Systems, technological or otherwise, reflect how reality isn't just *more* than appearance (and sometimes at variance with appearance) but also more complex than appearance. Navigating beyond appearance demands critical thinking because we have to discern multiple elements, causes, and interactions.

Quantum theory, in fact, strongly suggests (though the evidence is not definitive) that the universe operates in ways that are wholly at odds with how we perceive the everyday world. Subatomic particles, for example, can influence one another from afar—the deeply counterintuitive phenomenon that Einstein referred to skeptically as "spooky action at a distance." Scientists acknowledge it but don't fully understand it.[12]

Meanwhile, life as we know it offers plenty to think about beyond the visible. Other minds, emotions, values, personalities, social movements, the subconscious—these are among the things we seldom see fully or directly but can glimpse if we know where to look, things we can usefully call complex.

Complexity isn't always submerged, nor is simplicity always apparent. In history or science, for example, one of the aims is to identify simplifying patterns, laws, or regularities that underlie seemingly random or irregular facts or events. Such simplifying patterns are by definition less obvious, and in purely methodological terms, any digging is more complicated than not digging at all, just as a ten-step knot is more intricate than a three-step one. The models and the processes alike involve both complicating and simplifying. Critical thinkers need to look in both directions: from the simpler reality to the more complex one and vice versa. As logically inverse concepts, simplicity and complexity have inverse advantages and limitations. They only work in tandem.

Part of the job of critical inquiry, then, is to look beneath surfaces and explore the disparities between appearance and reality. That is how we discover constitutive elements, interconnections, or causal or other systemic patterns, which may have practical, intellectual, or moral implications. The unseen or the unobvious invariably complicates, and sometimes directly challenges, the more limited knowledge immediately available to our senses. There is no rule or principle dictating how deeply we should dig, and we don't all share the same appetite for complexity. That's where contestability comes into the picture. By and large, the more we dig, the more complexity and the greater the disparity with appearance we will find.

That human understanding goes beyond the obvious or the visible isn't news. It's reflected in the evolution of knowledge, especially over recent centuries. The great innovative thinkers of modern times—including Marx, Darwin, Freud, and Einstein—pioneered new avenues of inquiry by discovering ways in which reality differs fundamentally, even systematically, from everyday appearance. In doing so, they posited (or revealed) previously unimaginable levels of complexity: entire systemic substructures underlying what we know about society, nature, and the mind.

COMPLEXITY AND CRITICAL THINKING

All but the simplest forms of effective communication require some awareness of the simple-complex axis. Sometimes yelling "Stop!" or "Watch out!" or a physical gesture is sufficient, but usually we have to say more. Whether by simplifying or complicating (or doing both in succession) the aim of critical thinking is to find useful truths, shareable with readers, listeners, or the traffic cop who just pulled us over. What such critical thinking entails is not a commitment to complexity or simplicity per se but to *complexity management*—that is, awareness of the economies and trade-offs along the complexity axis and the need to balance nominally incompatible goals such as clarity and depth or breadth of communication.

Complexity is thus deeply embedded within the family of ideas that animate critical thinking and liberal learning. It is implicated whenever we think systemically and analytically, whenever we engage with history, human society, the mind, or other temporal phenomena. Whenever we argue about what is true, good, just, or beautiful, we're dealing with complex and conflicting interpretations of the world we ostensibly share.

To summarize: we defined complexity first of all as the logical opposite of simplicity. They aren't binary alternatives but define a spectrum. Whether in nature or the symbolic world of language and meaning, what is complex is more internally varied and/or externally related; that is why systems are paradigms of complexity. Natural and social systems tend to be "open." Mechanical and conceptual systems tend to be "closed," although language is in some ways both open and closed.

Again, the complexity axis can't be reduced to a single characteristic. Rather, it's a family of ideas, including multiplicity of parts or relationships, systemic structure, causal intricacy, analytic density, knowability, and opacity or deviation from the obvious.

We can scarcely avoid the complexity axis when we use language. How we describe the world, along that axis, is always partly object dependent, but it's often subject dependent as well, at least outside of science and closed systems. We make different choices, linguistic and otherwise, based on our subjective interpretations, worldviews, and appetites for complexity. Our values in art, morality, and politics reflect such choices. This is not to suggest that human values are formed entirely on the complexity axis, only that it is an important way of understanding and differentiating them.

As critical thinkers we model the world most effectively by commuting flexibly between the two perspectives that the axis represents. Each has benefits and limitations in the economy of knowledge and communication. There are trade-offs between clarity and depth or breadth, between what is easier to comprehend and what is more difficult, and between the obvious and the unobvious. We don't teach Kant or calculus to fifth-graders, but there's an audience for those subjects at a higher grade level. In case of fire, we need to know where the fire extinguisher is and how to use it, not the chemical composition of the flame retardant. But the manufacturers need to get it right.

Some scientists have theorized that the universe may be too complex for the human mind to understand. And so it may be, but we have no idea and seemingly no way of knowing. Indeed, it's not clear what it would mean to "know" that the universe is inherently unknowable to us.

Moreover, the overcomplexity conjecture poses a further conundrum, because the idea of complexity is *our* idea. It isn't a fact about the world but a tool for understanding the facts that are available to us. Our minds, and the tools we generate with them, are all we have, or are likely ever to have, for understanding what's out there and how it all works. So while there may in theory be truths about the universe or our place in it that lie forever beyond our reach, it may not be because they are beyond our mental grasp. If that were the case, in what sense could we still call them "truths"?

We'll get to truth soon enough. Meanwhile, in the knowable world, the axis of complexity and simplicity provides crucial traction for understanding things in systemic (and analytic) terms. Critical thinking about complexity enables more flexible boundaries, deeper understanding, and better communication. It also sheds light on our value differences, with direct application to the arts, to morality, and to politics.

Simpler worldviews tend to be partitional, stressing the individual and the particular, more rigid boundaries, and free will. More complex worldviews favor holistic over atomistic understanding, systemic thinking, greater disparity between reality and appearance, greater tolerance of ambiguity, and a wider causal web beyond the individual will. Our different ways of understanding, based partly on our different appetites for complexity, lie at the very heart of citizenship and democratic debate.

Neither tendency can be considered intrinsically superior; it is what philosophers call an "essentially contested" question. Whichever way we lean, flexibility is what matters to the critical thinker. Most democratic debate, and most intellectual discourse, is essentially a continuous referendum on complexity in society. As the sponsors of those debates, strong democratic institutions, whether of learning or governing, aren't biased toward either side of the complexity spectrum; they are where that spectrum lives.

NOTES

1. Julius Taranto and Kevin J. H. Dettmar, "The Secret of Good Humanities Teaching," *Chronicle of Higher Education* 62:5 (October 2, 2015): 68.
2. Primo Levi, *The Drowned and the Saved* (trans. R. Rosenthal). New York: Summit Books, 1986, p. 36. "Popular history," Levi continues, " . . . shuns half-tints and complexities: it is prone to reduce the river of human occurrences to conflicts, and the conflicts to duels. . . . This desire for simplification is justified, but the same does not always apply to simplification itself, which is a working hypothesis, useful as long as it is recognized as such and not mistaken for reality. The greater part of historical and natural phenomena are not simple, or are not simple in the way that we would like."
3. See Philip Goff, "Is the Universe a Conscious Mind?" *Aeon*, February 8, 2018. Retrieved from aeon.com/essays/cosmopsychism-explains-why-the-universe-is-fine-tuned-for-life.
4. What is invented and what is discovered is a version of the mind/body problem. For the present purposes, it suffices to say that we did not invent nature, but we did invent language and ideas as tools to model the world. Logic and math, as symbolic systems that are widely useful for such modeling, arguably constitute a third category, which it is futile to try to categorize as either inventions or discoveries.
5. C. S. Lewis, *Studies in Words*. Cambridge: Cambridge University Press, 1960, p. 175.
6. Ludwig Wittgenstein, *Philosophical Investigations*. New York: Wiley, 1991, §66.
7. Individuation can be difficult. Are Scotland, Wales, or the former East Germany nations in some sense? Did the nineteenth century end in 1900, or in 1914? These are cases where different elements, causal factors, and so on give rise to complex definitional boundaries, a.k.a. ambiguity.
8. John R. Searle, "What Your Computer Can't Know" (Review), *New York Review of Books*, October 9, 2014, p. 55. All systems may be (to use Searle's phrase) "observer dependent." But that doesn't mean they don't also exist in the world, insofar as what occasions them as mental events is both subject and object dependent. As Searle writes (p. 55), "All the literal information in the universe is either intrinsic or observer relative, and both are dependent on human or animal consciousness. Consciousness is the basis of information; information is not the basis of consciousness."
9. The weather, as Louis Menand writes (*The Metaphysical Club*, New York: Harper Perennial, 2002, pp. 207–8), "is a perfectly lawful, rather mundane phenomenon whose complexity nevertheless vastly exceeds our ability to understand it—and yet we freely pontificate about the causes of human unhappiness and the future progress of society, things determined by factors presumably many times more complex than the weather."
10. Karl Friston, "The Mathematics of Mind-Time," *Aeon*, December 24, 2017. Retrieved from https://aeon.co/essays/consciousness-is-not-a-thing-but-a-process-of-inference.
11. Todd R. La Porte, ed., *Organized Social Complexity: Challenge to Politics and Policy*. Princeton, NJ: Princeton University Press, 1975, p. 6.

12. See, for example, John Markoff, "Sorry, Einstein. Quantum Study Suggests 'Spooky Action' Is Real," *New York Times*, October 22, 2015. Retrieved from www.nytimes.com/2015/10/22/science/quantum-theory-experiment-said-to-prove-spooky-interactions.html?_r=0.

Chapter 11

Truth and Consequences

Tell all the truth but tell it slant—
Too bright for our infirm Delight
The Truth's superb surprise
As Lightning to the Children eased
With explanation kind
The Truth must dazzle gradually
Or every man be blind—

—Emily Dickinson

INTRODUCTION: WHAT IS TRUTH?

During the eighteenth century, combustion was believed to be caused by a substance called phlogiston, although there was no evidence for it, and no such fluid exists. Like phrenology or medieval alchemy, it was eventually revealed to be a false account of the world. A better understanding of combustion eventually emerged because scientists were interested in the truth of the matter—and also the truth about matter in general, and the nature of truth itself.

Truth is the gold standard of knowledge, even when it eludes us. Without it, we can't talk about "knowing" at all. Knowledge is inseparable from identifying, however provisionally, what is and is not the case. The "conduct of civilized life," Harry Frankfurt writes, "and the vitality of the institutions that are indispensable to it, depend very fundamentally on respect for the distinction between the true and the false."[1] All trust, all learning, and all democratic ideals rest on a concept of truth to regulate the quality of information. Truth isn't just useful in all those areas; it's essential.

But knowledge is complex, and so is truth. It assumes different forms, with different standards and methods for attaining it, and different levels of certainty. What we'll aim for here is a sense of the breadth and complexity of truth and its symbiotic relationship with critical thinking.

We can begin with what philosophers call the "correspondence" theory of truth: the conventional idea that what is true is whatever mirrors or adequately represents the world around us. A traffic light is either red or green; the United States has a constitution. It's only because we mostly agree on such things, and on how to use language, that we can have effective conversations at all. Yet correspondence gets us only so far, and truth, as a broad and complex gateway concept, goes further.

For one thing, logical and mathematical truths aren't mirrors of reality but statements about the validity of other statements. Definitions are conventional truths about meaning that are often vague and may evolve. Likewise, purported moral truths—such as "murder is bad"—aren't based on aggregating evidence directly from experience. They, too, are of a different order: social conventions that map shared values and how we use words.

For that matter, experience itself isn't immutable. It's at least partly constructed in our minds, based on our separate and limited perceptions. We don't simply assimilate things to our minds; we model them, and our models are limited, biased, and otherwise flawed. Everything we perceive is to some extent an interpretation, even things we agree about, because we don't share consciousness—and even if we did, such consciousness wouldn't be omniscient. We need the idea of truth as a matrix of agreement, but the truth or truths available to us are an infinitesimal part of what we call "reality."

That said, the idea of truth-as-correspondence has considerable explanatory power in everyday life, and there are certain obvious truths about the world beyond the merely trivial (for example, that I'm a human being, not a giraffe), the denial of which is a dead end for discourse. But nontrivial truths vary in their degrees of certainty, usefulness, obviousness, relevance, and so on. So it isn't enough to say that truth refers to what is the case or how the world is. We might rather say it refers to what is the case to the extent that we know what the case is, how we know it, how sure we are of it, and what, in a given instance, we mean by "the case." We'll try to steer clear of the deeper metaphysical questions here (though we can't entirely avoid them in talking about a concept as important as truth) in order to tease out how truth relates to critical thinking: why, in other words, truth is a gateway concept essential to all learning.

THE DUAL ASPECT OF TRUTH

One complicating fact about truth is that it is not just a neutral concept; it's also a value. Moreover, we value it in two distinct ways: as the intellectual value of truth seeking and as the moral value of truth telling. In both senses, it's a value that's widely but not universally shared. And in both senses, truth is aspirational: a perpetual goal of thought and behavior, not something we can acquire once and for all or store in the basement. It could hardly be otherwise, because truth seeking and truth telling are different aspects of the common process of trying to agree about the world. In both senses, truth sustains community and vice versa. The absence of either one degrades the other, causing communities to fray, shrink, or rupture.

However, the intellectual and moral dimensions of truth are less clear-cut than this initial distinction suggests. There's a moral dimension to truth seeking and an intellectual dimension to truth telling. Certain forms of truth seeking, such as scientific or other research, have more pragmatic than moral value (think of the Wright brothers' invention of powered flight). But then, all technologies have moral and political impacts, mostly unforeseen by their inventors; the Wright brothers could hardly have envisioned drone warfare. Neither dimension of truth is entirely neutral or entirely prescriptive.

Like nonviolence, truth telling is a basic moral lesson that we inculcate in our children as part of the glue of family and social life, and it's eminently teachable. It's also essential to all learning, formal or otherwise. Whenever we produce or consume information, even when gossiping among friends (unless in the presence of alcohol or other environmental factors that give a green light to bullshit), we more or less expect, and demand, veracity.

Even preliterate societies need consensus about shared facts in order to communicate and function. Unless we can agree on what my name is, how many fingers I have, and how many eggs are in my basket, we might as well not be talking. That's why truth is a gateway concept: We can scarcely interact on any level without passing through that gate of shared understanding about how our statements relate to the world. Language itself presupposes such a shared world; otherwise it would all collapse into babble.

But where do we go from there? The more we look beyond names, fingers, and eggs, the more complicated the idea becomes. The philosopher Paul Horwich writes that, "despite hundreds of years of looking [for a single definition of 'truth'], no acceptable answer . . . has ever been found. We've tried truth as 'correspondence with the facts,' as 'provability,' as 'practical utility,' and as 'stable consensus'; but all turned out to be defective in one way or another—either circular or subject to counterexamples."[2] Yet for all its complexity, the idea of truth hasn't been abandoned (except, in theory, by the postmodernists). It remains the moral and intellectual glue of discourse.

As with any complex concept, greater clarity about truth calls for critical thinking. But critical thinking isn't a guarantee of truth or a magic potion for correcting errors or dispelling illusions. It's a set of tools for minimizing them. And it begins with the points we've underscored thus far: that the concept of truth is necessary for noncoercive discourse; that it is both an intellectual and a moral value; that we distinguish truth in general from what we call, in a particular context, "the truth"; and that truth is prismatic but not wholly obscure or unobtainable. Thus, we can differentiate, in various contexts, between truth and error; between relative truth and certainty; between truth and fiction or imagination; between truth and propaganda; between truth and lies, deception, omission, or exaggeration.

> I think it is clear that while there is a universal human need for qualities such as accuracy (the dispositions to acquire true beliefs) and sincerity (the disposition to say, if anything, what one believes to be true), the form of these dispositions and of the motivations that they embody are culturally and historically various.
>
> —Bernard Williams[3]

As with the concept of complexity, there are crucial disparities between truth on the everyday level and truth at the quantum level of subatomic reality, where nature's ultimate secrets seem to reside. But it's comforting to note that, whatever the truths of quantum reality, the visible world is one of Newtonian stability. Apples fall and hit our heads; time and space seem distinct—and for everyday purposes, they are; we have calendars and atlases to measure them separately. Objects can only be in one place at a time, events have causes, and things can only happen in one way at a time. A ballplayer may either strike out or hit a home run, but not both in the same at-bat. And even when the causes of an event are multiple, obscure, or indeterminable, nothing is uncaused. At the nonquantum level, we can talk about how things are and how things happen in terms of "truth" and "the truth" and leave the rest to the physicists.

Even in the mundane case of throwing and catching a ball, however, what we call "the truth of the matter" is a vastly simplified and selective account. All knowledge and communication are limited by the powers of human perception and description. A complete or perfectly true account is neither possible nor necessary; we can't even say what such an account would look like. We don't need to examine the ball. But as the philosopher W. V. Quine put it, "No statement is immune to revision."[4]

If little is final or certain, we can still establish important truths, building useful if impermanent castles of understanding, as it were, on the shifting beach of reality. We hold people accountable for errors or omissions of fact, or for lack of due diligence in determining the facts—but not for failing to heap fact upon fact without end. Lacking omniscience, we still expect others to pursue and relate the truth based on their knowledge, resources, purposes, and audience. And (attention, critical thinkers!) that includes a sense of what isn't known, what can't be known, and what is merely probable.

THE VARIETIES OF TRUTH

Some kinds of truths are obvious or self-evident. Two plus two equals four, water boils at 212° Fahrenheit, and Boston is—until further notice—the capital of Massachusetts. Likewise, it isn't worth debating who won the 2008 presidential election. All humans are mortal, pigs can't fly, and mermaids and unicorns exist—in the human mind. These assertions are not what you'd want to call "arguable"; to deny any of them is to marginalize oneself from the conversation. Yet they are different kinds of truth statements.

The first one (that two plus two equals four) is a logical-mathematical truth, the kind on which all thought is predicated. The second (the boiling point of water, relative to air pressure) is a law of nature, at least in the known universe. The third and fourth (the 2008 election and the capital of Massachusetts) are social facts that brook no exceptions. And the last two (regarding human mortality and flying pigs) are, for all practical purposes, necessary truths about the world. In theory they're subject to revision, but only if we radically revise reality itself. In the same latter category are the truths that biological males can't bear children and that every human has exactly two biological parents, one male and one female. These statements are universally true in experience but not mathematical truths like those of arithmetic or logical truths like the proposition that parallel lines never meet.[5]

However, outside of logic, math, obvious facts, and universal laws of nature, what constitutes "truth" is often problematic and contestable. Unlike those more obvious forms of truth, empirical statements about the world often vex us. We struggle to reach agreement owing to our different subjective viewpoints, biases, and limitations. Some empirical truths are easily available and widely accepted as facts; others (such as the number of seagulls on the Jersey Shore at a given moment) can be imagined and expressed but can't be ascertained except by guessing or approximation. Still others are hypotheses, provable or otherwise.

The wider grooves of experience are similar for most of us. We all have bodies and minds, and we share the same planet. We broadly agree on what we mean by "Abraham Lincoln" or "World War I." But our knowledge of these is based on imperfectly shared facts, memories, images, interpretive schemes, and values—and limited by our general ignorance, or if you prefer, our lack of omniscience.

BEYOND CERTAINTY AND OBJECTIVITY

Certainty is the polestar of human cognition, sparing us the tedious business of doubting, wondering, guessing, arguing, or estimating probabilities. But certainty is in limited supply. Its various forms include logical and mathematical truths; conventions such as names, numbers, or alphabets; and demonstrable facts, such as Boston being a state capital, the outcome of an election, sports scores, or closing stock prices. Most of these latter can be called objective truths, and they fall under the heading of *accuracy*: the conformity of a statement to some objective prototype.

Quotations of printed or spoken words, for instance, are either accurate or they aren't. Verifiable statements of fact may also be deemed accurate: "I married the guy on Saturday—you can check at the courthouse." But facts, like quotations, can be misleading if taken out of context; was it a shotgun wedding, an arranged marriage, a marriage of convenience? And context, while crucial to all knowledge, takes us beyond the realm of objective certainty.

Even accuracy isn't always a purely objective matter. The accuracy of a translation can't be judged as easily as that of a direct quotation, although we still talk about its accuracy because it has an objective source. And translating poetry is even more problematic than prose—yet translate we must. Accuracy is prized in scholarship, education, journalism, science—wherever knowledge is publicly produced and shared. But leaving aside problems such as context and translation, it is limited to the correct reproduction of previously iterated expressions.

A different sense of objectivity refers to the neutrality of the observer rather than the thing observed. Like the accuracy of a translation, this kind of objectivity is aspirational. We pursue it as a social value, for example, as judges, umpires, or exam graders, but we seldom achieve perfection. Objectivity qua neutrality also contains pitfalls that call for critical thinking. It can be confused with the other type of objectivity—the type we equate with certainty. And it can create false or unrealistic expectations about fairness or perfection. No one is omniscient or unbiased, and relative impartiality is no guarantee of freedom from error.

These points about objectivity illustrate both the need for, and the limitations of, the subject-object distinction in dealing with the concept of truth.

The questions we ask, the ways we describe things, the unacknowledged and often unconscious interpretive frames we apply, are invariably selective and subjective. In the end, most useful knowledge, and most pursuit of truth, relies upon, but goes beyond, the realm of objective certainty. It involves uncertainties: inferences, generalizations, probabilities, educated guesswork, and intelligent doubt about what we don't know.

> Every year if not every day we have to wager our salvation upon some prophecy based upon imperfect knowledge.
>
> —Justice Oliver Wendell Holmes, *Abrams v. United States* (1919)

In most places, for instance, we can be fairly sure (although never certain) that the building we are in won't suddenly collapse, but in earthquake-prone regions, it's less certain. Pilots trust their instruments, not because those instruments are infallible but because they are far less fallible than the human senses. And so it goes: we live day to day by relying on pragmatic certainties—things it simply isn't worth doubting. We are all truth economists of daily life.

VERIDICAL COMMUNITIES AND THE SPECTER OF RELATIVITY

Numbers, identities, and formal systems (such as math, logic, codes, or alphabets) are among the accessible facts, or systems for organizing facts, that offer no room for disagreement; in these realms, the terms "certainty" and "objectivity" are appropriate. Science depends in part on unproved assumptions, untested hypotheses, and theoretical debates. But scientists agree about the basic laws of nature, at least the ones they're aware of. When we observe nature, or human-made artifacts such as machines, we're all looking at the same things, if from different perspectives.

But when we focus more broadly on human life and society—for example, through the lenses of the social sciences, the humanities, or the news media— the question of truth becomes murkier. There are factual anchors, but differences of values, perspectives, and interpretive styles complicate the project of reaching intersubjective agreement. Information is a social construct that we share imperfectly: a form of community that always falls short of shared consciousness or shared values. And what we can't agree on, once all available evidence has been shared, we can't talk about in terms of truth in an absolute sense. Or more precisely, we can talk about it, but within smaller communities of agreement.

> We may see the world, nature, science, in different ways; but we are looking at the same things. So a degree of workable consensus is at least possible. With values it is otherwise.
>
> —Jill Lepore[6]

This doesn't mean that truth is merely relative and untethered to reality or that ostensibly true propositions have no shared properties other than that some group of us happens to assent to them; having our own private realities is a nonstarter for any shared knowledge. Rather, it means that even in a shared world, our different histories and perceptions limit the pursuit of truth to what might be called *veridical communities*. Individuals can always choose, at whatever cost to themselves, to opt out of such communities. That the Earth isn't flat is a universal truth outside of the Flat Earth Society. But what we call reality is effectively the convergence of our separate perceptions. While we often agree on the facts, our subjectivity means such convergence can never be total.

In fact, majorities or significant minorities often believe things that are provably wrong, ignoring or innocent of evidence to the contrary. Galileo was right that the Earth moves around the sun, not vice versa. Barack Obama was born in Hawaii, infant vaccines don't cause autism, and global warming is real. These are facts for most of us—yet they are contested in political space. And Great Britain is an island, no matter what. I can show you a map—but I can't make you believe it.

> Thy truth is neither mine nor his nor another's; but belongs to us all whom Thou callest to partake of it, warning us terribly, not to account it private to ourselves, lest we be deprived of it.
>
> —St. Augustine[7]

Many other kinds of knowledge are elusive, however, and not just because some people ignore the obvious. Someone's state of mind, the nature of a human relationship, why an economy thrives or declines—we can only know such things up to a point, by finding patterns and clues in the available facts. Which we select and how we organize or prioritize them is another matter; and the larger truths we are looking for, the broader, more useful, more explanatory ones, are intersubjective. Thus, there's a superficial sense in which truth is relative. We can't force anyone to believe that the Earth orbits the sun. All we can do is share evidence and, when necessary, protect ourselves from the consequences of their erroneous beliefs.

But even such limited relativity comes with some critical thinking alerts. Our sense of what is true can't be based on who agrees with us. And the general commitment to truth is never a commitment to particular truths or to unjustified certainty. The more we know for certain, and the larger the veridical community, the better—though we could all be wrong. And we must also acknowledge what we don't know or merely believe to be the case. Critical thinkers reserve a margin of doubt about whether there's life on Mars, why a marriage dissolves, how World War I began, or who authored the Bible. And they also consider why these are difficult questions and in what sense they are knowable at all.

We tend to regard the truth as an absolute, something that is by definition observer independent. And on the nonquantum level, that often works. Intuitively we think what's "out there" is the same for all of us. Time appears to be linear, in fact monofilament, even if some physicists say that it isn't linear, is relative to the galaxy you're in, or doesn't exist at all. We can disagree about the meaning of the Constitution but not about what is in the Constitution. Incontrovertible facts form the core of what we understand as reality. When such facts are routinely denied, democratic or learning communities are weakened.

Yet complex events can be understood in competing, if not necessarily in equally valid or compelling, ways. We can disagree about how to describe, interpret, or contextualize events, what might have happened but didn't, or which facts or events to focus our finite human attention on. Sometimes it's unclear how much information we need, and how reliable it must be, to count as knowing. We are more certain that Lee Harvey Oswald shot John F. Kennedy than that he acted alone. As Adam Gopnik writes,[8]

> Any fact asserted can be met with a counter-fact—some of them plausible, many disputed, most creating contradictions that are unresolvable. But this is not a fact about conspiracies. It is a fact about facts. All facts in all inquiries come at us with their own shakiness, their own shimmer of uncertainty. The threads of evidence usually seem separate and sure only because life mostly comes at us in finished fabrics, and nothing requires us to pull the thread. When we do, there's a tangle waiting.

Science is a partial exception here, because unlike other forms of knowledge (such as pertain to human behavior, thought, or imagination) it appears to be governed by universal laws. There is one temperature at which water boils, and all objects fall at the same rate. Science is a unified enterprise with the common goal of understanding nature, and it is conducted using shared techniques, technologies, and methodologies.

Scientists, like all experts, disagree about many things and have rival theories, frameworks, and explanations. But in principle their debates can be resolved through further experimentation and fact gathering. Scientific truths, at least on the nonquantum level, aren't observer dependent. In this sense they enjoy a relatively secure status—at least until other truths come along to replace them. There remain big questions that science has yet to answer. We don't fully understand the origins or destiny of the universe or the exact nature of time, gravity, or consciousness. But we agree about what we're trying to understand.

TRUTH IS PRAGMATIC

Saying that truth is social, based on veridical communities, means that it's essentially pragmatic. Like rationality itself, it's a grammar of community: whatever works for societies, advancing their conversations about nature, building their bridges, or curing their diseases. In science, disagreements about what works are essentially temporary, in the absence of knowledge. (What forms of knowledge or inquiry count as "science" is another question.) But we don't argue about what it means for a bridge to stand or a disease to be cured. In this sense, scientific truths are different from the truths we debate in politics or in humanities classrooms.

Some such truths are beyond rational dispute, but most social facts don't exist as absolutes. They aren't "things" but shared ways of seeing things. In practice, we can only identify them as "facts" because we agree about them. You may see ghosts or flying pigs, but absent confirmation of the sighting, you're on your own.

An obvious objection here is based on the aforementioned intuitive notion that what we mean by "the truth" is precisely what's "out there," independent of what we may think or agree is out there or how many of us agree about it. We can call that realism. It's tempting because it accords with our common-sense understanding of "truth." In the world as we know it, things can only be, and events can only happen, one way at a time. Most scientific truths are of this realist variety. In one sense, realism is literally—if not tautologically—true: What is out there is out there, and not something else. It isn't altered by how we think about it. We can't communicate much if we can't distinguish the world as it seems to most of us from error, illusion, fantasy, and so forth. But "how the world seems to most of us" is an intersubjective idea, not an objective or subjective one.

The problem isn't that reality is a hall of mirrors but that realism doesn't always get the job done. It doesn't account for the inherently tenuous, uncertain, and nonuniversal ways in which we apprehend what's out there. It may be valid to say (in mundane contexts or with regard to simple propositions) that "truth" is knowledge that reflects some part or aspect of a fixed reality, but this approach begs important questions: How exactly is the world, and how do we know it is that way? In what sense is it one world, if we see it differently? In what way are our descriptions of it imperfect representations or models? Given our different perceptions, how can we form the consensus that we need in order to communicate at all? When do our perceptions conflict, and when do those conflicts matter? When do the words we choose matter—or rather, when *don't* they? For all of these questions, we need critical thinking along with facts.

It's enticingly simple to conceive truth in realist terms as an objective state of affairs. But for the concept to be useful as a basis for action and communication, we need to recognize that we can never see the world *exactly* the same way, and sometimes we need to talk about our differences. We don't need to abandon the intuition of a shared reality, apart from our separate and limited capacities for knowing it. But because such realism is of limited value for constructing and sharing knowledge, because we lack omniscience or shared consciousness, what is pragmatically true is what we can agree on and use as planks for shared bridges to other shores. And that still leaves room for mermaids and unicorns.

SKEPTICISM AND RELATIVE CERTAINTY

Saying that truth is a product of pragmatic consensus also doesn't mean that we can't identify certainties, or at least relative certainties: things it is irrational or imprudent to doubt. Many of the ostensible truths that get us through life are unconscious inferences or inductive bets based on past experience. It isn't a necessary truth that bathing makes us cleaner, that turning the doorknob helps to open a door, or that peer review produces better scholarship; it's just reliably and usefully true.

The search for truth is a search for facts, and larger factual patterns, while using the tools of critical thinking to keep our minds from misdirecting us. That process calls for skepticism, estimations of levels of certainty, and scrutiny of how we come to know what we think we know. But skepticism per se isn't knowledge; it's rather a state of epistemic limbo and a guardrail against false belief. If we make a fetish of either certainty or uncertainty, we lose our critical way.

Practically speaking, we can't afford to doubt everything any more than we can afford to believe everything. As Wittgenstein observes, "I can easily imagine someone always doubting before he opened his front door whether an abyss did not yawn behind it, and making sure about it before he went through the door (and he might on some occasion prove to be right)—but for all that, I do not doubt in such a case."[9]

Skepticism isn't ignorance, either. The philosopher Karl Popper exaggerated just a bit when he remarked, "We are all alike in our infinite ignorance."[10] He was right that we all lack omniscience, but we get by with what we know, or we wouldn't even be able to talk about knowing. Most of our useful knowledge exists in the space between certainty and nihilistic skepticism. "Indeed," as David Deutsch writes, "infallibilism and nihilism are twins. Both fail to understand that mistakes are not only inevitable, they are correctable (fallibly)."[11]

Finally, let's not forget subjectivity: the "I" that we distinguish from "thou," "us," and "them." This "I" is more than just a personal repository of ignorance and error. It's our self and the fragile seat of all our knowledge. And it occupies an important place in the universe of learning, not just in the humanities, where values and imagination are directly involved.

Morality is about reconciling the self with others—and so, in a sense, is art. Aesthetic ideas, like moral ones, are difficult to formulate as truths. In coming to terms with Ahab's white whale, a Cézanne painting, or French New Wave cinema, there's ample room for uncertainty, interpretation, and argument, as well as for subjective responses. Art, in other words, is partly about our subjectivity and our private truths. But like morality, it's also about a larger "I," a self that is (both biologically and culturally) indissolubly connected to the wider collective "us." It's about seeing through other "eyes" and seeing how other people's values, perspectives, and responses can deepen our own.

This isn't the radically subjective "I" who dreams at night and sings in the shower—and even that self is hardly a blank slate; it's a self with a history, genes, needs, habits, family, friends, and all the rest of what makes me that dreamer and singer. This larger self is the intersubjective "I": a self that takes the measure of its own ideas while reasoning with others, one that is learning and growing by reaching beyond itself.

THE BINOCULAR PURSUIT OF TRUTH

Let's try to summarize. The concept of truth is an essential and unavoidable gateway to the liberal arts. It permeates our thought and language because all useful knowledge requires such a concept to effectively model the world. When public truths are widely questioned and lies abound, mass confusion results and discourse is enfeebled. For all its importance, the concept of truth is complex and layered—but also transcultural and transdisciplinary. If we discovered aliens, or an isolated tribe, who had no implicit concept of truth, it would be virtually impossible for us to talk with them, or for them to talk with each other.

As individuals, we inevitably perceive the world differently, and our perceptions are fallible, limited, and biased. Yet they refer to what we can only conceive as a common world. We see the same train pulling into the station, no matter which side of the track we're on. The fact of our subjectivity doesn't alter what's out there, and it doesn't mean we inhabit private worlds. It means we each differently construct the single reality we presumably share.

At the same time, because of such separate construction, we must also reckon with our limited ability to achieve consensus about what is the case, what has happened, and what matters. In that sense, truth is pragmatic and communal rather than absolute. So, apart from the many occasions that call on us to look at different facts, or to look at them in different ways, we need, at a minimum, a binocular conception of truth.

"Binocular" here means a conception that recognizes both the realist assumption of a shared reality apart from those perceptions (what Kant called the *Ding-an-sich*, or thing-in-itself) and the many factual and normative conflicts to which our separate perceptions and interpretive habits give rise. In other words, we need to think of the world as "out there," but we also need to see how we construct it and how our constructions tend to diverge.

We're left with a bit of a paradox. We can't dispense with the idea of truth, or with the ways of learning, the forms of discourse, and the civic institutions that we associate with the pursuit and the telling of it. Yet critical thinkers feel some justifiable discomfort with generalities such as "the truth" and "the pursuit of truth." The terms sound at once too lofty and too uncomplicated, as if they identified things we could track down like a runaway pet. Too often that is not the case. In the short run, we need to discover and share facts as bases for further discourse. In the longer run, we pursue truth more asymptotically: aiming for pragmatically acceptable levels of certainty and consensus but seldom achieving either one perfectly or with finality.

Critical thinking provides the tools for dealing with the vexations of truth, enabling us to cut them down to manageable size, so to speak. It begins with recognizing that (a) we can't use language effectively without a concept of truth, (b) skepticism about the truth in a particular case isn't skepticism about truth per se, and (c) the pursuit of truth doesn't entail belief in absolute truth or discoverable facts that describe every possible state of affairs. "Agreement with reality" often comports with common sense, but it doesn't work in all instances given our separate and differently limited minds. And a pragmatic approach to truth isn't relativism—or at least, not the intellectually and morally nihilistic kind. Hostility to all truth is inimical to public life in open societies: to learning, governing, and conversation. Postmodernism was a well-traveled dead end.

Because our larger context here is the liberal arts, a final question lingers: What about the seemingly innate advantage of science as a truth generator?

Given that nature is essentially law governed, science can construct knowledge by accretion through discoveries, experiments, inventions, paradigm shifts, and endless theoretical refinement. It produces many useful "shiny objects," including the computer I'm writing on. But this doesn't make scientific knowledge "better" than other kinds. It rather marks it as a different kind of knowledge, where the goals and questions are more obvious than those we pose when looking at society, human nature, morality, art, or how we should think. We still have to look at everything.

Do truths accumulate over time in philosophy, or in the study of human behavior and society? Not in the same transformative way as in science. Yet those fields have also come a long way since Socrates and his forerunners. Wittgenstein enjoyed a wider conceptual vocabulary than Plato, but both offer powerful lessons in thinking. Hobbes, Locke, Rousseau, and Montesquieu helped to frame modern democracy. If science reaches formidable summits—curing disease, traveling to Mars, probing quantum reality—knowledge also accrues over time in history, psychology, or economics. Philosophy investigates truth at a different level, asking enduring questions that every generation must address for itself in order to learn how to think. That's one reason why we continue to teach and study all those disciplines. Another is that science and philosophy don't teach us everything we need to know to be citizens.

The pursuit of truth is both a moral and an intellectual keystone: it's how we regulate knowledge, identify false beliefs and false statements, and become more effective agents in the world. In most areas of inquiry, agreed-upon facts are essential pillars for larger frameworks of understanding. Truth is a complex ideal, differently defined and pursued relative to different forms of knowledge. Underlying all of these are the tools of critical thinking, which help us to understand what we know, don't know, need to know, and cannot know.

NOTES

1. Harry Frankfurt, quoted in Jim Holt, "Say Anything," *The New Yorker*, August 22, 2005. Retrieved from https://www.newyorker.com/magazine/2005/08/22/say-anything.

2. Paul Horwich, in a post on the *New York Times*'s "Opinionator" blog (March 3, 2013).

3. Bernard Williams, "Philosophy as a Humanistic Discipline," in A. W. Moore, ed., *Philosophy as a Humanistic Discipline*, 180–200. Princeton, NJ: Princeton University Press, 2006.

4. Willard Van Orman Quine, "Two Dogmas of Empiricism," *Philosophical Review* 60:1 (January 1951): 40.

5. There are subtle differences between these propositions. We can at least imagine pigs evolving wings, as other creatures on our planet have done. Similarly, that the sun will set isn't a logical or even a natural certainty. But such a world-ending event would also put an end to our thinking, whereas pigs having wings would merely astonish us.

6. Jill Lepore, "After the Fact" (Review), *The New Yorker*, March 21, 2016, p. 91–94.

7. St. Augustine, *Confessions*; quoted in W. H. Auden, *A Certain World: A Commonplace Book*. New York: Viking Press, 1970, p. 425.

8. Adam Gopnik, "Closer Than That: The Assassination of J.F.K., Fifty Years Later," *The New Yorker*, November 4, 2013, p. 105.

9. Ludwig Wittgenstein, *Philosophical Investigations*. New York: Wiley, 1991, sec. 84.

10. Karl Popper, quoted in David Deutsch, "Why It's Good to Be Wrong," *Nautilus*, May 23, 2013, p. 139.

11. Deutsch, "Why It's Good to Be Wrong." Fallibilism and nihilism, Deutsch adds, "both abhor institutions of substantive criticism and error correction, and denigrate rational thought as useless or fraudulent. They both justify the same tyrannies. They both justify each other."

Chapter 12

The Two Riddles of Causality

There's a divinity that shapes our ends,
Rough-hew them how we will.

— William Shakespeare, *Hamlet*, act 5, scene 2

INTRODUCTION: LIFE IS A CAUSAL BAZAAR

In *The Consolation of Philosophy*, the sixth-century Roman senator and philosopher Boethius envisions philosophy in the form of a woman. Writing from prison, and about to be executed on fabricated political charges, he consoles himself in a dialogue with his imagined priestess of thought. Among other things, Boethius asks "Philosophy" about the causes of "matters that lie hidden." She replies, "It is a question that can never be exhausted. The subject is of such a kind that when one doubt is removed, countless others spring up in its place, like the Hydra's heads. The only way to check them is with a really lively intellectual fire."[1]

The question and answer exemplify why causality is a gateway to the liberal arts. Like complexity and truth, causality is an idea that spans liberal learning and calls for a "lively intellectual fire." And it's a crucial portal to the moral dimension of the liberal arts, which we'll explore in the final chapters.

As with the other gateway concepts, our aim isn't to resolve the underlying philosophical questions about causality, though we'll need to confront them. The more modest goal is to survey the causal terrain and see why its riddles are not obscure or arcane but integral to critical thinking and liberal learning.

One doesn't need technical jargon or training in philosophy to engage with causality. The concept is intrinsic to almost every question about human agency. Whether in history, morality, literature, cognitive science or psychology, criminal justice, or the decisions we face from day to day, life is a causal bazaar. That is because we see causes and effects everywhere we look and because we can think and act to change them—or at least, we need to think we can. And note the word we use: be-*cause*.

How do we approach so broad a subject? As in dealing with truth (much of which is causal in nature), we must begin from an awareness of our relative ignorance. In fact, we are ignorant on two levels. One is epistemological: there's a lot we just don't know or can't know about actual causes and effects in the world. We have only so much time, intellect, and access to facts.

The other level is metaphysical—that is, it's about the nature of reality itself. There are different kinds of potential causality, based on their origin. Deciding which kind, or what combination, sheds the most useful light on human experience is a question that can be answered only if we spin a web of assumptions.

That said, causality may be complex, but it isn't a hopeless tangle. We can begin to sort it out by exploring three framing devices that lend some initial clarity: the distinction between causation and causality, the role of causality in human consciousness, and the logical dimension of causality.

CAUSATION AND CAUSALITY

First, there's a useful (if limited) distinction between "causation" and "causality." The terms are often used interchangeably. Both refer to causes and effects and the connections and distinctions we observe over time that define what we call "change." The distinction here reflects the two aforementioned limitations: our epistemological and metaphysical ignorance (or to put it more gently, our lack of omniscience).

We will use the term "causation" to refer to the actual geography of change: the mapping of what actually happens and why, or how one state gives way to another state over time. "Causality," on the other hand, refers to the larger question of *what kinds of ultimate causation there are*. Harkening back to the last chapter, we might say that causation is about "the truth" of what causes what, whereas causality is about "truth" in the wider sense of how we model the world. Although these two senses of cause and effect overlap, they represent different problems for human knowledge: a question of "what" and a broader question of "how" or "why."

Aristotle famously distinguished four types or levels of causation.[2] The *material cause* of something is the physical element that undergoes change: in the case of building a chair, it's the wood. The *formal cause* pertains to how that material transforms as the wood becomes the chair. The *efficient cause* is the agency that brings about such change: here, it's the carpenter who builds the chair. And the *final cause* is the purpose or reason for the causation: the chair is for sitting.

I'm talking about causation when I ask how you robbed a bank, including more or less specific causes, such as your motivation, method, and the chain of events leading up to the heist. I'm talking about causality in the more general or metaphysical sense when I question whether you could have not robbed the bank given that you're a sociopath or descend from a line of bank robbers.

Every one of us explores causation in daily life. In an endless variety of contexts, we apply practical rules of cause and effect based on experience. Infants learn that crying gets attention and that a ball when released drops to the ground. Children discover that touching a flame causes pain. Adults learn that adding oil to boiling water prevents pasta from sticking.

Probing more deeply, we look for lines and patterns of causation, and we use explanatory frameworks such as evolution, revolution, metamorphosis, metastasis, or economic, social, or natural cycles of growth and decay. In logic and math, certain propositions necessitate or "cause" other propositions to be valid because they function according to certain rules.[3]

Simple acts such as dropping a ball or touching a flame have obvious results. When it comes to more complex events, however, our ability to establish clear cause-and-effect connections diminishes as the causal horizon recedes—that is, as the possible causes of an event or phenomenon multiply or stretch backward in time.

What caused the American Civil War? We can cite a number of obvious triggers: the institution of slavery, *Uncle Tom's Cabin*, the Dred Scott decision, John Brown's raid on Harpers Ferry, the secession of the Southern states, the attack on Fort Sumter. But how exactly are those causes related, and what else do they relate to? Any complex event represents a convergence of multiple causal factors, including individual and group decisions, natural and social conditions, and seeming accidents. The limits of our knowledge are, to a great extent, causal limits.

We don't always need to look beyond the self or toward the causal horizon of an immediate event. I know who wrote this book and what led to the birth of my children. It's widely known that John Wilkes Booth shot Abraham Lincoln at Ford's Theatre. But what else shaped the aftermath of the Civil War? What did that war lead to? (Or perhaps we should say, What *didn't* it affect?) The questions are endless and the answers often vague.

Causation is problematic enough. But critical thinkers must also ask more general questions, not just about lines and levels of causation but about their ultimate sources. Broadly speaking, there are three such possible sources: human agency or "free will"; visible nature, as a web of causes and effects;

and nature on the quantum level, where subatomic particles appear to behave with sheer randomness. Herman Melville in *Moby-Dick* (without the benefit of particle physics) similarly spliced causality from three strands, which he labeled "chance, free will, and necessity—no wise incompatible—all interweavingly working together."[4]

LOGIC AND CAUSATION

However we approach the riddles of causality, one thing we can't escape is the rigor of logic. Here as elsewhere, logic doesn't solve any riddles or add to our knowledge. But as a form of rationality, logic helps by exposing contradictions and fallacies and by inviting us to think more deeply and clearly. While logic offers no surprises, it can help our causal reasoning independent of the facts.

To talk about cause and effect is to make statements or hypotheses of the form *A causes B*. In life, actual events seldom link up in neat, isolated chains. Indeed, the "chain" metaphor is misleading: The links we discover often intermingle, even to the point of obscurity. Although we can sometimes say, based on the facts, that A caused B, it's usually more complicated. Logic maps the broad possibilities.

Thus, A may have other effects besides B, or B may have influences besides A. Causal relations may also be bidirectional, with A and B influencing each other. They may be fraternal: A and B (my parents) caused both C and D (me and my sibling, who didn't cause each other). And the connection between particular causes and effects may be necessary, sufficient, neither, or both. It takes two parents and nothing else (without cloning) to make a child.

Logic further dictates that if A caused B, A must have preceded B (since that's what is meant by "caused") and that B cannot also have caused A. If slavery caused the Civil War, the Civil War must have come later and cannot have caused slavery. And just because A preceded B doesn't mean that A caused B. This is the well-known fallacy of "post hoc ergo propter hoc" (after that, therefore caused by that). Slavery didn't cause the Civil War just because it came first. It takes more than priority in time to ascertain a causal connection between things.

We can see from this example that while the statement "A caused B" may be true and useful, it seldom says everything that is causally interesting about A or B. That is why isolating causes and effects and ranking their importance is such a complicated business, and why logic is only the starting point for managing that complexity. But it's an essential starting point, because it establishes outer parameters for what we can say about cause and effect.

These logical parameters could be described as critical thinking—or in more obvious cases, as common sense. But our causal conundrums go far beyond logic's ability to police them. Logic only tells us how to begin and when we're wrong, but to talk coherently about cause and effect, that is where we must start.

CONSCIOUSNESS AND CAUSATION

Causal thinking also begins with this "hinge" proposition: awareness of cause and effect is an essential part of consciousness itself. We can't imagine existing as conscious beings capable of connecting thought and action to achieve ends without some awareness of causes and effects. To a great extent, consciousness *is* such awareness, or is predicated on it. Experience is coherent because we can individuate not just objects, properties, and relations but also events and change—the rearrangement of things over time—and because through our agency we can exert some influence over that causal flow.

Time is the mysterious dimension (one that we struggle to define) in which things change. Consciousness is also mysterious: a unified blend of perception, self-awareness, information storage and processing, and the ability to formulate ends and initiate actions that further them. Without some causal comprehension of how change occurs, and some ability to affect it, such conscious experience would be chaotic or impossible—and clearly it's neither. We understand what has happened when a cat swipes its tail on the kitchen table and causes a bottle to fall and break. It isn't uncanny.

Thus, we can't approach causation, or the more general problem of causality, without making certain background assumptions. Things exist and change in time and space, and things affect other things in ways we can at least partly understand and affect. In other words, things don't just happen willy-nilly; they happen for reasons, discernible or otherwise. We can't think about the world or live in it except on those terms.

An essential principle of science, as the study of nature, is the idea that every effect has a cause. Causation is also central to philosophy, which seeks to explain and organize it in general terms, going back to Aristotle; to history, in mapping how societies evolve over time; and to morality and politics, which depend on concepts of individual agency and responsibility.

In short, as part of the basic furniture of consciousness, causality figures in one way or another in every domain of knowledge, from the process of natural selection to the emergence of organized religion or capitalism, or the causes of chemical interactions or natural disasters. Life makes sense *because* events can be assigned causes, whether it's your cat breaking a bottle, the effects of these words on you, or the inductive truth that jumping off tall buildings almost always ends badly.

Again, establishing lines of causation means focusing on specific changes: who robbed the bank, under what circumstances, and with what results. The emphasis is on particular contexts and cases, with reference to types, phases, or larger patterns of change. But questions about the "what" of causation and the deeper "how" or "why" of causality frequently merge or overlap.

Specifically, whenever causation implicates more than one domain of origin—nature, human agency, or what we variously call "fate," "randomness," or "indeterminacy"—the larger question of causality arises. "Causation" and "causality" are both relevant to critical thinking because they're really two aspects of the same thing. We might call causation a factual scientific or social-scientific question and causality a philosophical one. But causality writ large can be viewed from either vantage point, precisely because it is relevant to all thought and action. It's about what happens and what kinds of causes are involved.

Things only get more complex when we consider the "causal horizon": how many different causes, or different types or levels of causation, we are talking about, and going how far back in time. The further back we go, and the more possibilities we consider, the cloudier that horizon becomes. With how much certainty can we describe causal relations generally and weigh their relative influence? Sometimes the answer is obvious: a ball hits a bat, resulting in a home run. But as the potential causes multiply (the count, the pitch, the batter's swing, the wind), the question can become obscure or downright imponderable.

The Civil War had more than one cause, although slavery was certainly the major one. The war's outcome, in turn, led to more than just the end of legalized slavery. We can make plausible assertions based on factual evidence, but the evidence is often limited, ambiguous, or conflicting and must be sifted and weighed to make those assertions, and we can never know or say everything relevant to the subject.

FREE WILL AND DETERMINISM: CAUSALITY BEGINS AT HOME

Having framed causality in relation to causation, logic, and consciousness, the next step is to look at metaphysical causality. We can begin at the personal level. Something—no doubt many loosely related things—just caused me to write this sentence. It could have been expressed differently, or not at all, without catastrophic results. But it makes sense to say that "I" wrote it, not someone else, and it certainly didn't write itself.

Never mind for the moment the influence of my genes, upbringing, education, peers, or what I had for breakfast. "I" am the causal nexus at which those and other influences converged to produce the sentence. Saying that I wrote the sentence also implies that I am at least somewhat responsible for it, whatever those outside influences may have been. Any critical judgments of it are properly addressed to me. But then, I'm also a product of my culture. I didn't invent language or the written word, and few thoughts are entirely original, however uniquely expressed. After all, the world is a causal bazaar, not a causal vacuum. Already there's a looming distinction here, if not a conflict, between free will (what "I caused") and necessity or determinism (what "something else caused").

Here's another case in point. Suppose I break an elegant wineglass at a friend's house. I feel sorry and apologize. It happened in what seemed like a millisecond, before I could prevent it. I certainly didn't want it to happen. Why do I feel guilty? Along with regret at the loss and sympathy for my host, there's a sense of authorship: I broke the glass after all, whatever the reason, and it makes at least some sense to say I should have been more careful. I can't go back in time—but if you want to Google "retrocausality," go ahead.

Maybe I can learn from the incident, but knowing myself to be absent-minded and accident-prone, I have my doubts. I don't think it was "within my control"; if that were the case, it wouldn't have happened. I'm not ready to give up on free will and responsibility, but a deterministic explanation makes a bit more sense while I'm picking up the pieces: the glass was slippery, my attention wandered, I lost my grip. That's my story, and I'm sticking to it.

In practice, if we're of sound mind, we individuate and identify with our "selves"; that's what it means to be a "self." And to that extent at least, we own our causal agency. But isolating the self is a (convenient or necessary) half-truth. We think of ourselves as distinct parcels of humanity despite our commonalities and all the causal factors beyond our control that help make us who we are. It would be tedious (if not redundant) to say, "I wrote this sentence, but with innumerable disparate causal influences, identifiable or otherwise, ranging from my genome to my current state of mind." In one sense we're all islands, causally speaking; but in another sense, none of us is an island.

The question is just how insular we are and how causally potent as free agents. That is the core dilemma that pervades liberal learning and everyday life. (Spoiler alert: It can't be solved, but there's a workaround: we need to have it both ways.) The fundamental schism between causal perspectives also lies at the core of our political differences.

Whether we believe causality is a realm of free will, determinism, or some combination of those (along with quantum indeterminacy), we know that life isn't just a random flow of unrelated events. Every event has a cause—or a complex causal history. Certain things follow certain other things; they don't just happen. Famine, plague, and war lead to death, not vice versa, and conception leads to pregnancy.

From a scientific perspective, nature is nonrandom—except at the all-important level of quantum physics, where it appears totally random. We experience nature as a plethora of caused events. Its laws are causal laws, and as far as we can tell they apply uniformly, at least in our universe. Following Aristotle, we can distinguish levels or phases of causation within nature: a leaf falls because the wind blows, because it's autumn and the leaf is dead, and as part of a natural cycle. People die due to age, disease, violence, or accident. It may seem random that it rained today, but rain only occurs when moisture and dust particles are in the atmosphere, and it never snows when the temperature is 80° F. In short, nature (on the supra-atomic level and apart from our putative free will) is inherently deterministic.

Subatomic particles are another story. Quantum indeterminacy upends the Newtonian worldview, throwing a monkey wrench into the causal equation. This unpredictable third domain roughly mirrors Melville's "fate." If quantum theory doesn't refute the idea that *anything* can be understood or predicted with certainty (the essence of scientific knowledge), it at least refutes the idea that *everything* can.[5] Nature, it turns out, is less lawful and accommodating to the human mind than Newton supposed.

Einstein found quantum theory strange, unsettling, and irreconcilable with his own scientific determinism, including his theory of relativity.[6] God, he famously protested, doesn't play dice with the universe. But that is exactly how subatomic particles behave. And yet, on the supra-atomic level, Newton's laws still apply. Balls drop when we release them, and apples continue to fall on our heads.

What are we to make of all this? Can we bypass "quantum weirdness" in forming a model of causality? We can't challenge the indeterminacy of quantum reality. Yet to understand human causality—not just free will, but how nature presents itself on the supra-atomic level—we need to at least quarantine it.

That's because we can't abandon either free will or natural determinism and still grasp the world as we do. Hence, the tacit assumption that determinism governs nature on the perceptible level, whereas human beings, while always subject to external influences, are in some measure free to choose their actions. That's what works. If free will is a delusion, it's a necessary one and an essential part of our reality.

The same is true for natural determinism. We still need it to explain how trees grow, oceans rise, and elk herds migrate in essentially Newtonian cause-and-effect terms. We couldn't even consider how quantum theory challenges traditional notions of causality without acknowledging how broadly those other causal schemes fit the visible world.

As noted earlier, the world is nonchaotic *because* we can experience it—and to some extent control it: because it's a web of at least partly discernible causes and effects, even if no complete causal maps are attainable. We know why tides ebb and flow, why today is sunny, and how Barack Obama became president. In some contexts, this causal understanding is a rigorous scientific process; at other times, it's based on available facts, inferences, or sheer educated guesswork.

Causation remains a riddle because the root causes of complex events are multiple, diverse, opaque, and elusive. They include the personal agency of individuals, often with obscure motivations, and also the effects of nature, technologies, social groups, movements, institutions, cultural conditions, and so forth, extending backward in time. *Causality* remains a riddle as well, because it's unclear (or disputed) which causal domain is predominant or how they coexist.

That riddle doesn't paralyze us, but it compels us as critical thinkers to acknowledge uncertainty, especially in the zones where free agency and natural determinism appear to intersect. Issues that hinge on it include our understanding of human nature and moral responsibility. Thus we need to think about the "why" and "how" of causality in general, and not just the "what" of causation in a particular instance or context.

Sam Harris is a rarity among modern thinkers as a radical determinist. "Without free will," Harris concedes, "sinners and criminals would be nothing more than poorly calibrated clockwork and any conception of justice that emphasized punishing them (rather than deterring, rehabilitating, or merely containing them) would appear utterly incongruous."[7] Yet he denies that we are the ultimate authors of our desires.

> What will my next mental state be? I do not know—it just happens. Where is the freedom in that?
>
> —Sam Harris, *Free Will*

Harris's argument is compelling. It's hard to conceive of the human mind as both a vast tangle of external influences and the sole author of its agency. Unless, that is, we redefine "agency" to mean not the ultimate author, but the cook who stirs the deterministic stew to come up with a unique dish and then serves it up to the world as the product of his or her free will.

As Harris notes, there is neuroscientific evidence that our brains make decisions before we are consciously aware of them, implying a less dominant role for free will. He's also right that we don't "make" our minds. As he puts it, "I cannot take credit for the fact that I do not have the soul of a sociopath." We don't pick our parents, gender, body, birth order, or when or where we're born. Key determinants of our lives are in place before our births. Even Jean-Paul Sartre, the existentialist and apostle of free will, writes in *Between Existentialism and Marxism* that "freedom is not what you do gratuitously. It's what you do with what's been done to you." Nevertheless, we persist in believing we are free agents. "We beat on," F. Scott Fitzgerald writes in *The Great Gatsby*, "boats against the current, borne back ceaselessly into the past." But it's we who beat on.

Where does the determinist's argument fall short? For one thing, we need to explain the different kinds of causality that we (rightly or wrongly) perceive as natural laws and free agency. We assume we have free will because that assumption fits with conscious experience, whereas radical determinism does not. Determinists, of course, would respond that it's all a delusion: we are simply programmed (that is, causally determined) to think we're free. But we can't apply the assumption that we're unfree, even if we believe it in theory.

One thing we can do is bias our explanations in one direction or the other—toward the self or toward the causal environment around the self—with important moral and political consequences. For example, we often look for a single or main cause in explaining events, when in fact most complex events have many causes. Rolf Dobelli cites this "fallacy of the single cause" as a common lapse of critical thinking. "A balmy Indian summer," he writes, "a friend's divorce, the First World War, cancer, a school shooting, the worldwide success of a company, the invention of writing—any clear-thinking person knows that no single factor leads to such events. . . . Still, we keep trying to pin the blame on just one."[8]

Dobelli shares Harris's deterministic bent. "Our actions," he argues, "are brought about by the interaction of thousands of factors—from genetic predisposition to upbringing, from education to the concentration of hormones between individual brain cells. Still we hold firmly to the old image of self-governance." Dobelli is right about this much at least: events have an indefinite number of causes, and often we can identify only the immediate or obvious ones. As the causal horizon of an event recedes, the more vague and speculative, and the less helpful, any explanation becomes. A balance must be achieved. But this is mainly a question of causation, whereas "self-governance" is a question of causality.

The sheer scope and persistence of the free will problem suggest the need for some kind of accommodation. Free will and determinism each have a firm purchase on different parts of reality and competing claims on the middle ground where human and natural causal forces presumably intermix. When I decide to dip my bare foot in a cool stream and feel the water between my toes, I don't sense a conflict between freedom and determinism. I do it because I like it. But it isn't clear that I freely chose to like it.

One thing seems clear (except perhaps to some physicists): although we can change our understanding of the past, we can't change the past. Whatever the causal forces working on us at a given place and time, we can make only one decision at a time. Hamlet couldn't choose both to be and not to be. When we act, we can only move in one direction in time (forward) and on one track (ours).

This sense of causal linearity can make past actions and events seem inevitable in retrospect. Yet the fact that one thing happened and not another doesn't mean that what did happen was preordained. Maybe it was just one of many possible outcomes. And yet, *something* must have caused that outcome and not others. So, in what sense exactly were the other outcomes "possible"? I don't claim to know the answer, but only a radical determinist would argue that I had to break my friend's glass.

The question lingers like a wine stain: What caused me to break the glass, and was that cause (or causes) internal to me, external, or some combination? In most cases, the common-sense answer is the latter. Most of us are implicit "compatibilists" or "soft determinists," if we think about it at all. That is, we tacitly acknowledge both determinism and free will and differ over how to balance them—most obviously when we judge the actions of others.

One version of the compatibilist view runs as follows: the unique set of causal influences that leads me to make my particular decisions, however far back those influences can be traced beyond my control, is just what we mean by having free will and a meaningful sense of self. This is the theory of the chef stirring the stew. All that matters is that this concatenation is uniquely mine—not that it could have been otherwise or that I could have chosen differently.[9]

Does this rescue the self? Or does it merely beg the question by identifying "me" as the nexus at which those deterministic forces converge? The question remains: What do I add that's uniquely mine—and what does it mean for something to be "uniquely mine"?

We have to ask that question, and there is no final answer. What matters is that we recognize the pervasiveness of the causal dilemma, the fallacies and illusions it engenders, and the practical need for all three causal models—free will, determinism, and chance or quantum indeterminacy—as modes of understanding. Adopting some form of "soft determinism" is a useful beginning, but it doesn't resolve the question. It just reframes it as a question of blending and balancing rather than choosing among alternatives.

Causality thus remains a source of endless debate on both levels—the level of causation and that of metaphysics—across the liberal arts and beyond. In fact, whether in nature, society, or the vagaries of history, human values, thought, or imagination, it's hardly ever *not* an issue.

HISTORY AND CAUSAL COMPLEXITY

In *War and Peace*, Leo Tolstoy wrestles with causality by asking, What is history? What makes things happen on the scale of the Napoleonic Wars? He addresses these questions directly in Part II of the epilogue, a disquisition on the complexity of history. Tolstoy doesn't argue that history is inscrutable, only that it isn't reducible to "great men" such as Napoleon. He invites us to think of it as a miasma of formal and informal power relations (including his spectacular accounts of Napoleonic battles), nature and geography, culture and family life, art, religion, economics, and so on. Warning against the fallacy of the single cause, Tolstoy writes,

> The totality of causes of phenomena is inaccessible to the human mind. But the need to seek causes has been put into the soul of man. And the human mind, without grasping in their countlessness and complexity the conditions of phenomena, of which each separately may appear as a cause, takes hold of the first, most comprehensible approximation and says: here is the cause.[10]

Sir Isaiah Berlin summarizes Tolstoy's view in this way: "No theories can possibly fit the immense variety of possible human behavior, the vast multiplicity of minute, undiscoverable causes and effects which form that interplay of men and nature which history purports to record."[11] History, in short, is a paradigm of causal complexity. Berlin goes on to say that "we shall never discover all the causal chains that operate: the number of such causes is infinitely great, the causes themselves infinitely small; historians select an absurdly small portion of them and attribute everything to this arbitrarily chosen tiny section."

Historians can't explain everything, any more than journalists, philosophers, mathematicians, or physicists can. Yet we still need to record and study history, just as we need journalism, which James Reston called "the first rough draft of history." We begin with factual evidence (using the logical frames of "who," "what," "when," and "where") and proceed by making plausible assumptions, generalizations, and inferences about what we don't know for certain: the more complex questions of "how" and "why."

There is no such thing as a "complete" account; we must select facts and make informed judgments about what is significant. But this doesn't diminish the importance of the historical or journalistic enterprise. It merely points to the complexity of the task and the critical thinking it requires. Causal gaps and mysteries remain, along with vast areas of contestability.

What caused the First World War? "The question is unanswerable," argues the historian Laurence Lafore,[12] "for the war was many things, not one, and the meanings of the word 'cause' are also many. . . . The study of history is always a study of patterns, of sorting out different hypotheses, of imposing different sorts of order on the confusion of raw facts." But, as Georges Clemenceau observed, "History will not record that Belgium attacked Germany."

For all of history's contingencies, one constant is that we see it only in retrospect. Like our own lives, we regard it as a singular, if complex, bundle of causes and effects that played out in exactly one way. The past can thereby acquire an appearance of necessity. Whatever might have happened, or almost happened, didn't happen. "The real problem of every philosophy of history," Hannah Arendt remarked, is "how is it possible that in retrospect it always looks as though it couldn't have happened otherwise?"[13] Meanwhile, the future seems opaque. We might call this "backward necessity" and "forward contingency."

One challenge for critical thinking is how to dispel that sense of backward necessity by underscoring the contingency of what has occurred. What does it mean to say that something "could have happened differently," when in fact it didn't, and we can't rewind the tape of events? If nothing else, it's a reminder of the vagaries of human affairs and the need for measured skepticism, as well as for making plausible assertions about things we can never know with certainty. And while the future is indeed opaque and unpredictable, it is shaped by the past and thus not entirely contingent.

CAUSAL COMPLEXITY AND CRITICAL THINKING

What all this means is that we need to think critically—rationally, logically, and analytically—on a number of levels. We need to do it on the level of causation whenever we make causal assertions beyond the most obvious. We need it on the level of causality to deal with the eternal dilemma of free will versus determinism. And we need it in all our thinking to avoid formal and informal logical fallacies, such as those arising from psychological or intellectual biases.

One example is the aforementioned fallacy of the single cause. Another is confirmation bias, which is the natural human tendency to believe evidence that conforms to our preexisting notions and to disregard or minimize evidence to the contrary. A third bias is our tendency to construe other people's actions as more deliberate and internally driven and to see our own actions as more compelled by external causes. From others we demand excuses; for ourselves, we give deterministic explanations.

A fourth bias, similar to the third, is seen when the weight of accumulated facts inclines us toward deterministic explanations. The more we know about the external causes of an event, the less we tend to ascribe free will to the individuals involved. As the French say, *Tout comprendre c'est tout pardonner*: To understand everything is to excuse everything.[14]

One explanation for this deterministic bias is that we have greater access to facts in the world than to facts about people's states of mind and motivations. As Berlin explains, "The more closely we relate an act to its context, the less free the actor seems to be, the less responsible for his act, and the less disposed we are to hold him accountable or blameworthy."[15] But can knowledge of such contextual influences, in and of itself, erode moral responsibility? Conversely, can other people's motives ever be fully understood apart from causal factors beyond their control?

Neuroscience notwithstanding, it's unlikely that the free will debate can be resolved by either science or philosophy. One reason it is irresolvable is that causality, like other forms of complexity, leads to contestability. There is always room for different explanations or emphases, both on the level of causation and in terms of free will. Yet, the very intractability of the causal dilemma attests to its importance. Engaging with causality remains an essential part of liberal education, applying to every subject from quarks to queer studies. It raises the most fundamental questions about the "what" and the "why" of history, human nature, morality, justice, and pretty much everything else. No question runs deeper.

Adopting a binocular approach—the assumption that both determinism and free will are indispensible frameworks for our thinking—doesn't solve the riddle. It is merely a first step toward thinking critically about causality. Binocularity reflects how we actually experience the world. This is what Ralph Waldo Emerson meant when he wrote, "If we must accept Fate we are not less compelled to affirm Liberty."

In sum, we assume that determinism and free will coexist, because causality must come from within us, from outside of us, or both, and the most plausible answer is both. They are not mutually exclusive, nor, given quantum indeterminacy, are they jointly exhaustive. But they compete as ways of understanding how things happen that involve both nature and human nature.

Both causal models are necessary, and neither alone is sufficient. Determinism explains rising sea levels, even if a chief cause is global warming due to human technology. But it fails to explain the autonomy we experience as conscious selves and attribute to others, not least in the realm of moral responsibility. There is no area of inquiry in which we don't struggle to determine what happens and why it happens, both on the factual level and the metaphysical. In every corner of the liberal arts, the two riddles persist.

NOTES

1. Ancius Boethius, *The Consolation of Philosophy* (trans. Victor Watts, revised ed.). New York: Penguin Classics, 1999, Book 4, sec. 6, p. 103.

2. Aristotle, *Physics* (II, 3) and *Metaphysics* (V, 20).

3. Douglas Hofstadter and Emmanuel Sander (*Surfaces and Essences: Analogy as the Fuel and Fire of Thinking*. New York: Basic Books, 2013, p. 411) distinguish between physical causality—processes that leads to some result in space and time—and "mathematical causality," the understanding of equations as expressing not just equivalence but rather "a calculation giving rise to a result."

4. Herman Melville, *Moby-Dick or, the Whale*. New York: Penguin Classics, 2003, ch. 47.

5. See, for example, Freeman Dyson, "What Can You Really Know?" *New York Review of Books*, November 8, 2012, pp. 18–20. (Review of *Why Does the World Exist? An Existential Detective Story*, by Jim Holt.)

6. Peter Pesic writes (*Labyrinth: A Search for the Hidden Meaning of Science*. Cambridge, MA: MIT Press, 2001, p. 146), "Quantum theory predicts correlations even between distantly separated particles; experiment confirms these effects, which do not involve transmission of information faster than the speed of light. Einstein was quite right that quantum theory is weird; nature just is that strange. This utter indistinguishability or identicality stands in the way of Einstein's determinism, which depends on the individual identity and distinguishability of each particle."

7. Sam Harris, *Free Will*. New York: Free Press, 2012, p. 1.

8. Rolf Dobelli, *The Art of Thinking Clearly* (trans. Nicky Griffin). New York: Harper, 2014, ch. 97.

9. This is what I understand to be the philosopher Daniel Dennett's view.

10. Leo Tolstoy, *War and Peace* (trans. Richard Pevear and Larissa Volokhonsky). New York: Vintage Classics, 2007, p. 987.

11. Isaiah Berlin, *The Hedgehog and the Fox: An Essay on Tolstoy's View of History*. Princeton, NJ: Princeton University Press, 2013, p. 20.

12. Laurence Davis Lafore, *The Long Fuse*. Long Grove, IL: Waveland Press, 1997, pp. 16–18.

13. Hannah Arendt, in "Hannah Arendt: From an Interview," *New York Review of Books*, October 26, 1978. Retrieved from http://www.nybooks.com/articles/1978/10/26/hannah-arendt-from-an-interview/.

14. In Ferenc Molnár's play *Fashions for Gentlemen* (Act II), a young shopkeeper explains to his mentor, The Count, "I just can't bear to see people suffer. If you look into another's soul, it's impossible to judge him." To which The Count replies, "So don't look!"

15. Berlin, *The Hedgehog and the Fox*, p. 28.

Chapter 13

Morality and the Liberal Arts

> Can you tell me, Socrates—is virtue something that can be taught? Or does it come by practice? Or is it neither teaching nor practice that gives it to a man but natural aptitude or something else?
>
> —Plato, *Meno* §70

THE MORAL DIMENSION

We can't talk about education as a stairway to productive citizenship, whether economic, civic, or cultural, without raising moral questions. For that matter, we can't talk about communities of any kind without seeing higher education as in some sense a moral enterprise. The ethical realm permeates education because learning is an interactive process, and human interaction is what gives rise to moral conflicts in the first place.[1]

There are no moral values or problems in a zero-person universe, or for hermits (except vis-à-vis animals). But put two or more people together in any context, and a moral dimension emerges due to the potential for conflict. Such conflict may assume the form of competition for resources (such as money, space, jobs, status, attention, honors, health, love, or opportunities), or it may involve harm or claims of having been harmed.

In one sense at least, moral thinking is unnatural to us. As individuals, we are directly attuned to our own needs, feelings, and goals and only indirectly to those of others. Instinctively, our own interests come first; even compassionate selves are selfish. Moral thinking urges us to look beyond our interests and consider others co-equally. In addition to such selfishness, our natural "groupishness" and affinities—to family, clan, tribe, community, nation, faith, profession, political party—can obscure the moral realities of other people and groups. Our psyches bind us to certain groups and blind us (in the formulation of Jonathan Haidt[2]) to others. Morality asks us to look beyond the bounds of the self and its tribes and consider the prima facie moral worth of all people. And part of that process is what we call citizenship.

Good citizens aren't just politically, economically, and culturally engaged. They are also moral citizens, at least in this limited but fundamental sense: they have regard for the interests of others, even when those interests conflict with their own. (No conflict, no problem.) They don't just obey the law; they consider the effects of their actions on others, recognizing that the law is a blunt instrument that can't regulate every facet of human conduct.

The very notion of a "citizen," in fact, has a moral component. Like language and critical thinking, it's essentially social: about what we do as members of communities, as opposed to what we do in our homes, on lonely forest paths, with other consenting adults, or in other private moments. If citizenship has a moral dimension, and education is primarily preparation for citizenship, education must have a moral dimension. So thought Plato, and most philosophers since.

However self-centered, we humans also have a seemingly innate sense of morality, whatever the source. If ants or primates act in ways we can describe as moral—such as caring for their young or protecting the group—it isn't because they think about right and wrong. Human beings can think about such things.

We also evolve morally—as individuals, as nations, and as a species. Such evolution is never linear, but adults are more ethically aware than five-year-olds, and for the most part, societies evolve as well. We don't tolerate slavery, exploitation, cruelty, or other abuses as much as in the past. Consider the slow and unsteady advance of civil rights in the United States for minorities of race, gender, and sexual orientation. Laws, norms, and cultures evolve slowly and imperfectly—but they do evolve.

So in what sense or senses, exactly, is education a moral enterprise, and where are the relevant boundaries? What moral differences can we tolerate, and what differences are intolerable, in the universe of higher learning? And—while we're on the subject—how, if at all, does learning make us better people?

We must consider the question on multiple levels. Moral concerns arise within the context of education generally, within the anthropocentric liberal arts more specifically, and within the value-centric humanities in particular. Questions of value emerge in different ways depending on whether they affect the student, the teacher, or the institution. This is because most forms of knowledge seek to elucidate human relationships, institutions, motivations, and the causes and effects of actions, practices, traditions, beliefs, resources, and so on. All such transactions involve the possibility of competition for resources or infringements of one person or group on the agency or interests of another.

Critical inquiry thus demands at least a general awareness of moral problems: how they arise and how they differ from nonmoral ones. It doesn't require or presume any particular way of responding to those problems. There is ample room for debate, as well as a need for agreement on certain key issues, including what we are arguing about, what we mean, and how we use language.

We each have our own personal moral thresholds, priorities, and tolerances, and we may place higher limits on ourselves than we do on others. Much of the time, our limits and tolerances overlap; it's when they don't that we have problems. Accordingly, we need to consider the complex, problematic, and fraught connection between higher education and moral thought and conduct.

SIX AXES OF MORAL ENGAGEMENT

There are at least six distinct axes along which higher learning and moral thinking intersect. Ranging from the general to the particular, they include the following: (1) *policy*, relating to the social and political context of higher education; (2) *communication*, based on the moral character of language; (3) *content* or subject matter, insofar as moral issues arise within the curriculum itself; (4) the *learning process* and its institutional setting; (5) the *student* as a moral agent and the question of individual character; and (6) the *mission* of liberal education, in terms of promoting moral citizenship and citizenship in general. And while all education is preparation for citizenship, we can't ignore the (sometimes competing) demands on, or by, students as simultaneous learners and citizens: demands in the form of public service, community participation, self-expression, and activism. We'll consider each of these in turn.

THE POLICY AXIS IN BRIEF

Questions of public policy and education are largely beyond the scope of this work. Our aim is not to open the Pandora's box of specific issues but rather to map their context and how they relate to one another and to the liberal arts and to suggest some broad parameters of moral citizenship. (We'll peek into that box in the final chapter.) But we should meanwhile acknowledge that the policy dimension of liberal learning is in many ways the most important one, morally speaking. As noted in chapter 2, politics literally governs the rest.

The policy axis embraces a host of urgent and contested issues and debates that confront any democracy: Who should pay for education, and how? Who should have access to it, in what form, and at what cost? How should learning be valued and distributed as a social good? What impact can or should critical inquiry have on society and class structure? How should liberal education be weighed vis-à-vis STEM, professional, or vocational learning? What are colleges' and universities' obligations to society, and how (for example) should they select their students and faculty, treat their waste, invest their endowments?

These are important questions. But it's worth recalling here that not all value differences can, or must, be finally resolved. The contestability of moral and political issues, not their closure, is the essence of democracy. Beyond a core of shared values, such as truth, decency, and fairness, we don't and cannot all agree on the scope of ethical constraints in general. Our values differ as to where boundaries should be drawn between the self and others or between the self and society, between freedom to perform actions and freedom from the actions that others may perform, between individual responsibility and seemingly exculpatory causal influences.

Ultimately these are political questions, because law establishes the baseline of public morality, and politics is about us. As citizens, we decide who makes the law. Even in an imperfect democracy, there is at least the potential for collective democratic self-improvement, for example, through structural change or by enfranchising previously marginalized groups.

The same condition of contestability that explains our moral differences affects the range of ideological views in a democracy; it's the reason why there is such a range and why we talk to (or past) each other and tolerate all but the most extreme views—that is, those that threaten civil discourse itself.[3] At best, we can hope to better understand and tolerate different viewpoints—not necessarily to embrace them or see them evaporate. That is a core goal of liberal education. And we can begin to understand why certain questions just won't go away: why we invariably can, and do, argue about them.

LANGUAGE AS A MORAL ARENA

Critical inquiry, as has been suggested throughout this book, is all about language. And as the vehicle of most thought, language is also the vehicle of most moral discourse. You may prefer to shake your finger at someone, make a facial gesture, or slap them—but these are expressions of emotion or assertions of power, not arguments. Why is language a moral enterprise? Because we argue with words, and words can do harm. We can use words to deceive or manipulate, withhold information, abuse language, or deceive our audience by lying, exaggerating, understating, ignoring context, or using rhetorical speech to imbue or to reinforce a belief. Public discourse, however logically or factually flawed, requires communication in good faith.

Visual images, symbols, and nonlinguistic codes also convey important information and make arguments, but students, scholars, and citizens still have to talk to one another. If controversial images are posted on the Internet or social media, or embedded in computer software, we need to discuss them.

All language isn't equally morally charged, and some of it isn't morally charged at all. (*Nice day, huh?*) But every utterance is a normative act of a kind: a claim about what it is important to know. (*You should know more about the Civil War—it's the greatest event in our history.*) Implicit value judgments tend to creep into our casual utterances—in the tone, if not in the words themselves. (*Nice day—turn off the TV and go outside. And by the way, what's with the sweater?*)

Language is seldom entirely value-neutral. Often, it's effectively inseparable from the actions that are its frequent causes and effects. We use words to assert, argue, forbid, demand, warn, wonder, scold, commend, prod, incite, and exhort, as well as to identify, announce, explain, or demonstrate. Speech is also selective and economic: it takes time and energy to say one thing and not another. Choices must be made, trade-offs acknowledged, priorities set. How far am I willing to go to explain Lincoln's views on slavery or the ambiguities in the ideas of honor, shame, or respect? How much of an explanation do I owe you—and how is that decision influenced by my values? How carefully do I choose my words, and with what effect?

We communicate to change the world or to keep it the same, as the case may be, by sharing information with an audience. In so doing, we may also intentionally or unintentionally offend or harm, encourage or discourage, approve or disapprove, empower or enfeeble, ignore or indulge, short-change, inspire, bore, or annoy. In fact, the whole point of communication is to manipulate: to share information for some effect. That is reason enough to watch what we (and others) say.

Critical inquiry, moreover, is based on ideas of community and rationality that are to some extent embedded in language itself. Reasoning involves a commitment to mutual understanding and transparency and to avoiding or offsetting the logical and moral pitfalls inherent in language. Like grammar, reasoning involves thinking and speaking according to acknowledged rules and conventions, and thereby sustains a kind of community that would otherwise deteriorate into rhetoric.

It has sometimes been argued that becoming a critical thinker involves not just developing certain dispositions but also becoming a certain kind of person: one who cites reasons and evidence and who values fairness, honesty, and open-mindedness, and, where appropriate, impartiality or objectivity.[4]

Such attributes are surely intrinsic to thinking critically. It may be difficult to decide at what point dispositions or habits become character traits, but at a minimum, critical thinking is a commitment to a set of intellectual best practices that are (like democracy itself) perfectible but never perfected—and accordingly, to a certain kind of community, linguistic and otherwise.

We may not "owe" it to each other to be critical thinkers—and sound thinkers can do bad things, while unsound thinkers may be saintly. But critical thinking enhances our powers of citizenship within the communities that are essential to democratic culture. It all starts with our choices in using language.

IN THE CURRICULUM: MORALITY AS A GATEWAY CONCEPT

A third moral axis of the liberal arts consists of the problems and conflicts that arise within and across the various disciplines. This axis is inevitable, because we're talking about a disciplinary spectrum that encompasses the study of nature, human nature and society, and the products of human imagination. Across that spectrum, questions arise about human decisions, interests, actions, and conflicts. They arise whenever we consider the consequences of economic or political choices or historical accountability, or when we study the mind, behavior, institutions, or communities.

Moral questions confront us most directly in the humanities, where the focus is on the arts and human values. They emerge in the lives and choices of fictional characters and in the ethical orientation of the artist or writer, in problems of crime, punishment, causal agency and responsibility, and on and on. But we also grapple with moral and political issues beyond the humanities.

What makes "terrorism" a pejorative term and "insurgency" neutral? What version of democracy is best, and which reading of the Constitution? Then there are the questions of income distribution in economics; authenticity and provenance in art; the ethics of research on isolated tribes or other social groups, or of psychological and medical testing and research; the global and community responsibilities of scientists. The historiography of the Civil War (to name one thorny topic) is replete with arguments about which approach properly apportions moral dignity to the various parties and participants.

Because questions of morality arise across the spectrum of liberal learning, it could arguably be considered a powerful gateway concept. It certainly can't be ignored. The problem with calling it a gateway is the difficult and shape-shifting nature of moral discourse itself. While moral questions are ubiquitous, they arise in different ways and in different terms, making morality not a simple window into the liberal arts but a complex conceptual frame.

Let me suggest two reasons for this shape-shifting. One is contestability. Moral issues divide rather sharply between those questions that we *must* contest, because there are legitimate but incompatible ways of viewing them, and those that we *cannot* contest, because disagreement effectively ends discourse. We can't argue productively about, for example, the morality of murder, assault, or slavery (as these are ordinarily defined), or the values of basic civility or truth telling. To do so undercuts the entire moral enterprise.

The other reason why morality is hard to reduce to an essence is that we encounter it in many different forms and contexts: as questions about truth, loyalty, duty, obligation, integrity, justice, honor, mercy, shame, remorse, forgiveness, and so on. It can't be *limited* to talk about rights and duties, or about resources, outcomes, human virtues and vices, or an overall conception of the public good—although the latter is especially important at the political level. Sometimes we need to talk about rights, sometimes about virtues, and sometimes (when human lives are at stake and there is no obvious or perfect solution) we even need to think like utilitarians, weighing possible outcomes against one another.

In short, the concept of morality is based on a family resemblance among a number of aspects of human conflict. Indeed, it would be hard to consider moral value as an overarching concept without broadening the rubric even further to include other forms of value, including political, spiritual, aesthetic, prudential, or psychological norms—to say nothing of the values of education and academic excellence, which span the spectrum of learning but apply in different ways to different parts of that spectrum.

THE LEARNING PROCESS AND MORAL COMMUNITY

Like all institutions, schools consist of individuals who share an ostensible common purpose but also have diverse backgrounds, roles, and aims. Wherever there is such potential for conflict, among individuals or between individuals and the institution, there is a moral community.[5] Unlike hospitals, prisons, or military organizations, however, colleges and universities are also laboratories of democratic life. They are intentional communities, each having a particular institutional character, focus, traditions, and student body.

Questions inevitably arise: For example, what information do we have a right or a duty to obtain, share, or withhold, under what circumstances, and what types of transparency or candor does critical inquiry require? And what does it mean in practice to respect differences?

Interaction among students and teachers, in and of itself, is an ethical process; it demands tolerance, a balance of restraint and self-assertion, and eagerness to teach and to learn. "More than achieving the competence to solve problems and perform complex tasks," writes Andrew Delbanco, "education means attaining and sustaining curiosity and humility. It means growing out of an embattled sense of self into a more generous view of life as continuous self-reflection in light of new experience, including the witnessed experience of others."[6] Delbanco goes on to quote Nathaniel Hawthorne, who said, "It contributes greatly to a man's moral and intellectual health, to be brought into habits of companionship with individuals unlike himself, who care little for his pursuits, and whose sphere and abilities he must go out of himself to appreciate."[7]

To be effective incubators of citizenship, learning communities must sponsor productive and civil conversations among diverse participants with diverse values. And they need to do this while recognizing that the primary role of students is to learn, of educators to teach, and of staff to facilitate that process. In almost any social setting, certain baseline forms of moral equality need to be observed, but this cannot mean that no one's values are challenged. Ralph Waldo Emerson opined, "People wish to be settled; only as far as they are unsettled is there any hope for them."[8] A recent study by the Association of American University Professors echoes Emerson's words: "The presumption that students need to be protected rather than challenged in a classroom is at once infantilizing and anti-intellectual."[9]

The idea of respect is a quintessentially moral one: a certain deference to or regard for others. But it's also a notably vague and vexing idea; it touches on what is deepest in us, but we have different notions of what respect means and how far it goes. Who doesn't want to be respected? Is respect something earned, or is it something we're all entitled to? What it means depends on the context.

In fact, there is a crucial ambiguity between several different senses of "respect." One sense revolves around a person's intrinsic moral worth. Another refers to a kind of moral credit: the acknowledgement of someone's having acted virtuously or earned a certain status. This includes the kind of respect we owe to those who have suffered or sacrificed on our behalf or in a worthy cause. A third sense of respect is more passive and limited: it's about granting mutual moral space and a concomitant willingness not to judge, or at least not to interfere—since nothing can stop us from thinking or judging.

Claims for "respect" sometimes obscure or exploit this ambiguity, implicitly demanding approval or recognition when what is actually warranted is tolerance. Freedom of speech entails our noninterference; it doesn't compel us to agree with whatever we hear or to withhold criticism. The failure to make this basic distinction is a common lapse of critical thinking in the public sphere. Civility and controversy must coexist; any democratic community requires both.

Inevitably, there are further complications. Many moral boundaries are inherently fuzzy and contestable and thus difficult to stipulate, let alone to regulate. Even truth telling can be problematic; there may be uncertain boundaries between, for instance, borrowing and plagiarizing, proper and inadequate citation, or legitimate criticism and needless offense.[10] Such boundaries tend to be embedded in a particular community or culture and not in particular rules, codes, acts, or utterances. Climates of engagement are vague and implicit, and they change over time. Moral climate control is difficult, and that's one reason why we never run out of things to argue about.

CHARACTER AND CITIZENSHIP: THE STUDENT AS A MORAL AGENT

Another point of intersection between morality and liberal education is this vexing question: How, if at all, can we learn to be better human beings and better moral citizens? Can we expect a liberal education to improve us in some particular way? This question of character (to use that vague umbrella term) is perhaps the most problematic facet of the prismatic relationship between the moral life and liberal learning, and it's one that raises a number of subsidiary questions about ethical development.

Can we, in fact, learn to be good—or at least better—moral agents? The idea of education as a route to moral improvement has a long, if at times dubious, history. Higher learning has traditionally been seen as a rite of passage of character, with theology serving, roughly from medieval times to the nineteenth century, as the primary vehicle of moral engineering. Indeed, faith and virtue in the Judeo-Christian tradition have seldom been viewed as separable ideas.

The question of moral education is central in Plato's *Republic* and again two thousand years later in Rousseau's *Emile*. More recently, scholars such as Claude Lévi-Strauss have written about the incremental stages of intellectual sophistication, while Lawrence Kohlberg and others have explored the phases of moral awareness through which we pass from childhood to adolescence and adulthood. Students, writes Delbanco, "still come to college not yet fully formed as social beings, and may still be deterred from sheer self-interest toward a life of enlarged sympathy and civic responsibility."[11]

Nevertheless, the idea of moral education is ill-suited to our times. We generally understand moral character as something that is largely formed long before one reaches college age. Heredity, early development, parenting, peers, authority figures, and other formative experiences all arguably play a role in that process. Except for sociopaths, most people understand that inflicting gratuitous harm is wrong before they show up for class. What remains to be learned—or unlearned—about basic decency, fairness, or truth telling?

Still more objectionable is the implicit notion that higher education (any more than, say, religious devotion or public service) confers some sort of ethical advantage or status that the less educated or less faithful don't enjoy. We've come a long way since President Woodrow Wilson called college "a nursery of principle and honor."[12] Daily headlines tell us of people whose moral orientation—whether measured as law abidance, civility, altruism, or otherwise—doesn't correlate with their background, professed faith, political orientation, or level of education.

Studying moral philosophy doesn't help either. For the most part, it doesn't purport to make us better people, but it invites us to think more clearly and deeply about moral issues—which is not the same thing. Moral theory (with some exceptions, such as problems involving lifeboats, hijackings, and runaway trains) isn't about *what* we consider right and wrong but *why* and on what basis we distinguish right and wrong as we do. There is a great deal of actual moral consensus, at least where egregious acts are concerned. Again, we don't debate the ethics of murder or sexual assault but rather what count as instances of these. It's mostly the hard cases that preoccupy us.

What does raise moral standards is anyone's guess—and one guess, following Hawthorne, might be this: exposure to different points of view and to problems that one has to solve along with others. These, to be sure, are signatures of liberal learning.

On the other hand, however, saying that we learn nothing of moral value through higher education (or through religion, scouting, sports, or any other presumably socializing activity) isn't satisfying either. It implies that we are uniquely influenced (if not causally determined) by our genes and early influences and that at some point our capacity for moral growth stops. Being part of a learning community, from this perspective, is inevitably a growth process and thus also one of ethical development: a process of learning to get along, to share classrooms and dorm rooms, to defend our views and expose them to challenge, to allow our opinions to evolve, and to accept irresolvable differences. Don't we go to college, after all, to grow—intellectually, emotionally, and in some sense ethically, by becoming more conscious of the needs, desires, and dignity of others?

To this the moral education skeptic might reply, "What exactly does one gain from the experience of higher learning that couldn't be gained from working in a diner, a coal mine, a hospital, or a submarine?" The skeptic has a point; we no longer want to say that a college education improves our characters. And yet, like those other activities, we don't want to think of it as morally inert either.

This much is clear: virtue isn't simply based on acquired knowledge. An illiterate person may be more decent, peaceful, or altruistic than someone with a Ph.D. Likewise, the values of primitive tribes may be more humane than those of more complex communities. Animals, too, display various types of intraspecies affection and cooperation as well as competition, although interspecies it's more often dog-eat-dog. Humans' only clear claim to superiority is that we can at least *think* and *talk* about being nice to each other, and we can organize our moral consensus through democratic institutions.

But if moral decency doesn't correlate with education levels, neither is it inborn. If we were all born good, we wouldn't need parents or other role models (at least not for moral purposes); nor would we need laws, prisons, or moral discourse.

One way of mitigating this dilemma might be framed as follows. Our fundamental characters aren't changed by higher learning per se. We may or may not become more ethically aware as we grow and move through various socializing communities, including family, schools, activities, jobs, and civic and cultural organizations. Having roommates and classmates doesn't make us better human beings, but like other experiences, it can mobilize our preexisting moral resources to make us better moral citizens. It isn't necessarily character building—but it's citizen building.

One might further argue that our preexisting ethical condition and our innate capacity for growth influence the use we make of such citizen-building opportunities. The potential for civic education isn't just a structural effect of being in school. It also depends on the background and motivation of individual students and what they make of their learning experience. And it can be realized in other forms of communities as well. The first-century Roman writer Seneca expressed a similar idea about the catalytic moral potential of the liberal arts in his eighty-eighth epistle to Lucilius:[13]

> "Why then do we educate our sons in liberal studies?" Not because they can confer virtue but because they prepare the mind to receive it. Just as what long ago used to be called basic grammar . . . does not teach the liberal arts but prepares the ground for them to be acquired in due course, so the liberal arts themselves do not lead the mind to virtue but clear the way for it.

We might amend the last phrase so say "civic virtue." Critical inquiry doesn't provide ready solutions to moral problems, but it creates foundations for civic empowerment. Liberal education, in other words, is not a substitute for basic socialization, nor does it compensate for the lack thereof. Its ethical function is not to make us good (or better) people in our daily lives but to promote moral literacy: the ability to recognize, have informed opinions about, and participate as co-equals in, moral discussion; to separate fact and opinion from principle and the consensual from the contestable; to work in groups and communities. Like critical thinking, such moral literacy, while difficult to define or codify, is an essential civic skill set for the three broad kinds of citizenship.

TRUTH, CIVILITY, AND THE LIMITS OF NEUTRALITY

Our beliefs, as factual understandings of the world, should always evolve and be subject to revision. But we are under no similar obligation to revise our core values. The question thus arises: Does the need to acquire the shared skills of citizenship entail a kind of moral agnosticism on the part of the student, the teacher, and the school? One answer is: yes—up to a point.

Moral communities are based on common ground. A measure of agnosticism (or tolerance or respect) creates a safe space for our beliefs and those of others. But again, it doesn't shelter us from challenge or exposure to different views. And there are other important qualifications to moral agnosticism in the educational context, as there are in parallel democratic communities such as legislatures, courtrooms, newsrooms, and conference rooms.

One such qualification is the overriding need for tolerance and civility, and civility means talking, listening, not insulting, not personalizing, showing due respect—meaning respect of the important but limited kind. But if civility is a precondition of effective teaching and learning, it is not without its own boundary problems.

Words matter here, and they need to be treated with care. Some words have encoded derogatory meanings, and some have meaning or intent that is debatable or different to different ears. Yet arguing over particular words can also miss the larger points. Political correctness is a two-way street: it can be a bulwark against incivility or a shield for bigotry—and we can't always read other people's minds and hearts. Clarity is almost always preferable to vagueness. But we should heed Hobbes that words are "wise men's counters, they do but reckon with them, but they are the money of fools." Individual words ("racist," for example, or "moderate" or "radical") seldom fully define people or situations. Even when their use is appropriate, we shouldn't ask too much of them. They demand analysis and context. The blunt inadequacy of particular words can only be offset by discourse—that is, by more words.

Another qualification is that the conjoint values of truth telling and truth seeking are paramount and non-negotiable (however much we need to argue about what is the case and what truth is). As both a moral and an intellectual value, the pursuit of truth is the basis of all trust and all intellectual rigor. It is something we owe to one another in any community of learning. There can be no arguing about lying, cheating, or plagiarism—only about when they occur.

And while committed to truth and civility, we can't leave our moral principles in the hallway when we enter a classroom or laboratory. We aren't automatons, fortunately, and learning isn't a robotic activity. And as citizens with moral agendas, we also have political agendas; indeed, in any coherent worldview, political agendas *are* moral agendas. Both are about fundamental power relationships involving one's role in society and one's rights and duties vis-à-vis other people, institutions, and government.[14]

Critical thinkers understand that political ideology drives the democratic process. Democracy is a system for managing and reflecting our ideological differences, not for suppressing or eliminating them. (Terms like "agenda" and "partisan bickering" are often used to suggest otherwise—an example of uncritical thinking in the public sphere.) Political gridlock isn't caused by partisanship; it's caused by inadequate institutions, including constitutional and electoral systems, that are unable to manage partisanship and produce consensus.

If we can't avoid moral questions in the learning environment, neither can we avoid political ones. It's often appropriate or necessary to bring one's values to bear on, say, theories of human behavior, works of art, or accounts of the past. Facts are where we start from, but they are not always sufficient. How we select, frame, and interpret them is often just as important, and it is never completely value-neutral.

Can one discuss Picasso's *Guernica*, the causes of the Great Depression, or the 2008 economic collapse from a standpoint of absolute neutrality? Could one examine slavery without condemning it? And if we condemn slavery, what about human trafficking, exploitation of children, racism, sexism, homophobia, religious bias, or the panoply of lesser oppressions? Can we agree on how bad these are, what the appropriate remedies might be, or how much to emphasize them in the curriculum? These are all contestable issues.

At the same time, unyielding political agendas are also antithetical to critical inquiry, especially when they ignore or cherry-pick facts, inhibit opposing views on contestable matters, or obscure larger truths. Higher education is about expanding our worldviews, not entrenching them. It's about locating the regions of contestability more than it is about contesting that terrain. But we can't pretend that such terrain can only be contested outside the classroom.

SPEECH IS SPECIAL

One final contentious question (noted in chapter 2) cannot be ignored here. Uninhibited free speech is as crucial in higher education as elsewhere in an open society. Speech is nevertheless a particularly fraught issue on campuses, and has been at least since the 1980s, as demands for "political correctness" (mostly from the left) and assaults on it (mostly from the right) have divided the academy and the wider culture. It is about how we talk but also what we say. And that's a slippery combination.

Speech in general, and certain words in particular, can do emotional as well as other types of harm. That's why there are laws against perjury, libel, defamation, and public endangerment. Depending on the context, words may jeopardize someone's safety, dignity, legal status, reputation, opportunities, pocketbook, and so on. So freedom of speech can never be absolute. But intellectual discourse is a public highway, not a private driveway. Traffic needs to move freely in all directions. Speech that we disagree with or find abhorrent must be protected for its own sake, as well as to keep the discursive traffic moving.

Attacks on political correctness often defend vile speech, but intolerance of intolerant speech does the greater harm. Prior restraint, censorship, or suppression through formal speech codes or trigger warnings is not the democratic answer, and it doesn't prepare students for the unregulated rough-and-tumble of a democratic society. Criticism—answering speech with speech—is. Bigotry or vile speech must be censured, not censored.

Attempts to restrain or punish offensive speech, rather than respond to it critically, are the counterpart to the uncritical idea that freedom of speech somehow entitles us to be shielded from criticism. Shutting down specific words reflects a lack of faith in an institution's channels of discourse to ensure a proper airing of ideas. It also ignores the wide variety of contexts in which particular words may be used and the variety of intended meanings they may have. At the same time, there is no place for verbal abuse. What's "offensive" and what's "abusive"? Discuss among yourselves.

If there's one overriding lesson to be drawn from the United States' long struggle toward a "more perfect union," it's that speech, not silence or censorship, lights the way. Nothing is absolute—not even the sanctity of human life, in cases where all of the alternatives are catastrophic. But only in extreme cases should we limit what people can say. Libel and slander, child pornography, dire threats to public safety or national security: these are the kinds of things for which suppression of speech is sometimes justifiable. Otherwise, we do better to consider which freedoms the Founders chose to enshrine in the First Amendment to the Constitution and why.

NOTES

1. Following common usage, I am not distinguishing between "morality" and "ethics." The terms are mostly used interchangeably. There is a useful distinction in certain contexts, for example, Ronald Dworkin, in *Justice for Hedgehogs* (Cambridge,

MA: Belknap Press, 2011), differentiates between moral third-person reasoning (what one expects of others) and ethical first-person reasoning (what one expects of oneself). But the distinction is not widely observed, and it potentially obscures the more important connections.

2. Jonathan Haidt, *The Righteous Mind: Why Good People Are Divided by Politics and Religion*. New York: Pantheon Books, 2012.

3. Our moral differences are magnified when viewed through the political lens. This is in part because there is room to differ ideologically over the role of government, the economy, income distribution, and so on. Democracies are systems for managing those differences, not for resolving them. But the essential questions are the same: Where do my rights stop and yours begin? What do I owe the community, and what does it owe me?

4. See, for example, Harvey Siegel, "The Rationality of Science, Critical Thinking, and Science Education." *Synthese* 80:1 (1989): 9–41.

5. Here we see the ambiguity between the descriptive and prescriptive senses of "moral." To speak of a "moral community" in this sense doesn't mean an ideal or virtuous community but one in which conflicts potentially arise.

6. Andrew Delbanco, *College: What It Was, Is, and Should Be*. Princeton, NJ: Princeton University Press, 2012, p. 47.

7. Delbanco, *College*, p. 54.

8. Ralph Waldo Emerson, "Circles." Carlisle, MA: Applewood, 2016.

9. American Association of University Professors, "On Trigger Warnings," August 2014. Retrieved from www.aaup.org/report/trigger-warnings.

10. "Truth telling" here is distinct from the educational process we have referred to as "truth seeking." It's not about locating elusive facts about the world or explanatory models but about specific information that one is morally obligated to disclose.

11. Delbanco, *College*, p. 44.

12. Woodrow Wilson, speech at Swarthmore College in 1913; quoted in Darwin H. Stapleton and Donna Heckman Stapleton, *Dignity, Discourse, and Destiny: The Life of Courtney C. Smith*. Newark: University of Delaware Press, p. 81.

13. Seneca, "Lucius Annaeus, Moral Letter #88," in C. D. N. Costa, ed. and trans., *Seneca: 17 Letters*. Oxford: Aris and Phillips, 1988.

14. Any political theory implicitly presupposes a moral view, but the converse is not always the case. Because morality is first of all about how we interact directly with others, we all have a moral orientation, even if unconscious or by default. But no one needs to have a conscious political orientation; one can choose to remain apathetic regarding the larger world beyond one's immediate moral universe.

Chapter 14

Democracy and the Liberal Arts

> To ask what college is for is to ask what life is for, what society is for—what people are for.
>
> —William Deresiewicz

THE LIBERAL ARTS IN CONTEXT: "PATHS OF LAUDABLE PURSUIT"

We will conclude this exploration of the liberal arts and critical thinking with some brief observations about their wider public context. That context consists of democratic society as a whole: the political, legal, cultural, and economic milieu in which liberal learning and citizenship take place. In preparing people for citizenship, liberal learning both shapes and is shaped by the culture of which it is a part.

Let's begin by recalling some of the main theses of this book. A robust democracy depends on citizens who are critical thinkers. Without them, the best constitution is useless paper, just as great education is useless without motivated students, or great journalism without media-literate news consumers. All of these are ultimately demand driven. Democracy is a form of community, and so is language and the rational thought and conversation on which democracy is predicated. Citizenship is essentially triangular, with economic, cultural, and civic dimensions that overlap and interconnect. And all forms of education are of value both to individuals and to society as a whole.

We have explored aspects of the inner workings of the liberal arts to show something of how the clock works, not to claim its superiority over a watch or an iPhone. Different forms of learning, like different forms of chronometry, are right for different people—and for their families, their community, and society.

The liberal arts are not a substitute for STEM, vocational, or professional training. But they are unique in that they are instrumental to the entire triangle of citizenship. We study the humanities because we are human. We study the social sciences because we live in societies. We study science because we exist in nature. These are the bases on which we've explored the meaning of the liberal arts and critical thinking.

Brevity is in order here, first of all, because we have focused on the intellectual dimension of higher education and not the political; and second, because the cultural environment is a Pandora's box of contestable issues that go far beyond the questions we've been addressing: what we mean by the terms "liberal arts" and "critical thinking." Yet we have also seen that the intellectual dimension inevitably leads to the moral and the political.

Another reason for brevity (beyond its intrinsic value) is that the public dimension of the liberal arts has been explored in recent years by a number of eloquent writers and educators.[1] Many of those works defend liberal learning, and that is fitting, because many Americans don't fully appreciate its value. It is literally indispensable to democracy. This book has not been a defense per se, but rather an explanatory map of the territory. And yet, such an undertaking can't help but amount to an oblique defense.

Why say more? Mainly because the cultural and political dimension is the proverbial elephant in the room—or rather, we should invert the metaphor and say it's the room occupied by the liberal arts elephant we've been examining. Like other sectors of public life—government, business, nonprofit institutions, media, or the arts—higher education is both essential to the system as a whole and in potential conflict with those other sectors. And its very function and definition relate to those other sectors.

Finally, I want to leave you with some provocations. If you've read this far, you've been burdened enough, and I won't presume at this point to add to the sum of your knowledge. But students and educators, in particular, need and deserve to understand the political context of higher education, because it is the space they inhabit.

Peeking into it, we encounter hard political and economic questions about how people are selected, or self-selected, to study the liberal arts, the STEM disciplines, or other forms of education; what that selection process means; and how society pays for it. These aren't just urgent questions for students, parents, and colleges and universities; they're also directly related to how we educate future citizens at the primary and secondary levels. What could be more important than that? Education is the broadest avenue of class mobility and citizenship, and it is a crucial determinant of a person's income, status, and economic, civic, and cultural productivity.

This is inevitably a class issue, pertaining to who gets what. Am I raising the specter of "class warfare" here? Absolutely—because no matter where you stand, virtually all democratic politics is class warfare in one form or another. Crying "foul" at the mere mention of class warfare is a polemical move, falsely implying that democratic political arguments aren't fundamentally about economic opportunity and equality. Politicians and pundits who disdain talk about class are not critical thinkers.

This doesn't mean that everyone should go to college. Some of us don't need it, don't want it, or aren't suited to it. But as the number of Americans with a college degree has soared from a few percent to about 37 percent over the past century, so has our overall national prosperity (however unequally shared), cultural wealth, and human capital. We have formed a somewhat more perfect union. No one should feel inferior for being less educated, and everyone deserves the chance to go as far as their talents and interests allow, in whatever direction. That is the American creed. Abraham Lincoln put it best, in his first message to Congress after the outbreak of the Civil War, on July 4, 1861:

> This is essentially a people's contest . . . a struggle for maintaining in the world that form and substance of government whose leading object is to elevate the condition of men—to lift artificial weights from all shoulders, to clear the paths of laudable pursuit for all, to afford all an unfettered start and a fair chance, in the race of life.

THE LIBERAL ARTS AND STEM REVISITED: COST, CLASS, AND INEQUALITY

To pursue Lincoln's ideal, we need to have several national conversations about education moving forward. For one, we need candid discussion of higher education, mobility, and class: how the United States educates, whom it educates, who learns what, and who foots the bill. If everyone deserves a fair chance to reach their potential, education must be an equalizing and a mobilizing force in society, a democratizing force rather than one that perpetuates differences and barriers. In a knowledge-based economy, learning is the main gateway to the American dream of a secure life in the middle class. As such, it matters how people are given or denied opportunities to learn, and there are real, contestable questions—core political questions—about how broadly the concept of opportunity should be construed. If a measure of class warfare is a natural function of democracy, so is the ideal of "an unfettered start and a fair chance."

To have these conversations, we need to reckon both backward and forward, using the gateway concept of causality. Backward, to understand how history, culture, law, economics, individual circumstances, and primary and secondary education shape and limit opportunities (a problem that goes well beyond the role of the liberal arts). Forward, to grasp the implications of different educational pathways for long-term mobility, well-being, and citizenship, as well as for immediate employment.

In an economy that favors specialized entry-level skills, STEM learning undoubtedly offers a more direct route to employment after graduation. The same holds for vocational training and undergraduate service learning. This fact puts added pressure on less-advantaged students to be more risk-averse and to avoid the liberal arts. Yet, depending on the field and individual talent, these may also be routes to careers with lower reward ceilings in terms of income, civic engagement, or overall self-fulfillment.

> [The] focus on college as job training reflects not only a misreading of the data on jobs and pay, but also a fundamental misunderstanding of the way labor markets work, the way careers develop and the purpose of higher education.
>
> —Steven Pearlstein[2]

To be sure, a college education of any kind is only an imperfect leverage point for entry into the middle class, and widening the higher-education gateway is a complex problem. But the near-term advantages of specific marketable skills, and the cost of a liberal education, continue to skew students' choices. In this way our system of higher education contributes to the reproduction of class barriers rather than their erasure. "The stark truth," Andrew Delbanco observes, "is that America's colleges—with . . . notable exceptions . . . have lately been reinforcing more than ameliorating the disparity of wealth and opportunity in American society."[3]

In the interests of national prosperity, cultural wealth, and civic well-being, the United States needs to get more young people into college, and it also needs to get more of them *through* college by increasing graduation rates, especially for students who tend to underperform relative to their potential. We also need to achieve more diversity in the selective colleges that confer career and leadership advantages. The United States used to rank first in the world in college graduation; now we are twelfth. That's a political problem and a solvable one.[4]

> What is a primary marker of likely success in the contemporary American economy? The answer in one word is education.
>
> —Thomas Edsall[5]

The main qualification here is this: While higher education plays a crucial role in promoting social mobility, it's a limited and complex role. Colleges and universities can't dictate tax policy, income distribution, economic conditions, cultural attitudes, or the quality and availability of K–12 education. In fact, colleges and universities aren't naturally suited to be agents of change. They are conduits to opportunity and engines of citizenship, not blueprints for transforming society. Their core mission is to teach. In fulfilling that mission, schools must pursue a bundle of often competing goals: rigor and academic excellence; meritocracy; campus diversity; a civil and harmonious community that is wide open to controversy, criticism, and questioning; and opportunities for social engagement. Colleges, after all, don't manufacture citizens; they just supply the tools.

Schools can provide models of just communities—albeit limited by the educational and administrative hierarchies that are intrinsic to all formal learning. They can prepare students to pursue their own conceptions of the good life and the just community. But while serving society as a whole, they cannot make society whole or impose on it a single vision. You say you want a revolution? Making higher education accessible to all is just the first step.

Higher education can't remove every personal or social obstacle, every stratum of differential success, or every self-perpetuating elite in society. Nor is education the sole determinant of people's lives or the only mechanism for achieving equality in ways that count, but it counts heavily. So students need to know where they're heading and why, in order to make informed decisions and travel as far as they can toward "laudable pursuits" of their choosing. That's what democracy is rightly about: not class resentment, envy of those above or fear of those below, not equal outcomes or fates but radical equality of opportunity and robust debate about everything else.

Which brings us to another unavoidable conversation, about the broader implications of education for citizenship. It begins with recognizing the value of all paths of learning: science and technology along with liberal, professional, and vocational education. These paths are not mutually exclusive; business and computer science majors can, and often do, also study history, literature, and psychology. Yes, we need STEM and vocational learning and more community colleges; and no, not everyone needs a four-year degree. (According to one study, 65 percent of jobs will soon require some postsecondary training, but only 35 percent will require a four-year degree or more.[6]) But the liberal arts should not be the province of the more privileged. That gateway must widen too.

That is why, as we noted in chapter 1, W. E. B. Du Bois argued for broader liberal learning for African Americans, while Booker T. Washington urged skills training. It is why Thomas Jefferson founded the University of Virginia, not the Vocational or Agricultural School of Virginia, stating, "This institution will be based on the illimitable freedom of the human mind." What laws, policies, or institutions are needed to advance Jefferson's, Lincoln's, and Du Bois's vision? That's for you, the reader, to decide. But you can't decide properly unless subjects such as opportunity, outcomes, mobility, elitism—and class, race, gender, and everything else that divides (and connects) us—are up for discussion.[7]

SCIENCE AND LIBERAL LEARNING

Again, liberal learning is important because critical thinking and citizenship skills are the foundations—and the only possible foundations—of a robust democracy. "Liberal learning" here emphatically includes the sciences. This is not just because science is part of virtually every liberal arts curriculum, nor is it because scientific method is a paradigm of rationality, or because technology is a growth sector in the knowledge economy. The sciences are crucial to liberal learning and vice versa, because all scientists are citizens, all citizens are affected by science, and no comprehensive approach to education can leave nature out of the equation.

Thus, we need science-literate citizens as well as civic-minded scientists who are also good communicators. Too many of us don't understand the basic underpinnings of personal and public health, scientific discovery, technological innovation, the politics of research, or the impact of nature and technology on all of us—to say nothing of atoms, molecules, or gravitational waves. Think of energy or climate change; pandemics, overpopulation, or the politics of scarcity; health care, pharmacology, information technology, or the costs and benefits of space exploration. Consider physiology, sexuality, genetics, or meteorology. Is there a remote corner of science without some bearing on our lives or the life of our community?

To be sure, technology is seldom a panacea, even in the crucial sphere of human health. Technology's benefits (take the Internet, for example) tend to come with less obvious human costs, and its foreseeable consequences with unforeseeable ones. Technologies' relationship to other social systems is often real but unobvious. Yet the leading questions here are nonscientific ones: What are the costs and benefits, and for whom? Technology in a postindustrial world (including information technology) is a key economic multiplier, and the benefits, like the costs, tend to distribute unevenly at first but also to diffuse over time. (How's that iPhone working for you, those antilock brakes, that ATM?)

Critical thinkers are skeptical but not cynical. They collect facts, look for patterns, consider the big picture, and make judgments. They shun scientism, the uncritical worship of science as the epitome of all learning and progress, but neither are they Luddites who fear new knowledge. They ask what's connected to what, what leads to what, who benefits and who pays, and what are the priorities. While we need to be more science-literate, we also need to be more technology-critical.

> Science and technology are providing us with the means to travel swiftly. But what course do we take? This is the question that no computer can answer.
>
> —Glen Seaborg[8]

More than other areas of learning, our understanding of nature progresses incrementally and produces technologies that are often widely, but not universally, beneficial. Yet science is not, for that reason or any other, of unique or transcendent importance. In fact, the practical, cumulative, and occasionally paradigm-busting nature of scientific knowledge doesn't just fail to weaken the case for other kinds of learning; it strengthens that case.

The more technology advances, and the more it permeates our private and communal lives, the more we citizens need to understand it, control its uses democratically and in our personal lives, and see its connections to everything else. We need to appreciate the awesome potentials of science as well as its limits and dangers in a democratic culture and its impact on other realms of life. We need to distinguish real science from pseudoscience and make intelligent public and private choices about the uses and effects of technology. And we might also heed Thoreau, who said, "All our inventions are but improved means to an unimproved end."

Science, then, must always be part of the democratic conversation—but not the whole. And it must always be part of a liberal education, but not the whole. The STEM disciplines are vital to productivity and national security, and so is the rainbow of human knowledge and the ability to think "broadly," "flexibly," and "critically," to "communicate effectively," "work in teams," "adapt to change," and be a good citizen. Scores of writers on the liberal arts have stressed these common aims, often using those exact words.

In a world that is increasingly, in Thomas L. Friedman's words, "hot, flat, and crowded" due to global warming, interconnectivity, and population growth, just how important are the liberal arts? Well, the need for sound thinking may explain why universities around the world have recently begun to embrace the liberal arts ideal that American education has done so much to promote, even as some among us question or attack it. It's why American business leaders, scholars, and educators at specialized schools such as culinary institutes and military academies insist that students gain the breadth and sophistication that only comes with exposure to the liberal arts.[9]

Consider the United States Military Academy, where cadets are now exposed to liberal learning for the most practical of reasons: preparation for military leadership.[10] Curricular reforms at West Point have included immersion in foreign cultures and languages, a more interdisciplinary approach focusing on "educational experiences that transfer learning from one context to another," "collaborative reflection," an emphasis on students' "leadership and ethical decision-making capabilities under stress," and the ability to "minimize the unintended second- and third-order consequences of their actions." In other words, like all effective citizens, twenty-first-century soldiers must learn to see their own perspective as conditioned and limited. They must think in terms of causal and cultural contexts that span the sciences, social sciences, and humanities, and adapt to unforeseen challenges.

More fundamentally, we need to pursue other kinds of truth besides scientific ones to protect ourselves from technology and its shiny objects. To put it most bluntly: if all we had was STEM learning, then (through no fault of scientists) we would still be living with every manner of human hell: slavery, feudalism, totalitarian rule, famine, war. Think: Orwell's *Nineteen Eighty-Four*. Critical thinking, moral thinking, and liberal learning are the bulwarks of democratic life that stand between us and the darkest side of human nature, including the worst predations of technology.

THE VIEW FROM THE CAMPUS GATE

Imagine now that you're a prospective student touring a liberal arts campus for the first time. You ask the admissions dean that perennial question: "What kind of job will I get after I graduate?" It seems like a fair question. One answer is: maybe none that is both immediate and well-paying. But over time, as the dean might point out, the average liberal arts graduate earns as much as or more than the STEM graduate. Sean Decatur, former president of Kenyon College, notes that "the economic argument on the value of a liberal arts education is clear. Data shows that philosophy majors . . . out-earn business majors on average in the long term."[11] And Stephen Hume adds this:[12]

> Studies in both Canada and the United States show that while graduates in the applied sciences enjoy an initial recruitment and wage advantage when entering the workforce, this advantage evaporates over time. Once career midpoints are achieved, wages even out while those with technical skill sets are more likely to be unemployed and for longer periods than those educated in the liberal arts.

Another response to "What can the liberal arts do for me?" is that it's the wrong question. The liberal arts are not a form of job training, and colleges and universities don't shape the job market. They impart intellectual skills that are essential for many jobs, useful for others, and pertinent to citizenship for everyone. It has never been the mission of liberal education to make students immediately or maximally employable. At the risk of repetition, we also need clear-thinking, socially aware nurses, welders, first responders, and home health aides. One doesn't need a college education to be a good citizen, or a critical thinker for that matter. Good citizens also tend at bedsides, collect trash, fight fires, tell folk tales, mind the young, and give in many ways of their time and resources.

Even for those students and parents who recognize the risks and rewards of a liberal education, it isn't an easy call. We certainly need to make college more affordable and debt-free and to improve K–12 education. And we need to teach young people to think of jobs, careers, service to their communities, and fulfilling lives as interconnected goals. But more than anything, we need to think critically about education, and that means first of all exposing myths and misconceptions about college in general.

Many Americans, for example, still believe that a college education is a bad investment, and student debt is a major reason why they think so. But they are wrong. According to the *New York Times*, "American workers with a college degree are paid 74 percent more than those with only a high school degree, on average."[13] Yale president Peter Salovey, citing the American Council on Education, further notes that "many Americans believe that the economic value of a college degree is declining, although that is not true. Likewise, they think that colleges are charging more in tuition than it costs to educate a student. And many say they do not believe graduates with a liberal-arts degree will have good job prospects after graduation. These assumptions all contradict what we know about our institutions and our graduates: The value of a college education is greater than ever."[14]

Another disconnect with reality is the failure to recognize that public spending on education (as, for that matter, on infrastructure or basic research) leads not only to more opportunity and more equality but also to greater overall prosperity. We're not always good at seeing the connections or distinguishing reality from appearance.

Education—of any kind—does more than just serve the individual student. It serves the nation and the world, by fostering economic, civic, and cultural prosperity—maximizing human capital—and correlatively diminishing poverty, isolation, ignorance, and fear, with all their attendant costs. A democratic society needs work done at every level, from raking to rocket science, and citizens at every level who are critical thinkers. You say you want to drop out and start a software firm or a hedge fund? Go ahead. But read *Moby-Dick*, *Huckleberry Finn*, or *The Great Gatsby*, and you will understand the United States better, and maybe even yourself.

In sum, there are no easy solutions to the problems in the cultural and political landscape I'm describing. But three conclusions are abundantly clear. These are political problems with political solutions; college pays, both for the student and for society; and college is about much more than financial reward.

LAST WORDS

A final point about the role of education in the United States reprises a central theme of critical thinking: that words matter. There's a lot of talk about elitism in our political culture, most of it coming from the so-called populist right. ("Populism" is another among the many terms we overuse and underanalyze.) The anti-elitist critique resonates powerfully, but too often for the wrong reasons. It is fundamentally (often blatantly) anti-intellectual, demonizing educational elites.[15] It is also preposterous.

The word "elitism," as Marilynne Robinson writes, "has a new and novel sting in American politics. . . . There is a fundamental slovenliness in much public discourse that can graft heterogeneous things together around a single word."[16] In fact, the abuse of the term epitomizes what Hobbes meant when he warned of words being "wise men's counters" but "the money of fools." Fools use words in place of actual analysis and argument.

Similar contradictions infect vague or ambiguous terms such as "partisanship," "ideology," and "class warfare" when used uncritically for rhetorical purposes—used, that is, for effect, not for meaning. Such buzzwords are toxins of democratic discourse. They don't so much mean as insinuate and obscure. If critical thinking and liberal learning are about freeing the mind, Ground Zero is freeing ourselves from the abuse of uncritical language.

Any morally coherent vision of higher education in the United States is an anti-elitist vision of education open to all, requiring no special qualifications and resulting in no special privileges. Yes, some of the more highly educated among us have more power than the rest. But a diploma isn't an extra vote, a bank account, or an automatic seat at the tables of power. It is economic elites and institutions, and supporting laws and cultural attitudes, that are the real obstacles to mobility, not the ladder of education itself. Attacks on education are perverse.

If the liberal arts are an incubator of economic elites, that's a reason to expand access to the liberal arts—and to stem or eliminate the pernicious forms of elitism. If connecting to the world to become better citizens is elitist, we need more of it. Education is never the problem; reviling knowledge is never the solution. Demonizing education only obscures the real problems of our democracy and delays their resolution. In fact, like demonizing the media (as opposed to particular institutions or examples), it's an attack on democracy itself.

Just as a liberal education isn't for everyone, neither is it all things to anyone. It constitutes a crucial and potentially transformative phase of intellectual development, with lifelong results. Critical inquiry is not, and cannot be rejiggered as, a skill-based, careerist curriculum. It isn't about job training but about mind training, and it doesn't require four years on a bucolic campus.

The college or university campus is indeed a place apart, in location and function, as it must be. That's why it's called (however dismissively) the ivory tower, not the ivory cellar. But it's no more isolated or irrelevant than a maternity ward, a legislative chamber, a space station, or a factory floor. And make no mistake: the potential view from that tower isn't inward. It's a panoramic view of the world—past, present, and future—and how we usefully model it.

Every student in fact climbs a separate tower of their own devising. But every such stairway winds around the common intellectual pillar of critical thinking. To make that ascent is to become a more empowered citizen, ready to earn, serve, share, create, enjoy, and continue to learn: to occupy one's mind and thereby embrace a wider world.

NOTES

1. Recent authors on the subject include Andrew Delbanco, William Deresiewicz, Andrew Hacker and Claudia Dreifus, Louis Menand, Martha C. Nussbaum, Michael S. Roth, and Fareed Zakaria.

2. Steven Pearlstein, "Meet the Parents Who Won't Let Their Children Study Literature," *Washington Post*, September 2, 2016.

3. Andrew Delbanco, *College: What It Was, Is, and Should Be*. Princeton, NJ: Princeton University Press, 2012, p. 122.

4. See, for example, Paul Tough, "Who Gets to Graduate?" *New York Times Magazine*, May 18, 2014, pp. 26–41. As Tough writes (p. 41), "The data show that today, more than ever, the most powerful instrument of economic mobility for low-income Americans is a four-year college degree."

5. Thomas B. Edsall, "The Great Democratic Inversion," *New York Times*, October 27, 2016.

6. Georgetown University, "Recovery: Job Growth and Education Requirements Through 2020," Georgetown University Center on Education and the Workforce," 2013. Retrieved from https://cew.georgetown.edu/cew-reports/recovery-job-growth-and-education-requirements-through-2020/.

7. For a thoughtful set of proposals for higher education reform, see Andrew Hacker and Claudia Dreifus, *Higher Education? How Colleges Are Wasting Our*

Money and Failing Our Kids—and What We Can Do About It. New York: St. Martin's Griffin, 2011, pp. 237–43.

8. Glen Seaborg, testimony to a U.S. Senate committee in 1965. Seaborg was the head of the Atomic Energy Commission and served on the Commission on the Humanities, which established the national endowments for the humanities and the arts. Quoted in "The Heart of the Matter," Report of the Commission on the Humanities and Social Sciences, American Academy of Arts and Sciences, 2013.

9. In a survey of 318 business leaders by the Association of American Colleges and Universities, 93 percent agreed that "a demonstrated capacity to think critically, communicate clearly, and solve complex problems" is more important than a candidate's undergraduate major. Quoted in Jon Marcus, "The Unexpected Schools Championing the Liberal Arts," *The Atlantic*, October 15, 2015; see also Edward J. Ray, "The Value of a Liberal Arts Education in Today's Global Marketplace," *Huffington Post*, July 24, 2013.

10. See Bruce Keith, "The Transformation of West Point as a Liberal Arts College," *Liberal Education* 96:2 (Spring 2010): 6–13.

11. Sean Decatur, "The Myths and Realities of a Liberal Arts Education," Aspen Ideas Festival Blog, June 30, 2016. Retrieved from https://www.aspeninstitute.org/blog-posts/myths-realities-liberal-arts-education/.

12. Stephen Hume, "Three Cheers for the Liberal Arts," *Vancouver Sun*, September 7, 2012.

13. Eduardo Porter, "Equation Is Simple: Education = Income," *New York Times*, September 11, 2014, B5.

14. Peter Salovey, "How to Sway Higher Ed's Skeptics," *Chronicle of Higher Education*, March 16, 2018, A40.

15. As a Harvard-educated former senator, Rick Santorum, pronounced to a cheering crowd in a stump speech (February 25, 2012), "President Obama . . . wants everybody in America to go to college. What a snob!"

16. Marilynne Robinson, "What Are We Doing Here?" *The New York Review of Books*, November 9, 2017.

About the Author

Jeffrey Scheuer is the author of two previous books on media and politics, *The Sound Bite Society: How Television Helps the Right and Hurts the Left* (1999, 2001), a *Choice* "Outstanding Academic Title," and *The Big Picture: Why Democracies Need Journalistic Excellence* (2007). He lives in New York City and West Tisbury, Massachusetts. A selected bibliography is available at www.jeffreyscheuer.com.

www.ingramcontent.com/pod-product-compliance
Lightning Source LLC
Chambersburg PA
CBHW022013300426
44117CB00005B/158